WHERE THE EVIDENCE TAKES US

WHERE THE EVIDENCE TAKES US

A Memoir of a Scotland Yard Detective

KEVIN O'LEARY

ROWMAN & LITTLEFIELD
Lanham • Boulder • New York • London

Published by Rowman & Littlefield
An imprint of The Rowman & Littlefield Publishing Group, Inc.
4501 Forbes Boulevard, Suite 200, Lanham, Maryland 20706
www.rowman.com

86-90 Paul Street, London EC2A 4NE

British Library Cataloguing in Publication Information available

Library of Congress Cataloging-in-Publication Data
Names: O'Leary, Kevin (Criminologist), author.
 Title: Where the evidence takes us : a memoir of a Scotland Yard detective / Kevin O'Leary.
 Description: Lanham : Rowman & Littlefield, [2024] | Includes
  bibliographical references and index.
 Identifiers: LCCN 2024010890 (print) | LCCN 2024010891 (ebook) | ISBN
  9781538174852 (cloth) | ISBN 9781538174869 (ebook)
 Subjects: LCSH: O'Leary, Kevin (Criminologist) | Great Britain.
  Metropolitan Police Office. Criminal Investigation Department. |
  Police--Great Britain--Biography. | Crime--Great Britain--Case studies.
 Classification: LCC HV7911.O334 A3 2025 (print) | LCC HV7911.O334 (ebook)
  | DDC 363.2092 [B]--dc23/eng/20240607
 LC record available at https://lccn.loc.gov/2024010890
 LC ebook record available at https://lccn.loc.gov/2024010891

To Jane and the kids. This is why I was often home late.

Contents

CONTENTS

PREFACE

Confirmation bias is the tendency to process information by looking for, or interpreting, facts that are consistent with someone's existing beliefs. It is, to a detective, what kryptonite is to Superman—toxic to survival. For this reason, during press briefings, detectives will often use the phrase, 'We're keeping an open mind, and we'll go where the evidence takes us.' More than impartiality, it signals a journey of exploration and discovery that describes events that shaped my career.

I kept no diaries during my thirty years of service as a London police officer. This book is drawn from memories of my adventures. Some of the events I witnessed left somatic markers—emotional tattoos of thrills and excitement as well as sadness, anger, and frustration that I was exposed to throughout my career.

The term 'career' makes it sound like I followed a deliberate pathway, but I had no intended plan to become a detective or a senior officer, spending almost half of my service as a constable in front line roles, working shifts of earlies, lates, and nights in uniform and sometimes in plainclothes operations. One fortunate opportunity led to another, first becoming a detective, and then rising through the ranks in a late career sprint where I was exposed to undercover operations, kidnap negotiations, and a leading role in policing the Olympic and Paralympic Games.

Undercover police tactics, by their very nature, include methods referred to as 'tradecraft' that would be of great interest to criminals who are trying to develop measures to avoid detection. Therefore, I've excluded those details that might put the safety of individuals or the effectiveness and efficiency of operations at risk. I also considered including accounts of some investigations and incidents that were sensitive at the time, only to realize that I'd be giving things away that require me to take those secrets to the grave. There are two key principles at play here: 1. Never tell everything you know.

Everything written is based on my experience, my knowledge, and true events. I have disguised some facts and names to protect those involved as a professional courtesy or in one or two examples to avoid further damage to reputations in resolved issues. In describing some of the cases I was involved in, I've also anonymized some of the names of offenders as they were young. Though interesting, these cases were not high-profile at the time. Acknowledging that the offenders may have turned their lives around, I can tell the story and let sleeping dogs lie.

Other case studies I share in this book are well known, and the names of those involved are readily exposed with the lightest of research efforts, making it less useful to anonymize. In some cases, I have used open sources of material to fact check my own recollection of events, supplementing my knowledge with news reports and unclassified documents to aid my memory and accuracy.

CHAPTER I

Operation Zebra

ON A SUMMER EVENING IN LONDON'S FASHIONABLE NOTTING HILL, A tired and battered dark green Ford Transit van parked on a residential street there might have looked out of place, but they were a common sight at the time. Hiding in the back were half a dozen detectives waiting impatiently for the action to begin.

We'd borrowed the van from the friendly fleet manager of a construction company and knew that we couldn't make it look any worse than it already was after several tough years of serving the road building industry; it was a perfect Trojan horse. The back of the van smelled of road tar, an assault on the nostrils, especially after a long day parked in the hot sun. Every panel of the bodywork warm to the touch.

The tree-lined street was giving way to the sweet, refreshing cooler evening air. There were just a few people walking by with purpose yet casually. They all seemed to have somewhere to go for the evening, perhaps a beer garden or to sit outside at a busy eatery, I imagined with envy. Cars were driven with windows down sharing the reverberating bass of their stereos with the world. It was the typical London summer vibe of the time.

A few spaces down the road from our road builder's van sat an equally tired Volkswagen Golf GTI. It was an unmarked police car that was also at the end of its service, and we'd dressed it down a little to make it look the part. We took off one of the plastic bump strips on the passenger side door, removed all the wheel caps, and replaced the car's aerial with a bent coat hanger. When new, this car would've been quite desirable, but it now offered the appearance of someone who couldn't have afforded to have one then and could barely afford to run one now. An aspirational old beater car, if ever I'd seen one.

It was just turning dark as the undercover officer in the driver's seat of the VW sat nervously waiting for his target to turn up. Aaron was young, arrogant, and late, as usual. He was also a very active street robber with a flair for violence who liked to threaten women with a knife before relieving them of their valuables. Like a predator stalking its prey, he'd look for those wearing well cut office attire, carrying designer handbags and expensive, killer shoes. He knew they'd have something worth taking and would be unlikely to cause any trouble, unlike some of the more streetwise sports shoe-wearing savvy commuters who might try to run, or even put up a fight.

Aaron's modus operandi involved following lone women as they left underground stations and, when they were in a quieter side street, he'd pounce and hold a knife to their throat and frighten them into handing over whatever they had. Purses, bags, cash, watches; he'd take anything of value. The victims would get over their material losses, but all were shocked and upset by the experience to the extent that they weren't very good witnesses. No one could identify him from mug shots and reactive investigations to build a case against him failed every time. It was frustrating because we had various intelligence sources and so we knew it was him, but we couldn't prove it. Other teams had mounted surveillance operations, static observations on the tube stations he stalked, and had even tried a using an undercover officer as a decoy to catch him in the act, to no avail. Police teams would have to be very lucky with their timing and such techniques were time consuming, resource intensive, and expensive. The odds were on his side.

I was a detective sergeant on the Central London Crime Squad and oversaw Operation Zebra. It was standard practice to give investigations a code name to avoid compromising confidential information about people and places. A clumsy, overheard reference to the name of an individual criminal or gang is all it takes to screw up a job that could've taken a lot of time, effort, and resources to pull together. An intelligence unit at

HQ was responsible for allocating operation names and Operation Zebra just happened to be the next one on the list.

Aaron was one of several active criminals that fitted the remit of Operation Zebra, the purpose of which was to arrest violent street robbers who could be targeted in a covert operation to combat street level drug dealing. While it is very difficult to catch a robber in the act, it's far easier to catch them if they're willing to commit an imprisonable crime in the presence of someone they don't know is really an undercover police officer.

A few days earlier, Aaron answered a call on his burner phone—a cheap, off-the-shelf phone with an unregistered 'pay as you go' SIM card that could be thrown away after a week or two to reduce the chances of detection. Our undercover officer gave a reasonably convincing story of who he was and what he wanted, with cash at the ready. Aaron arranged to meet, and the first deal was made without incident, establishing evidence of his readiness and willingness to supply. We'd need at least a couple more transactions to be able to demonstrate to the Crown prosecutor and, eventually the court, that Aaron was more than a casual, one-off dealer among his immediate circle.

Tonight, the third evidential deal would result in his immediate detention, or buy-bust, as it was known. He was calling the shots and had no time for social niceties; he knew you were there to buy his gear because you had no better option. It was a seller's market and you put up with his attitude or went without—he'd turn up when he was ready, and you'd pay his market price. Take it or leave it.

Disquiet broke out in the back of the builder's van as someone had farted, and vocal complaints from the others were threatening to blow their cover. Accusations and denials flew around amid the stink, with no firm suspect identified. A fellow detective sergeant leading the attack team hiding in the van hushed them up and gave them a whispered angry command to shut up as Aaron, already over half an hour late, approached the VW. The fart would have to be recorded as an unsolved 'silent but violent' crime against humanity.

I watched from a second storey observation point overlooking the street and ordered radio silence as our man walked up to the car and got in alongside the undercover cop. Whether the undercover officer in the car was genuinely nervous or putting on an act I was never sure of, but he looked sketchy and desperate for a fix. Perfect.

Aaron was as calm as the officer was nervous. Taking a plastic bag from his pocket, Aaron pulled out a ball of crack cocaine the size of a fist along with some prewrapped deals that were exchanged for cash. There wasn't much conversation, but the whole thing was successfully caught on hidden devices in the car with both audio and video recordings. Previous buys with Aaron had tested positive for crack cocaine at the laboratory, so we knew this was the real deal. After the transaction, and as Aaron prepared to get out of the car, the least covert sound of a rough diesel engine spluttered and propelled the van toward him. The 'go' signal was given by the undercover officer, and I called out in full dramatic mode on the radio my *cri de guerre*, 'ATTACK, ATTACK, ATTACK!'

Not surprisingly Aaron put up a fight, but detectives seemed to come from everywhere and within seconds our suspect was on the ground, handcuffed and being searched. The ball of crack cocaine was a bonus, as we'd be able to present this as further evidence of the extent of his drug supplying enterprise. I joined my colleagues on the street and enjoyed the satisfying moment of introducing myself and telling him he was under arrest. I read him his rights and he replied simply 'Fuck you, c**t!'

My team set about the various post arrest routines, one of which included a search of Aaron's home, which was a council-owned flat in a tower block on the outskirts of Notting Hill. Like many of London's districts, Notting Hill was home to multimillionaires in grand houses and mansions, living cheek by jowl next to high-rise blocks occupied by those on lower incomes in social housing. The romantic worldview presented was that everyone seemed to rub along together. I wonder.

A call from a colleague during the search brought news of finding our suspect's brother, Kaden, up to his elbows in crack cocaine and in the process of bagging it up into deals. Sitting next to this cottage industry of crime was a healthy pile of banknotes that would be seized as the proceeds of their criminal enterprise. Killing two birds with one stone was an unexpected result and now both brothers would spend a night in the cells, though neither for the first time.

Both were interviewed with their lawyers present the following morning. I collected Aaron from his cell, where he greeted me with, 'What do you want, c*nt?' I suppose he was still bearing a grudge, perhaps understandably. Aaron declined to answer most of my interview questions, but when confronted about dealing to the occupier of the VW Golf he chose to give his version of events in which he described the other guy as the dealer, explaining that he was only holding it for him because he was scared of him and was acting under duress. It was quite an act and verging on a tearful performance in front of his lawyer. I let him tell his lies, asking follow-up questions to get a full and detailed account of events surrounding this relationship that put him under so much duress. I'd heard enough and decided it was time to show Aaron just what a 'c*nt' I really was, and so revealed to him that the driver of the VW was an undercover police officer who had video evidence of buying drugs from him three times that week. Aaron's face dropped and his legal representative advised him not to answer any more questions, though the damage was already done.

I could only imagine how his robbery victims might have enjoyed that moment. Now it was his turn to feel the disbelief, then horror, of understanding what was happening to him. It was all over for him and his brother who had remained silent throughout his interview. Both were charged and sent to court, without bail.

When the time came, they pleaded not guilty, electing for jury trial rather than accepting the overwhelming evidence against them in the hope of a lighter sentence. The trial was held in a Crown Court, which is a higher court with a judge who has powers to sentence the convicted to longer terms of imprisonment than the lower courts. The courtroom was one of imposing traditional design with wood paneled walls, an impressive elevated bench where the judge sat facing the dock (a place in the courtroom designated for the defendants) and eye to eye with the accused at the opposite end of the room. I gave my evidence from the witness box, looking at the jury and making sure I gave them more eye contact than the judge or barristers. The judge would tell the jury that his job was to advise them on matters of law, and it was for the jury to use their life experience and judgment to decide on the evidence and whether the accused were guilty beyond all reasonable doubt. If the jury was not certain, they should acquit.

For me, I always thought of the jury as the audience rather than the legal professionals in the room. My role wasn't to impress the judge, but to help the jury by making my evidence clear and unambiguous. As I explained what had happened and the evidence we'd collected, I'd look at the accused brothers in the dock occasionally to be met with their snarling faces in reaction to my revelations, which also helped to show the nature of their character to the jury.

The judge, in this case, was straight out of central casting. He was as old as they came with a thin, wrinkled face and white, bushy eyebrows above half-moon glasses that rested on the end of his nose. Beneath his judge's wig I imagined a completely bald head, which we never saw. He would peer over the top of his glasses when addressing the barristers, often to regale them with an anecdote of his own from a long career in law, which would always begin with the phrase, 'I'm reminded of an occasion . . .' from which his story would unfold. Everyone seemed to indulge this quite charming old boy and I think he added a delightful touch of English eccentricity to the proceedings.

Regardless of the quality of my performance as a witness, the jury didn't have to take my word for it because they could watch the covert video recordings for themselves and make their own minds up. When we heard news that the jury was ready to come back into court to deliver their verdict, we all returned to take our places. I sat behind the prosecution barrister and immediately in front of the dock, where the defendants were brought back into court to await their fate. I looked back at them, and Aaron snarled at me, calling me 'c*nt' one last time before the jury returned to their benches and we all stood to the call 'All rise!' as the judge entered from his chambers and took his seat.

The judge, lawyers, clerk of the court, and ushers went through the performative and procedural steps to invite the foreman of the jury to deliver the verdict, which was guilty on all counts for both defendants. For once, Aaron was silent, and I resisted the temptation to turn around to face him.

Each case must be heard by the jury on its merits and so, unless exceptional circumstances apply, they are not told about any previous convictions to avoid prejudicing this impartial assessment of the case against a defendant. After the verdict, it was the turn of both barristers to address the judge, with prosecution going first to reveal that both defendants in this case were no strangers to the criminal justice system.

The defendant's barrister did their best in difficult circumstances to mitigate and plea for a more lenient outcome, but the judge was having none of it and sentenced them to five years in prison. Both brothers became vocal in their disbelief at the thought of going away for a few years and I couldn't help turning around to witness the agitation in the dock behind me to see Aaron snarling at me. I couldn't stop myself from asking him, 'Now who's the c*nt?' mouthing the words just enough for him to interpret them. He moved forward as if he was going to jump out of the dock but was restrained by the security officers who were there, ready to take him down to the cells, which is where he went, kicking and screaming, until the door to the court closed and the noise faded away.

In an unexpected turn of events, the judge called the court to order and chose to announce that he was formally commending me and my team for a successful, professional, and determined investigation to rid the streets of dangerous drug dealers. In his wonderfully eccentric way, in relation to the undercover sting he commented, 'What the first defendant must have found particularly galling was that he was taken in by a mere copper!' I've had a few commendations in my career, but I think this is the one I enjoyed the most.

There was something very satisfying about Operation Zebra. It felt like we were deservedly bringing the right people to justice and making the streets a little safer, one robber/drug dealer at a time.

I have a special dislike of street robbers, for reasons you might understand. They are bullies and cowards and are among the lowest form of criminal. I loved locking them up.

CHAPTER 2

Recruit

As he ran toward me, my eye caught the shine of the blade in his hand, and although it seemed to happen very quickly, my memory of it plays in slow motion. There were four of them, but the guy with the knife was the main act as he grabbed at the handlebars of the only significant possession I owned as a fourteen-year-old boy—my Carlton Continental alloy frame, fifteen-speed racing bike that I went everywhere on. I'd saved up money I'd earned from my newspaper delivery round to buy that secondhand bike from a friend. I picked a bad day that summer to become the victim of a late afternoon knifepoint robbery. I thought the knife was a bit over the top—it wouldn't have taken all four of them to overpower me. I stood in disbelief as I watched them take off, with the guy with the knife riding ahead of the other three culprits.

I ran to a house where I knew the family who lived there and called the emergency number, asking for the police, telling them the direction my attackers had made their escape, and explaining how they could still be caught. I was told to go home and that an officer would come to report the crime. The response seemed to be less urgent than I'd expected. With this, I experienced my first disappointment with policing at that young age. I went home and an officer duly came to the house to take some information for his report. I told him what had happened, and he immediately got on his radio and changed the status of the incident to robbery, not just a bike theft. That sounded a bit more important and went some way to correcting the lack of urgency from the officer I'd spoken with on the phone earlier.

A few days later, I met a detective from the local police station who took a statement from me. He was very attentive and sympathetic to my ordeal but didn't hold out much hope of finding the culprits, or the bike, ever again. I gave a description of events, the suspects, and my bike, which I remembered had my friend's initials and the year he bought it painted on the underside of the saddle.

A couple of weeks had passed when I saw in the park a group of lads that looked very similar to those who'd robbed me. At first, I thought I was just reacting to the trauma of the robbery, except one of them was on a racing bike that looked like mine—but it was blue and mine was green—except he did look a bit like the guy with the knife. After I shared my thoughts with the park keeper, he went to his office and called the police saying to me, 'Better to be safe than sorry, son.'

An unmarked police car drove into the park and, as luck would have it, the detective who'd taken my statement stepped out, accompanied by a colleague. They stopped the youth on the racing bike, and as I watched from a distance, the detective picked it up and turned it upside down, presumably looking for my friend's initials under the seat, which I'd described in my statement. I expected him to return the bike back to the rider and drive off, but he put the rider in the back seat of the police car and the bike in the boot. They'd recovered my bike and nicked the robber. Result!

When I got home, I told my parents that 'I think I'd like to be a police officer.'

I was a fresh-faced youth in 1983 when I applied to join the Metropolitan Police and was invited for an interview at the recruitment office next to Paddington Police Station. My Dad gave me £100, which felt like a small fortune back then and with it I bought the obligatory suit from Burton's Menswear in readiness. I learned from another applicant that those who returned from the interview with an information pack were successful and those who failed went to a side room with a staff member carrying a file. He knew because this was his second attempt.

At my interview I met with an inspector and a chief inspector who put me through my paces: Who is the home secretary? (I knew that one: Willie Whitelaw.) If I was accepted, which part of London would

I prefer to be posted to? One with a higher level of ethnic diversity or a white, working-class area? Yes, the questions were this obvious. There were a few other questions too, but these I can still remember. I came out of the interview and was handed an information pack and sent back to the waiting room for a medical. I could hardly contain my excitement. The chap on his second attempt was accepted too.

I'd borrowed my dad's dressing gown for the medical and, as instructed, went into a cubical and stripped, apart from the gown, which hung off my skinny frame like a towel on a rake. I went into a large consulting room and was directed to stand on a rubber mat with white foot shapes printed on it. Sitting behind a long table about ten feet away was a panel of three doctors. The doctor sitting in the middle barked the order 'Disrobe.' I obeyed, dropping the gown and standing there in all my naked glory while they wrote notes. One said, 'Turn around and touch your toes.' I wasn't sure what they were looking for but hoped I had 'it' if it was something they wanted or didn't have if it shouldn't be there. 'Come here, O'Leary,' another said. I started to waddle backward toward them with my arse in the air, until corrected by a doctor who said I should stand upright and put my robe back on. 'You haven't signed the form in both places. I hope you'll be better at paperwork when you're in the job.' I apologized, signed, and beamed at the thought of being 'in the job.'

HENDON

My joining date came through, and in October 1983, I was off to Hendon Police College in North London. I presented my joining letter at the security gate and stood before the entrance to the campus, which was dominated by three large accommodation tower blocks built in the 1970s from preformed concrete panels, giving them an appearance closer to Soviet era brutalist architecture. The campus was made up of several separate sections, buildings, and facilities, with the police cadet school at one end next to the driving school. Decommissioned Rover police cars were driven at impressive speeds and sideways between the two skid pans, which were covered in oil and sprayed with water. As a new recruit, I was in awe whenever I saw them used for training.

Further along the campus was the uniform stores, the gym and swimming pool complex, and then the classroom blocks, which provided training accommodation for recruits, detectives, and all manner of specialist courses, often attended by overseas officers walking around in their national uniforms. Behind the classroom block was a mock police station, complete with cells and training roads with old cars and a bus. This is where practical lessons were conducted, which included everything from a case of drunk and disorderly to a simple traffic accident where the drivers were having a punch up. Some people hated role-play exercises, but I quite enjoyed them as a way of putting knowledge into practice.

The accommodation blocks were designated so that men occupied A and C blocks with B block strictly for women. Training school romances were frowned upon, and we were warned that anyone found in a room of the opposite sex would be dismissed, but they still happened. I can neither confirm nor deny being a participant.

The recruit training course was about assimilating to our new personas as police officers. We were often reminded that we were a part of a disciplined force who were to always act and behave appropriately, on or off duty, as our lives now came with many restrictions. Officers were required to live within twenty-six miles of Charing Cross, the most central point in London, could not associate with (or marry) undesirables, and needed permission to grow a beard as it might necessitate a change of warrant card photo. The ubiquitous Form 728 would become our way of requesting or reporting anything for which the thousands of other proformas did not provide a solution. These reports were to be signed off with 'Respectfully submitted,' followed by name, rank, and number.

Despite the disciplined environment at Hendon, which was enforced by a fierce drill sergeant who put the fear of God into us recruits, there were still some rule breakers. It was not uncommon to hear of some poor recruit having the furniture taken from their room if left unlocked for five minutes. Then it would appear in the lift, going up and down until discovered by the victim. There were daredevils who would climb out of their window in the accommodation block and edge their way along the outside of the building, many floors up, to terrify an unsuspecting neighbour by knocking on their window.

Turning in one evening, I'd been in bed for about twenty minutes when I felt my bed levitating to the sound of someone imitating a ghost. 'Whoooo . . . woooh!' I leapt out of bed to find a classmate in stitches as he released the edges of my bed frame. It seems he thought of this prank when he saw me leave my room just before lights out.

We worked hard but also had the time of our lives. There was plenty of learning to do about legislation and procedure. Academically, I was a good B+ student. I could work hard and get an A or at a pace that meant I would pass comfortably and enjoy all aspects of this eighteen-week immersion into my new life. Economy of effort was my chosen path but all students were warned that firearms week was a key milestone and that struggling students found it a challenge as the law was quite messy. As far as I could gather, the law was that if you were of a certain age with a certain firearm, you could walk along Piccadilly with it over your arm. If you were a different age with a different weapon, you'd likely be shot on sight. This was just one example of unfathomable legislation I'd have to navigate in my new career.

Some wouldn't make the grade and firearms week was the one that would weed people out of the course. I studied hard to make sure that I passed; there was no way I was going to get kicked out of police college for a lack of trying. It was a lot of work committing to memory the various definitions, ages, weapon types, and so on. I got an A.

The following week, I read the various definitions of fraud, burglary, and deception, but otherwise enjoyed it and got a B+. Screw all that dedicated time committing definitions to memory. I'd found my level. I'm a B+ guy, I say now a little ashamed of my lack of industry.

Staying at the police college during weekends was like being on holiday with your mates. Most recruits went home and although I did some weekends, I liked staying on campus with a few recruits from different intakes and struck up friendships with a handful of people from groups ahead and behind my course. We wouldn't go far: Hampstead, Golders Green, sometimes into London's lively West End. I was having a great time and enjoying the company of my new friends.

During training, there was a parade every morning in the area immediately in front of the statue of the first police commissioner and creator of the Metropolitan Police, Sir Robert Peel. When on parade we were expected to turn out in pressed uniforms, cleanly shaven or with neatly trimmed beards (like I could grow anything other than fluff!) with shoes shined to a mirror finish on the toecap, or 'bulled' as they were called. To be properly bulled, a small amount of polish is applied to a cotton wool ball with some water or good old-fashioned spit, and then rubbed on the toecap in repeated tiny circular movements to bring the surface to a glass-like shine. Many an hour was spent in the ironing rooms of the accommodation blocks by small groups of recruits pressing uniforms and bulling shoes. It seemed rather pointless at the time and something never to be repeated after graduation, but it was, of course, an exercise in discipline and a shared commitment to high standards. We all did it and those who struggled were helped by those who knew how to do it. Those little tokens of teamwork were all part of the experience I cherish.

There was a physical element to the recruit training course that took place in week eight. It was known as the 'bottle test'[1] and included jumping off the high board at the swimming pool and boxing training all in the same week. The PT instructors were either ex-military hard cases or just your normal everyday psychopaths. One of them was a former professional boxer and this was his week to identify talent for the Metropolitan Police Boxing Team. Standing five foot ten and a half and weighing in at 10.5 stone (if I had some coins in my pocket), I was an unlikely candidate. Boxing was compulsory only for the men (It was 1983!) and so we were told to partner up with someone our own weight and height. Clearly, there had been some preplanning that I hadn't been party to and many had already chosen their dance partners. I was left with the six foot two, broad-shouldered, 14-stone Nigel, which seemed a bit one-sided to me. However, in a moment of subconscious recognition in my reptilian brain, I assessed that he wasn't too keen on this either. The bigger they are, the harder they fall, I told myself.

The bell rang and I went in with everything I had. If it went badly for me, I wanted to hear the words 'plucky little bugger' or something similar to assuage my hurt feelings. After about a minute, the instructor stepped in. He was wiry, athletic, and had a broken nose, every inch the image of a PT instructor and former boxer. I had no idea what was happening during that furious minute, as I'd had my eyes shut for most of it and was giving Nigel a good hiding. Or not, as it turned out.

The instructor said to us, 'Well, you're certainly throwing a lot of punches. Unfortunately, very few are making contact. Try less wind-milling and more boxing.' With that, he beckoned us back together to resume. I looked straight into Nigel's eyes. BANG! Right on the nose. Mine that is. I was seeing stars until it came to a merciful end what seemed like an hour later but was probably only thirty seconds. And with that, my boxing days were over.

I made it comfortably through my recruit training and we all went to a restaurant in Golders Green for the obligatory end-of-course booze-up. One of the course instructors, a sergeant who thought he was funnier that he actually was, told me that I'd make a good police constable (PC), but nothing higher. He was 50 percent correct. I did turn out to be a good PC.

Our families came to our passing out parade, bursting with pride to behold the sight of our course in their No. 1 dress uniforms, complete with ceremonial white gloves. The rain came with perfect timing as we marched past the Peel statue, giving us a good soaking. We'd spent hours getting our uniforms ready and our shoes bulled to perfection, but we looked bedraggled and smelled of wet dogs and regret—surely a fra-grance baked into the blue serge uniforms in the manufacturing stage to motivate all coppers to seek shelter in the event of rainy weather.

Figure 2.1. O'Leary on graduation day. Photo courtesy of author.

CHAPTER 3

The Early Years

THE METROPOLITAN POLICE DISTRICT (MPD), AS ITS TERRITORIAL boundary was known, was divided into twenty-four districts, each designated by a letter of the alphabet. The exceptions were I, O, and U, which were not used for districts. U was assigned to the Special Patrol Group and I to the Air Support Unit helicopter, known by the call sign India 99. Heathrow airport made up the twenty-fourth district, known for some reason as AD. Everyone dreaded being sent there as a new recruit as it wasn't thought of back then as a proper district. I don't know why.

I'd been assigned to Y District, which took in the North London boroughs of Hornsey, Haringey, and Enfield and from there I was posted to Edmonton division within the borough of Enfield, as PC 948Y. I was posted there with Budgie, a nickname earned because he admitted to breeding them as a hobby. He was issued with the warrant number consecutive to mine and we worked the same shift for the first couple of years. He remains a friend to this day.

My mum had given me a few ornaments for my new home to make it a little more . . . well, homely, I suppose. I added a boombox and a coffee maker. I tossed this assorted jumble into a cardboard box and packed my clothes in a suitcase. My worldly possessions were thus contained as the drill sergeant came to supervise our departure from police college. I'd already loaded my suitcase into the bus and was just about to add the cardboard box when he bollocked[1] me for having spent all my money on having a good time instead of buying a proper suitcase. 'A bloody cardboard box?' he grunted in astonishment.

We left Hendon Police College in a bus that snaked its way around London, north and south, dropping us off at our district headquarters to meet our area commanders, the senior officer, and head of one of the twenty-four districts of London's police territory.

At Y District HQ we were also met by our street duties instructors who taught a twelve-week course of induction for new constables under the supervision of more experienced tutor constables, led by Jon, an avuncular, funny, and friendly sergeant. After our stern talking to by the commander, we loaded our possessions into a van and, in my case, wrestled a suitcase and a cardboard box, into the boot of a marked Ford Escort police car. They decided to take me straight to my living quarters to unload. They'd never had a recruit turn up with a big cardboard box before and recommended I use Pickfords removals company next time.

I was allocated a room in single quarters in Northumberland Park Police Section House, Tottenham, which would be my home for the next two years. It was a great way to start out. Free accommodation for new officers of similar age who were all in the same boat.

I stepped out into the streets of North London and was 'puppy walked' by Joe, a constable with eleven years' service. He was as an experienced area car driver (considered the fighter pilot of frontline policing), taking a break from earlies, lates, and night shifts to tutor some rookies during mainly daytime hours.

He had a deadpan, serious appearance and was God-like to us probationer constables. His downturned expression, framed by a handlebar moustache, added to the impression that he was barely tolerating you just so he could get some time off the arduous shift pattern. As we walked through the suburban streets, passing row upon row of 1930s semidetached homes bordering the busy A10 highway, he asked me to give our location. I had no idea; I'd just been walking around looking for something I could leap on to impress him. 'If you needed urgent backup, how would you radio for help?' He had me there. 'Always know the street you're in, at least. If you're going to get beaten up, it helps to know where to send the ambulance.' A point well and truly made. I felt incompetent and suspected he thought he could spend his time more productively if he didn't have this 'wet behind the ears' probationer in tow. We walked

Figure 3.1. Edmonton police station, early 1980s. Photo courtesy of Rowan Healey.

some more, and I clocked every street sign at every turn from that moment on. It was a useful lesson.

Joe explained that there were some landmarks in Edmonton that every copper should know. It helps to get to know the community and understand its needs and issues, he said. As we turned one corner, he told me about the dogs of Edmonton. I was hanging on his every word, my sensei teaching me the secrets of policing wisdom.

He explained that the pair of matching dogs was a well-known site of special interest as police had been called to an incident a year or two before in which one of the dogs had been destroyed. As we reached the exact place, he pointed out two ornamental poodles adorning the gateposts of a very well-kept, semi-detached house. One of the poodles had been re-created following the incident, and it looked as though a young child had made it from papier-mâché.

The head was disproportionately elongated, it had a badly formed snout, and one of its marble eyeballs was higher than the other. I looked in amazement and was trying my hardest to hold back from laughing. I turned to Joe with a look of bewilderment, and he stared back with his deadpan expression, until he broke first into an uproar of laughter. It was like a different person was revealed and we both started walking away giggling like schoolboys at the mangled dog statue. He said he felt bad that a procession of coppers might be noticed turning up here every now and then falling into fits of laughter at the householder's craftwork. It was quite a clever move by Joe. We'd been walking in silence for a few minutes and the wonky dog story broke the tension.

From that moment on, Joe and I got on like a house on fire. He was the funniest person I knew, and I ended up being posted to his shift, along with the avuncular sergeant. Result!

Pranks were part of the informal induction process back then. We were expected to understand and appreciate that if you can't take a joke, you shouldn't be in the job. Modern policing is different and most of this is folklore of the bad old days. It would be against any corporate bullying policy now, but back then we took it as part of the rites of passage that meant we'd be seen as good sports for taking it in the spirit intended. It was about being accepted.

Here of some of the popular pranks of the time, especially designed to fool naive rookies new to the station:

Pharmacy: The custody sergeant would hand the officer a sealed envelope and send them to the pharmacy to collect a prescription for a prisoner in the cells. The victim of the prank, in full police uniform, would hand the envelope over at the pharmacy the note inside reading: 'I'm a little embarrassed to ask, so could you please supply me with a pack of condoms? I'm on a promise tonight. Thanks.'

Advanced cyclist: The police driving courses were very sought after, with the pinnacle being the area car drivers, or advanced course. This was a plum post for a uniform PC on the divisional frontline and the course was known to be exacting and difficult. Part of the training includes several sessions on the Hendon skid pan to hone the skills of car control and, otherwise, driving the length and breadth of England in a fast car, being taught by the very best instructors.

Re-created, in part, in the police station yard was the completely fictitious advanced pedal cycle course. Those being pranked would be told that only the people who qualified would be able to use the station's bicycles. Candidates would be assessed on their ability to control the bicycle through the skid pan, which was a hosed down area of the police station car park. The test consisted of cycling through the wet area at speed and slamming on the brakes. There were also extra marks available for anyone who could cycle up the ramp and into the back of the police van, but I never heard of anyone succeeding.

Counting the ducks in the pond: This was a survey by the Royal Society for the Protection of Birds (RSPB), so we were told, to assess the population of migrating ducks. It was a challenging task when they were all swimming around the surface or flying off. Police would assist the RSPB by helping with the national duck audit and the new officer, notebook and pen in hand, would be tasked with tallying the number of ducks in the park pond, submitting a typed report afterward.

The Heathrow airport contingency plan: Edmonton police station underlies the flight path from the east toward Heathrow airport in the west. One unfortunate new officer was told to climb the fire escape during the evening to implement the contingency plans to assist aircraft in finding the airport as the automatic beacons showing the way had shut down. For around an hour, they waved all aircraft along the route toward Heathrow with a service torch in each hand.

Prisoner's property: This was not a prank for recruits but a testament to the continuity of practices elsewhere that was told to me by a friend and colleague who was a custody sergeant at a different station. This was a routine he used with drunks after they'd spent a night in the cells. He would get them to sign for the return of property taken from them for safekeeping at the time of their arrest and then hand over an old, huge TV set, along with their wallet, change, keys, and any other belongings. The soon-to-be freed detainee would be aghast and in a state of total confusion in their hungover state. Denying the TV was theirs, the sergeant would counter, telling them they had it with them when they were arrested and watch their incredulous expression. Priceless!

The life of a probationer meant they were to expect 'opportunities for development and experience' to come their way. Any officer working the shift while a street duties training course was running would gladly hand over certain tasks to you so that you could learn from them. It was a way of transferring unattractive tasks thinly veiled as a training opportunity. We were expected to accept them with gratitude.

Shoplifters: From every granny that was at the end of her pension and who'd nicked a tin of beans to keep her going, to professional thieves who would fill a trolley and walk out with barefaced cheek. Thanks for the opportunity.

Sudden deaths: Police are required to attend any unexplained death not certified by a doctor to ensure there are no suspicious circumstances or evidence of corporate manslaughter. This was always, for me, an unpleasant and sorrowful task. From every sad, decomposed, lonely, aged death to those taken unexpectedly in their youth. Thanks for the opportunity.

Drunks: These were plentiful, and most would move on when asked by a copper in uniform, but some would be persistent, resistant, or insistent that they were sober. They could be funny or infuriating, from the laddish who'd had one too many to the career drunkard who'd wet himself and lay stinking in a heap. Thanks for the opportunity.

Road accidents: From a minor bump to a serious accident that needed someone to manage the carnage and write the report. Thanks for the opportunity.

These and many other jobs that were weary or involved lots of paperwork would be pointed in our direction. There were always things for the new in service to do that those who were time-served would avoid like the plague.

To ensure we were always in a state of readiness, should we be needed, there was a constant requirement for a cadre of uniformed officers to be trained to deal with riots. The first wave response would be the Special Patrol Group (SPG), a central department with a controversial reputation in the media, but one of admiration among the ranks. If the SPG came to your division for a posting, the criminals went very quiet as they were bound to be nicked. These were very experienced, active, and fearless officers who would ride around in transit van personnel carriers. They did not suffer fools gladly and epitomised robust policing of the time.

There were additional District Support Units that were recruited from the divisions to work full time in a similar role. They were seen as a junior version of the SPG and were the second wave.

Then there was the third wave—the officers who worked at police stations on shifts, or in various other roles, who could be called upon to jump into the spare personnel carrier and become the riot police of last resort. To qualify for this third wave role required officers to be 'shield trained.' If you could carry 17lbs of Perspex with a handle mounted on the back and run ten metres while being pelted with wooden bricks, you'd pass.

Edmonton was considered an 'outer London' posting and the officer demographic was somewhat older than that of an inner London police station. Proximity to the safe and quieter suburbs and home counties where family housing was cheaper meant that there were far fewer officers who wanted to be in a riot situation and were thus adept at avoiding the training. For youngsters like me and my cohort it meant that we attended more shield training than was our share, just so that the division could fulfil its quota. In those days, we went on a miserable journey to a disused warehouse in Greenwich on a personnel carrier from Edmonton, via other divisions, to pick up some more overtrained younger officers. It was to become very familiar. I was going there fortnightly at one stage, and it seemed like I was preparing for Armageddon.

There was a fleet of personnel vehicles, or 'battle buses' as we called them. They were said to have been a cancelled order from somewhere hot and dusty overseas that had discovered their personnel would be likely to fry in them. Air conditioning was still a rare luxury in 1979 when they were registered, and it wasn't fitted to these vehicles. They were quite uncomfortable, noisy, and slow, hot in the summer and freezing in the winter. These vehicles had the aerodynamics of a small house and those who drove them described the steering like setting a course by sail and the gearbox like wiggling a stick in a bag of washing. We went everywhere in them.

When officers are drafted to assist with big events it is known as mutual aid, or just 'aid.' Many aid events, such as protest marches and rallies, take place in Central London, though most football matches were also considered as aid. Battle buses were filled and sent on an awayday from their normal duties.

It was summer 1984, and President Ronald Reagan was on a state visit to the UK. It was my first big 'aid' assignment. I was posted to a line cordon in Piccadilly, and the cavalcade was about to pass along my stretch of the crowd. The atmosphere was electric, and the crowds were out in force to catch a glimpse of Reagan and Thatcher as they drove by. The cavalcade was approaching when my attention was drawn to one of the police outriders about one hundred yards away who was off his motorcycle and wrestling with someone on the ground. His bike was on its side, and I thought he'd been knocked off by a protestor. I later learned that these officers are trained to drop their machine and tackle whatever needs dealing with. It was indeed a random protestor who'd

Figure 3.2. Bedford personnel carrier (Battlebus). Photo courtesy of Lorraine Wyld.

launched himself at Reagan's car, and the outrider had leapt into action. It felt like quite a moment for a naïve probationer officer to witness. Just at that moment, my aid sergeant shouted at me to face the crowd, not the entertainment. My job was to look for threats and deal with them, not to spectate. I turned my head to the crowd. 'Yes, Sarge.' That was quite a public bollocking, and some of the spectators in my section of the crowd were quite amused to witness a policeman being admonished.

The political atmosphere in the UK at that time was quite volatile. Prime Minister Margaret Thatcher decided to take on the striking coal miner's union and their leader, Arthur Scargill. The UK's police forces were going to be deployed to ensure that the law was upheld on the picket lines. Those on strike were allowed to speak to any worker who wished to cross the line and go to work, but they were not allowed to harass or jostle them. The derogatory term 'scab' was shouted by the strikers toward anyone who went to work during the strike. It became intimidating and occasionally violent—a trend that would escalate and require a huge number of police to keep the peace.

At first, only constables who had completed their probationary period of two years would be sent on mutual aid to police the strike, but after a few months that rule was relaxed as they needed numbers. It was going on far longer than had been anticipated and the novelty was wearing off for some officers who'd been away on several tours of duty to police the picket lines. Those who'd been the early pathfinders said they'd enjoyed a reasonable rapport with the miners, as police officers saw themselves as working people, just as the miners did. However, as the atmosphere became more militant and violent, lines were drawn and the miners began to hate us. Especially the 'white shirts,' so identified by the miners because our uniform shirts were white rather than the pale blue of junior ranks in other forces at the time. I'm sure some of my colleagues weren't as well behaved as they should've been. They had no stake in the community and wouldn't have to police these towns and villages when the strike came to an end. There were stories of police officers lighting cigars with banknotes as they drove past the miners in an obvious act of provocation. Police were earning plenty of overtime while the miners were on low strike pay and using communal feeding halls. Some jokes don't age well, and we now know how families suffered during the strikes.

Within our serials (as each mobile unit was called), there was a great team spirit and, for most of the time, a bit of a laugh during the boredom, which was punctuated by occasional outbursts of violent protest. During one of the postings, we were billeted in a military dormitory and the canteen was in a huge marquee where we were fed and watered before being sent out to work. I'd overslept by just a few minutes and hadn't heard my colleagues plotting to teach me a lesson. They'd borrowed some industrial-sized cling film from the catering staff and before I knew it, I awoke to the conspiracy taking place: wrapping me tightly to my army issue camp bed. I was powerless as they lifted me up, bed and all, and carried me aloft into the marquee, which was full of about two hundred officers from different forces around the country awaiting deployment. A cheer went up as I, the sacrificial probationer, was offered up to the voluptuous canteen lady who approached with a large carving knife and made a cut in the cling film directly where it would reveal my embarrassingly small manhood (they all go like that where we're terrified, apparently). In her best pantomime style, she asked the audience 'Shall I?' 'YEEEEESSSS' was the obvious and loud reply. Again, she asked, 'Shall I?' clearly hamming it up now. 'YEEEESSSS' was the even louder reply at which she inserted a can of instant whipped cream and gave it a good squirt. There were people who'd pay good money for that in London's red-light district, I thought, trying to take my mind off the humiliation. As the cheers died down, I was freed from my cocoon to cries of 'Good sport, mate' as if in any part of it I'd been a willing volunteer. I never slept in again.

Later that day, things were getting a bit lively on the picket line. It had been tense from the start of the day and the miners looked and sounded up for a scrap. A single-decker bus was used to pick up working miners from a secret rendezvous point, which changed each day. This vehicle looked like something from a *Mad Max* dystopian movie, with makeshift metal screens along the entire length of both sides to protect the windows from the inevitable shower of bricks, bottles, and stones that would greet it as it drove across the picket line. It arrived at speed and ran the gauntlet of missiles and angry jeering by the mob that lay in wait.

Police closest to the action had been hit by collateral missiles that missed the bus and showered them instead. They moved in to make arrests and it all kicked off.

There were so many miners and so many cops, it was like having a fight in a crowded train carriage, everyone squeezed in a small space together. Missiles started flying. We were wearing ordinary beat helmets with the straps down to keep them in place in order to protect our heads from the projectiles. We all had one eye on what was happening in front of us and one eye above the crowd so that we could duck the missiles when they came our way. Then, suddenly, and seemingly in slow motion, a plastic bag was coming toward me through the air. It twisted and rolled through the sky, and I thought it might miss me, but as it continued in flight, I was locked shoulder to shoulder with my colleagues. All I could do was bow my head slightly so that the top of my helmet took the impact, which it did. The gold and red print logo of the Sunblest bread bag passed before my eyes and released its cargo of fresh, warm urine all down the back of my neck. A distant cheer went up, obviously from the missile launcher and assumed recently relieved miner and friends. It was one of those days.

I spent eight weeks policing the miner's strike before it came to an end. It started as something of an adventure but soon lost any sense of fun. I was glad to get back to a routine shift pattern at Edmonton.

I was living in single quarters in Tottenham, known as Section House SQ34. Populated by a mix of mainly younger officers, with the occasional domestic refugee pending a divorce, the section house was a residence for police officers where the rent was paid in lieu of an allowance that would otherwise be part of the pay packet. Many residents, like me, were not from London, hence the need for digs. Everyone had their own room, though we shared bathrooms, communal TV lounges, a gym, and a canteen. It was a great place to live for a couple of years, and with many girlfriends and boyfriends taking up informal residence it was something of a frat house. Parties would be arranged at the slightest excuse and were well refreshed, both in liquid offerings and the constant new arrivals of people coming off shift to join in. One such party came to an end when someone got carried away and lit fireworks. Indoors. Idiot!

After a couple of years in the job I was posted to Southgate, the leafy and rather wealthy suburb of Edmonton division. For a young man keen on fighting crime and saving the world, it was deathly quiet sometimes. On the upside, I'd passed my police driving course so would be mobile now. Three weeks of driver training and a couple of exams at the driver training school at Hendon were necessary to qualify you to drive a marked 1.0 litre Austin Metro (known as panda cars), or an unmarked saloon car such as an Astra or Cavalier in those days. Every PC wanted to get this course under their belt as it meant more freedom. The course itself was run by skilled instructors who were actually very good at driving progressively, yet safely.

What I couldn't understand was the reasoning behind our marked pandas not being equipped with a blue light. Some out of touch policy wonk at the Yard had decided that too many standard course drivers were trying to emulate the more qualified advanced area car drivers, so one way of putting a stop to it would be to delete safety equipment. There were many occasions when a blue light would've helped to keep us safe on our way to a call or at a scene, but it was better that we all were denied that than punish the few that broke the rules, eh?

One early foggy Sunday morning shift in Southgate I was on patrol in my panda when a couple in a car coming the other way drew up alongside me and reported that there was some kind of parade where children were being marched along the road. They'd noticed just in time to avoid a collision. Who in their right mind would walk kids along the road in the fog? I relayed the information on the radio, in case there were any other units nearby, but knew it was unlikely on a Sunday morning as we were thin on the ground. Try as I might, I couldn't catch up to get in contact with this march. It was too foggy to drive fast, especially as I knew what I might meet ahead. I had no blue light, no siren, just some stripes along the side of the car and a police sign on the roof. I was desperate to get to the march to put a stop to it but couldn't.

I eventually caught up with the march as it came to a halt and was relieved that everyone made it safely back to the church, from where the march had been arranged. There were thirty or so children of ages from about six upward.

I spoke to the church leader to offer some advice and was told that I was being arrogant and unreasonable. One of the congregants told me he was a retired detective and that I didn't know what I was talking about. It was exasperating that they couldn't see what the problem was. I submitted a report about children coming to the notice of police, but never heard anything about it ever again.

A couple of months later, there was a tragic accident in Birmingham where a group of children had been marching on a road in good visibility, when a speeding car hit the tail end of the parade. There were fatalities and serious injuries. It haunted me for a while that the same situation could've happened in my foggy scenario, to the extent that I had a recurring nightmare in which I couldn't quite save them from the same fate.

SUDDEN DEATH

One day shift, I was called to a very nice address in Southgate. The house looked like that of an accomplished professional: well presented, a neatly trimmed lawn out front with seasonal flowers, and pruned roses around the arch of the front porch—it was middle-class suburban perfection. This houseowner was a man in his late fifties or early sixties. He explained that his son had been suffering from mental illness for more years than he cared to remember and now, in his early twenties had taken his own life. We talked for a bit. Dad was emotionally under control, and it almost appeared that he was relieved the constant torment had ended, but of course, he was devastated as any father would be.

I was shown into the son's room. It was like walking through the wardrobe into Narnia. Leaves from the tree outside had blown in through the open window and the thin ends of the branches extended their reach across the windowsill and into the room, which looked like it hadn't seen a lick of paint in years. The walls were adorned with scribblings and messages in small writing and drawings were everywhere.

The young man hung from a thin rope attached to the window frame, reaching to his bed where he lay half upright. It was such a sad sight. I looked back at the dad and his expression was enough to suggest 'See what I mean?' Dealing with death is part of the job and to be expected, but it's different when it happens to young people. I attended quite a few deaths of elderly, and it was easier to manage the thought process of dealing with those scenarios where a person has lived a full life, but the memorable ones I dealt with were those young people taken way before their time. I remember them now, decades later.

RINGERS

Keeping myself busy and proactive, I'd learned about the prevalence of stolen cars driving around with false number plates, which are known as 'ringers.' A slightly more thorough roadside check could surface the true identity of these vehicles. I'd stopped a car and called the control room for the chassis, or vehicle identification number (VIN), to be checked on the Police National Computer (PNC). The well understood phrase from the radio operator came over the channel, 'Yankee sierra three one, are you free to speak, over?' I stepped slightly out of earshot while my partner kept an eye on the driver. 'Go ahead, over.'

'PNC shows it as stolen from Tottenham two weeks ago.' That was my first direct stop arrest for a ringer, but it wouldn't be my last.

I was posted back at Edmonton for a few weeks to balance the teams across the division as a few officers were on leave or other postings for a while. I was radio operator (front seat passenger) in call sign Yankee Four, Edmonton's area car during the 3:00 p.m.–11:00 p.m. late shift. Gary was my driver, and he spotted a local hot list criminal drive past. We turned around to follow him and he sped off. Lights on, siren on, and we were in pursuit. I was giving a commentary over the radio so that other units could hear where we were headed and converge, but no other units were close enough by the time the chase ended, just a few streets away. We stopped in a car park of a tower block on one of the local estates and as operator it was my job to get out and apprehend the driver, which I did with enthusiasm. POW! It was boxing week at Hendon all over again. I never saw the punch coming. It floored me. By the time I got up to give chase, he'd ran into the tower block and behind the buzzer-controlled door.

Other units started appearing, including a District Support Unit van with full crew. We found out very quickly who our boxer was and raided his flat in the tower block. He wasn't found, so I went back to the car and searched it to find a huge Rambo knife on the passenger seat. It was sharp, had a serrated edge, and was ready to use. My black eye emerged over the next hour and I was grateful he'd decided to punch me, rather than stab me.

Months later, at Crown Court, he was charged with assault and possession of an offensive weapon but was acquitted by the jury. Police officers accept the fact that they might be assaulted now and then, but we expect in return, that those responsible will answer for it. The job sucked that day.

Riot!

Some of the residents at the section house worked at Tottenham Police Station, the division next door to mine, and they were bringing back stories of increased tension on the Broadwater Farm Estate. Built in the late 1960s by the local authority, the estate is a series of brutal concrete buildings linked by labyrinth walkways, alleys, and decks providing places to gather. The buildings are named after World War II airfields such as Tangmere, Lympne, Manston, and Northolt, among others, I assume as a nostalgic and patriotic nod to the brave pilots and crew of the Royal Air Force.

Within a couple of years of opening, by the early 1970s, severe problems were starting to emerge such as water leaks, pest infestations, and electrical faults caused by poor design and lack of maintenance. Prospective residents refused offers of accommodation and existing tenants were desperate to move out. A government review of the Broadwater Farm Estate condemned it as such poor quality that demolition was the best option. Residents became increasingly confrontational with the local authority, who tried a half-hearted redevelopment plan that was underfunded and confirmed the estate's terrible reputation.

Buildings were linked by elevated decks where shops and amenities were located. This design reduced flood risks from the nearby river, but also meant that no one walked around at ground level, decreasing a sense of community. These walkways and decks created dark, isolated areas that became hotspots from crime and robbery, providing an easy escape route for criminals, which led to an increased police presence, including the Special Patrol Group, sent in to confront the robbery problem.

There was around a fifty-fifty mix of black and white people, but the resident's association was all white and was seen as distant from the day-to-day challenges of the whole community. A youth association was established and supported by black residents, especially in its challenge of the police in relation to perceived harassment of local youths and black residents of the estate. Rival associations were established by different groups with assumed, undefined authority to represent the community.

Of nearly four thousand residents, the unemployment rate was over 40 percent and children living there were underachieving. Several improvement initiatives were launched and achieved little.

In the summer of 1985, some of my coresidents at the section house who were permanent beat officers for the Broadwater Farm Estate reported that residents were feeling nervous. Small incidents were blowing up out of proportion. Assaults on officers were increasing and trouble was brewing.

Meanwhile, in South London, it all kicked off in Brixton. Over the next few days, police in vast numbers were sent in personnel carriers to provide riot-trained serials to quell the rioting and, eventually, it calmed down. I found myself on an aid serial to supplement patrols in the area immediately after the riots had ended.

There was a quiet eeriness about the streets of Brixton, and you could've cut the tense atmosphere with a knife. We were given very short walking beats to patrol, and it was more about providing a visible police presence than anything else. A car cruised by with every seat occupied— young men staring at me with contempt. There's something not right about them, I thought, so I called up on the radio suggesting they might be worth a stop to find out what they were up to. A few minutes later an inspector was walking toward me, and he didn't look too impressed. Oh, hang on, I thought. I remembered him as the sergeant who gave me my first bollocking during President Reagan's visit. He'd been promoted to inspector and proceeded to admonish me for saying 'well worth a stop' over the radio. 'Don't you understand the tensions? This is a tinderbox; it could go up again at any moment,' he said. 'I was just doing my job, guv. I genuinely thought they deserved a pull,' I replied, as if that made a difference. It didn't. I was to do little policing, if any. Just be there and that's it.

I wondered if he'd remembered me from the Reagan visit, or whether he was always admonishing junior officers. Now that he's an inspector, doesn't he have a sergeant to issue his bollockings? Maybe he just likes doing it? Of course, his judgment of the situation was right, and I vowed to do, or say, nothing for the rest of the posting.

Back at the section house, my friends were bringing back more stories of increased tension on the Broadwater Farm Estate in Tottenham. One of the doorstep milk delivery drivers reported that he hadn't had any empty bottles returned for a while and the beat officers found crates of empties stashed in a bin storage area on the ground floor of one of the residential blocks. The dedicated beat officers for the estate kept a daily diary in the station, but it went missing, and the PCs felt it had been deliberately removed by senior officers for political reasons as it gave a clear daily audit of the increased tension on the estate, which had been going on for weeks.

The following day, one of my section house mates, who was one of the community beat officers, was badly assaulted as he patrolled near the estate. He had responded to a call from the public, which was an ambush. When he arrived, a gathering of young men surrounded him, and he was badly beaten. He was taken to the hospital and underwent emergency surgery to remove his spleen. We all knew that the inevitable riot was coming.

It was a quiet, sunny Sunday afternoon in early October, and I was the late turn radio operator on Yankee Three, the area car for Southgate. I was barely into my first hour on duty when one of the sergeants called me over the radio directing me to get over to Edmonton with my riot kit. The third wave had been invoked and I was to be part of a serial being sent to deal with a riot that had just blown up on the Broadwater Farm Estate.

A local young man by the name of Floyd Jarrett, who lived a short distance from the estate, was arrested having given a false name when stopped in a car with a forged tax disc. His home was later searched by four officers, during which his mother, Cynthia Jarrett, collapsed and died.

There was a small demonstration outside Tottenham Police Station the following day and it passed off largely peacefully, apart from a bottle thrown at the station window. However, later that day, police officers in a van attending an emergency call on the Broadwater Farm Estate were ambushed and attacked in an incident that triggered the largest riot in UK history at that time.

I was twenty-two years old and four days away from two years of service, meaning that I was still a probationer constable. I was in a transit van with a team of shield-trained officers from Enfield and Edmonton divisions. We rode toward Tottenham in silent, nervous anticipation. We knew we were headed for danger, thinking about it the whole way there. No one spoke much except for the minimum perfunctory discussion to check we all had our kit and would be ready to join the fray.

We pulled up on a street just outside the Broadwater Farm Estate, next to a few other police vehicles near the front line. We could hear the commotion as we kitted up in black, heavy, flameproof overalls and our dark-blue NATO-style riot helmets. We each grabbed a full-length shield as we headed toward the action. As we turned the corner, we saw, heard, and felt the ferocity of the riot. We were on the junction of the main entrance to the estate and saw hundreds of people in maximum riot mode. The sounds were almost medieval: shouting, the clashing of stone against shields, and fire whooshing up from the petrol bombs that landed around us. As we were trained to do, I locked shields with one of my crew to form a three-man squad next to other three-man squads, creating lines with formation gaps between the ranks.

The rioters seemed to have an endless supply of material, ripping up paving if they needed more. Many of those missing milk bottles made their appearance as Molotov cocktails that lit up the scene as evening turned to dusk and then full darkness.

A senior officer blew his police whistle to order a charge, irritating the rioters who increased their intensity of throwing stuff at us. Police whistles were, I thought, a quaint traditional novelty of a bygone era kept for decorative reasons. I'd never heard one used in anger before.

I was on the very front line, and saw an officer to my right fall forward, the crowd surging toward him to attack. The group of officers nearest to him countercharged, and my squad moved forward in support. Those officers took some stick and were beaten and pelted by rioters. I remember thinking how brave the officers were right in that moment as they were clearly outnumbered, had nothing to throw, and were most certainly all in danger. The countercharge had made the crowd retreat just enough for the PC to be rescued by dragging him back behind our lines, even though the rioters tried to get to him right until the last moment before he was safe.

One inventive rioter had taped a machete to a long, flexible pole and was taking swipes over the shields to aim at whatever he could reach. *CRACK!* It dug into my riot helmet and felt as if he was tugging it off my head as he pulled it out and over the heads of the rioters, taking another swipe. We had no means to go on the offensive against the rioters, just the shields to protect ourselves from the material they were throwing at us, and they were well-stocked and well-prepared. Our role was to contain the crowd and hold the line.

I took a slab of concrete to the back, and it knocked the wind out of me. I wanted to collapse as it felt like a heavyweight boxer had landed a kidney punch on me, but I'd already seen the danger of being vulnerable to attack on the ground. I gasped for air and held on to the handles of the riot shield.

CRACK! The shield was almost shattered, and I didn't quite know what it was. *CRACK!* I thought it sounded like pellets rebounding off the shield. *CRACK!* Not pellets, that's shotgun fire. I could see the shooter on the first-floor deck of the block in front of us and saw the flash from the barrel as another round was set off. A millisecond later, and the shot reached us again. Some officers were hit, and there were some journalists behind the police serials who took shotgun pellets to the head and body, one of them losing an eye.

As this continued, an officer appeared suddenly beside me, kneeling down and using my shield to give him just a little cover for his shoulder. He was holding a baton gun and was pointing it toward the shooter. 'I have clear line of sight and I can take him, guv,' I heard him say on his radio. There was no action. He repeated this call two or three times before withdrawing and leaving us, disappearing back from wherever he came. It would've been the first time that baton rounds had been fired on the UK mainland and the commanders wouldn't give the order. We suspected that it was because it would represent a watershed in the history of policing in the UK and they didn't want to be associated with such a significant turning point.

At around midnight, we were relieved by another serial, and we got back to our van and drove to the command operations base at Y District HQ, Wood Green. There was row upon row of police vans full of officers awaiting their turn on the front line. I saw the commissioner, Sir Kenneth Newman, for the first and only time in my service, speaking with a bunch of higher-ups. I hoped they had a plan. Sir Kenneth was previously chief constable of the Royal Ulster Constabulary and had plenty of experience in managing public order in Northern Ireland.

After several hours on the front line, we were offered refreshments at the catering van, but they only had limited supplies left. I remember drinking lukewarm instant chicken soup and eating custard cream biscuits as I tried to find a phone to call home. Mum would've seen it on the TV, and I wanted her to know I was OK. I told her I was on standby and unlikely to be used as this kind of thing is done by trained riot squads, not local officers like me. I hoped she was reassured by my little white lie.

We went to a police stores lorry and were told to hand in our shields and helmets, all of which were damaged. The storeman looked at my helmet and said, 'You were lucky' and then showed me the top of the helmet, which had a deep cut from the machete. It was so damaged he was able to flex the top of the helmet open at the point of impact. He gave me a brand-new replacement and I swapped my pockmarked long shield for a new one. I was glad to have done my bit and was pleased we'd been stood down. Or so I thought.

Instead, were sent back to the front line. I was at a loss to understand why, after several gruelling hours, that another of the plentiful rested and fresh units weren't despatched. An error by the commanders in the fog of war, perhaps.

News was spreading that a serial had been attacked on the other side of the estate and that there were serious injuries and an officer down. 'There, but for the grace of God, go I,' someone said.

We went back to the same spot on the front line. Maybe it was a coping mechanism, or just a very rapid example of conditioning, but there seemed to be a rhythm of intense attack with bricks, bottles, and petrol bombs, followed by a senior officer blowing their whistle to order us to press forward and then retreat when it became too intense again. It wasn't as terrifying as it had been, probably because I'd become used to the back and forth, the noise, and the physicality of it. The hours went by very quickly.

Dawn broke to bring daylight back to a now dystopian scene. Cars were burned to their metal frames and the air was thick with the acrid smell of melted plastic that caught the back of your throat. A house on the junction we'd been holding was burned, its roof and windows totally blown out. With every step there was a crunch underfoot from debris and broken glass. Paving slabs had been pulled up to provide ammunition for the missiles that had been thrown at us.

Our faces were dirty and clammy, and it felt like sweat was steaming off our backs, such was the physical exertion we'd endured all night. I was exhausted but didn't feel the slightest bit like I needed to sleep, probably because of the adrenalin still running through my body, shocked by the experience, and of the urban battlefield before me.

How was the area going to recover from this, I thought? Later that day, I would be able to go back to my room at the section house, but for residents of the estate this was where they lived, and they would have to suffer this in the place they called home. I don't mean the rioters, but the elderly, the families. Where would things go from here?

I noticed a fresh serial in a pristine personnel carrier arrive at the entrance to the estate where we'd spent the night containing the rioters. As a policewoman in riot gear stepped out of the van, the press swarmed around her. In the mid-1980s, it was still quite novel to see women officers in some of the male-dominated areas of police work, and the press knew a story angle when they saw one. No criticism of the officer, but I doubt anyone would take a second look if the same thing happened today, as women officers serve ably in all roles and ranks policing has to offer.

During the night, we'd heard about a serial on the other side of the estate getting into trouble when they had gone into the main block to protect firefighters who were tackling a blaze. There were about fifty rioters who rushed the scene, chasing firefighters and the police officers from serial 502, who ran for their lives, but PC Keith Blakelock fell and was surrounded by a machete and knife-wielding mob who set upon him. When his colleagues saw what was happening, they turned back and went to rescue him, along with the firefighters who joined them. When they found Keith, he had been stabbed over forty times and had a six-inch knife embedded in his neck.

Others in his serial were attacked too, leading to life-changing injuries for PC Richard Coombes, who had his neck cut open, suffered a five-inch-long cut to his face, and broken upper and lower jaws. More than thirty years later, he was still suffering the effects of the attack, including constant pain, poor hearing and eyesight, epileptic fits, nightmares, and memory loss that renders him unable to read or drive.

Another officer, Michael Shepherd, was assaulted with a metal spike. He had collapsed next to Richard using his shield to protect them both from part of the crowd who were attacking them ferociously. Firefighter Trevor Stratford received spinal injuries, and PC Max Roberts had been stabbed.

During the rescue, police and firefighters confronted the rioters, who dispersed, allowing them to help their injured colleagues to safety. However, Keith was already fatally injured and died in the ambulance on way to the North Middlesex Hospital.

Sergeant Dave Pengelly, who single-handedly fought to hold the crowd away from Keith and Richard after they fell, said that when he and the other officers got back to the safety of their van, 'We just sat there, numb with shock, and life was never the same again for any of us.' He would later receive the George Medal, awarded for acts of great bravery in recognition of the way he conducted himself with total disregard for his own safety on that night. All members of the serial and firefighters were awarded the Queen's Gallantry Medal, posthumously for Keith.

The local MP, Bernie Grant, would remark later that the police got a well-deserved 'bloody good hiding,' though he later backtracked on this saying he was quoting what others had said. The feeling within the police community was that this was wholly insensitive in the context of a murdered officer. Keith was a community beat officer, husband, and father. He was a brave public servant and deserved nothing of the sort.

A couple of weeks after the riot, someone thought there should be counseling provided to the officers, but there were few, if any, trained therapists to do it. It fell to one of the divisional sergeants back at Edmonton. He was a very likeable chap who cheerily greeted me and asked if I was one of those who were on a serial that night. I confirmed I was, and he said, 'You're OK aren't you?' to which I said that I was. Therapy complete. Today, there would be much more attention to well-being and mental health, but that was how it was back then. I've no complaints and certainly have no criticism of the affable sergeant, given such an unenviable task.

After the riots, a dedicated incident room was established at Southgate police station to investigate the long list of crimes that had taken place. Detectives were drafted from other divisions, and even other forces, to assist. I was on desk duty at Southgate one day, covering the public counter, when an out-of-town detective presented himself to report to the incident room. I did a double take and remembered him as the very same detective that investigated my bike robbery some years before when I was a kid. I'm pretty sure he didn't remember me, but he took the time to have a chat with me, after which I blamed him for my career choice, and he seemed quite flattered. Small world, eh?

In the subsequent reviews carried out after the riot, one of the lines of inquiry examined strategy and tactics for public order policing, where they discovered that the front line riot officers were trained in techniques, drills, and tactics, but senior officers were not. There was a vague assumption that seniority of rank equated to wisdom in all domains of police leadership, which was such an outdated way of thinking, but it helped me to understand why the senior officer on the ground that night persisted in blowing his whistle to command a charge of the crowd when our training had required containment as the main objective.

The outcome of the review was to establish a transformation in the training of public order commanders so that only those trained and qualified to lead in such situations were able to take command. Another outcome was the introduction of the gold, silver, bronze command model.

This command structure is not dependent on rank but gives the gold commander responsibility for setting the strategy, silver for commanding the tactical response with bronze commanders responsible for tactical areas of command, such as crime, intelligence, specific territories, community liaison, and so on.

This command structure is still in place today across all emergency services and replicated in other public and private businesses involved in emergency response.

BACK TO BUSINESS AS (UN)USUAL

Among police legends, on average, an officer will catch a burglar during patrol once in nine years. Mine came early. I was in uniform with Dick on night duty, but in an unmarked car. We drove through the well-kept residential streets of Winchmore Hill and had just pranked a colleague on foot patrol by stopping short of him, turning off our lights, and darting down a side street. Naturally, he thought we were suspicious, and he called up excitedly on the radio, describing the vehicle and occupants. I replied, 'Were the occupants particularly handsome? Over.' There was a short silence on the radio, followed by, 'They looked like a couple of complete bastards. Over,' appreciating he'd been had.

As the excitement of the false alarm passed and the radio became silent again, we meandered slowly through the streets and came to a halt at a junction. We stared at two figures walking toward us and then stop. As our eyes adjusted to the darkness, we saw that one of them was carrying a TV . . . at three o'clock in the morning! It was like a Mexican standoff, but they blinked first, and the TV was dropped to the ground as they legged it away. With the advantage of a Ford Escort to give us the first twenty yards, they were caught, and we discovered, before the homeowners did, that the burglary had been executed silently nearby. Amazingly, the TV still worked, and they were reunited with it in exchange for a statement over a cup of tea. The prisoners were handed over to the burglary team the next morning and admitted to several other break-ins, helping the clear up rate for those interested in the performance figures. We had earned our corn that night.

Apart from our burglary arrests, the rest of night duty that week was painfully dull. There was an old song called '123 O'Leary,' made somewhat more well-known by the musical crooner Des O'Connor back in the 1960s. Once, when bored, as a bit of a wind up, I typed out a 728 (a general report form) asking if I could change my number from 948 to 123 to strike a more musical tone with the public and do my bit for community relations. It was supposed to go to my sergeant in the expectation that he should ask whether I had anything better to do and add a little light reading to his otherwise mundane pile of paperwork. Knowing the tune, he said it had given him a chuckle, but had indeed made him wonder if I didn't have anything better to do.

Back on day duty, I was on the area car with Gary again. He was an active copper, and I knew we'd be in for a good day, being proactive to find our own work if the calls weren't keeping us busy. However, before long there was a call for assistance from an officer who'd responded to a robbery at a pharmacy by a suspect armed with a knife who was now threatening everyone in his way. We were on our way in the area car, blue lights and siren blaring, like Moses parting the sea of traffic in our path. Over the radio an update came in that a policewoman had just encountered the robber a few streets away and he'd tried to stab her before he made off through a nearby alleyway. We arrived and all the responding units, in an impressive demonstration of teamwork, surrounded the area where we thought he might have gone to ground.

Gary and I started to search the rear yards of a row of shops, opening one back gate at a time, like a terrifying game of hide-and-seek. Suddenly, we opened the right gate (or wrong gate, depending on your disposition) and our suspect made a leap forward from his hiding place, pointing the knife at us and lunging toward us with it.

I was armed with only a light wooden truncheon, which had only been used, so far in my career, to break a window at a sudden death situation where an elderly person hadn't been seen for a few days. On this day, it would be used to smash a knife-wielding robber across the hand, elbows, or anywhere I could cause him pain.

I was unaware at that moment that I was doing my Hendon boxing windmill again—lots of blows, few of which hit the target. I decided to abandon the useless truncheon. As Gary grabbed one of the suspect's arms, I grabbed the other and we managed to get him to the ground. He was strong and desperate to get away—it felt like he had the strength of a dozen men, but we managed to get the knife out from his grip, and I saw it spin across the yard out of his reach. Now we could focus on restraining him, but he was too strong for us to get an arm into a position to handcuff him. Suddenly, a black, shiny toecap joined the struggle and stepped on the suspect's arm pinning it to the ground. The cavalry had arrived, and other officers moved in to assist us in restraining him. Eventually, he was under control and led away in handcuffs to the station van. We recovered the knife and our breath as Gary and I congratulated each other with mutual thanks and backslapping. Except, Gary said, about the truncheon, 'You must've hit me on my arm a dozen times, you nutter. You were like a mad dog.' And so, for a while afterward, I was known as Mad Dog O'Leary.

I returned to Southgate and was back on day duty a couple of days later and received a call to a serious accident. I was in a single crewed in panda car and quite near, so I made my way. It was a clear and sunny day in this well-to-do suburb. I was about two hundred yards out from the accident when I spotted the mayhem and the remains of two vehicles as if they'd been ripped apart by an explosion. As I got little closer, I could see bodies on the ground and noticed people standing in the road looking toward me, waving. I knew they would feel a sense of relief at the arrival of the first vehicle from the emergency services and from seeing a police officer who would take charge, which I did. Everyone was upset, excitable, and frantically calling out with information about what had happened, who was hurt, where the driver was last seen, explaining this was a hit-and-run. One of the cars had jumped the red light and the driver and sole occupant had run away. My copper's instinct was to catch the bad guy, but there were bodies everywhere. A car coming the other way on the green light had been hit side on, at speed, by the offending vehicle, wrecking both cars. There were people trapped in the victim's vehicle, and they were silent. There was no fire or smell of fuel. Traffic had stopped in all directions and the scene was fairly safe from moving vehicles.

I prioritized the casualties and checked the driver's pulse—they were dead. I checked the front seat passenger—also dead. Two younger occupants had been thrown from the car. One of them was badly injured, but there was pulse, and she was breathing. Someone was trying to provide first aid, so I ask them to monitor her breathing and pulse while I checked others. Another young body was on the ground, being tended to by people who'd stopped to help. I couldn't find a pulse, so I decided to give CPR a go and began with three short breaths followed by heart compressions. Once you start you must continue, and I'd been there for a few minutes when the ambulance arrived. By then, others in my team had arrived as well, and all three blue light services were dealing with other aspects of the scene. I was stood down from CPR by the ambulance crew and started the routine of taking accounts of witnesses and writing notes about what I'd seen on arrival. Postaccident efforts began to return the scene to normality and the debris was cleared away. Three souls were lost that day. My efforts at CPR hadn't made a difference, but I tried. The driver of the other car was arrested a couple of days later by colleagues who tracked him down.

Working in an outer London division meant that serious road accidents went with the territory, unlike inner divisions where the traffic was slower and high-speed accidents less likely. Edmonton division was crisscrossed by A10 Great Cambridge Road and A406 North Circular Road. Both had mainly forty mile per hour speed limits but were open to some very fast driving and spectacular crashes.

On one night duty shift, it had poured with rain, leading to several serious and two fatal accidents. I was in my panda car and attended a fatal single vehicle accident on the North Circular Road. It was a seventeen-year-old lad in his first car who had lost control and hit a tree on the central reservation. I went with the ambulance to the emergency treatment room in the North Middlesex Hospital where they worked frantically to save him. I stood to the side and out of the way but remained for evidential continuity, which meant that the same officer who saw him taken from the scene was witness to the doctor declaring him deceased, but only about an hour after they had started their battle to save his life. I noted the time and otherwise said nothing. I was the outsider in the room, a metaphoric grim reaper standing in the corner, all black in my police uniform.

His parents were away on holiday somewhere on the south coast and I thought of the poor bugger who had to find them and break the dreadful news. The following morning, when the parents had returned from their holiday, I arranged to pick up the father and take him to the mortuary to identify his son. No parent should be faced with this. A combination of poor communication and a lack of experience on my part meant that the mortuary wasn't ready for the visit. The deceased was in a body bag, and to my horror, was wheeled out on a trolley. Dad looked at his son and with quiet dignity made the legally required confirmation to me that it was the body of his son. We drove the father home in absolute silence. I had no words, but it's burned forever in my memory as one of the saddest events I dealt with. That poor man.

Some policy wonk at the Yard decided it would look like we had more police officers than we actually did if they were dressed in high visibility yellow over jackets when on aid. I liked our smart dark-blue uniforms and thought the now ubiquitous 'hi viz' jackets made us look like road sweepers. I have nothing against road sweepers by the way. They do a great job. It's just that they're not expected to carry authority by the smartness of their appearance.

It was a Saturday and that meant football duty, which some would see as a perk of the job. I wasn't as keen as it all seemed a bit too emotional for what should've been a day of sport.

There's nothing better for taking the fun out of things like a threat from one set of supporters to kick the other supporters heads in and make every effort to keep their promise. It's so tiresome. I wasn't in the mood, and it was now policy to wear the yellow jackets so that the bosses in charge of policing the match could see where their officers were. Perfectly reasonable, I know, I just wasn't a fan of any of it and I was grumpy. The officer in charge of policing that day was a legendary chief superintendent who was not to be messed with. I was petulant with one of his inspectors who had ordered us to put barriers out because the people who were supposed to do it had just stacked them on the road and gone for tea. In my foul mood, full of self-importance and judgment, I muttered something along the lines of 'looking like a road sweeper and acting like a manual worker,' which the inspector heard and reported me to the match commander. A bit of an overreaction I thought, and the match commander had little patience with it, asking why the inspector was troubling him with it. 'If you can't deal with him, send him back to his division,' he said. I was the first officer in memory of an Arsenal game to be sent back to division in disgrace.

A colleague from Edmonton came to fetch me in a panda car. I went into the control room to present myself to the sergeant. Luckily, it was the avuncular street duties sergeant who laughed it off saying that the inspector was well-known for being a no-good shiny arse[2] and to forget it. It would all blow over, apparently. But not before some proper ribbing from everyone on my shift about me throwing a childish hissy fit at being asked to move some barriers. I just had to suck it up.

The following Monday, I was summoned to see my chief superintendent for a top grade bollocking. I entered his office and stood straight to attention like a soldier about to be court-martialed. He looked at me as if I was a curiosity at a museum. 'Relax, man. It's not that bad,' he assured me. He invited me to sit down and then spent a few minutes asking me how things were on the front line and that my shift inspector had told him that I was a good and highly motivated officer with a good arrest record, etc. I was quite pleased to hear that, and it seemed to balance the chief's opinion of me. He said he'd spoken with the match commander, who was an old friend of his, and that the inspector on the day had been struggling to cope with some of the pressures of the job. I wasn't to think too badly of him, and it had been suggested that we all put this behind us and forget it ever happened. This was turning out to be the best bollock-ing ever! We chatted for a few more minutes about the job and where I saw my career going. He was very supportive, and I was thankful for not being on a discipline board and for the opportunity to have a tête-à-tête with the boss. As I got up to leave, he said as a by the way, 'Your request to change your divisional number. 123 O'Leary! Des O'Connor wasn't it? Great idea. Get some numerals from the store and change it right away. I'll get the admin staff to do the paperwork.' It seemed that my sergeant had the last laugh on this one and had submitted my prank report as if a serious request.

My inspector was waiting, somewhat nervously, for me in the canteen. I emerged with a look of confusion on my face. 'Well, what's going to happen to you?' he said. I recounted the experience and thanked him for putting in a good word for me. That day I became PC 123 O'Leary. The job works in mysterious ways.

I was sent on another driving course to enable me to drive the station van, which amounted to a few days at Hendon mainly spent on driving a transit van backward with precision through cones. I got top marks and returned to division as a qualified police van driver. The movie *Top Gun* was a recent hit and one of my colleagues started calling me 'Top Van.' in recognition of qualifying with distinction. In case any Hollywood bosses read this and want to shoot a movie about an old van driver going back to training school to teach some youngsters how it's done, I am available for casting.

I was on night duty with Dick, again. We were in plainclothes in an unmarked car and decided to go looking for trouble, which is a challenge in the quiet suburbs. In the posh streets of Southgate and Winchmore Hill is a street called Broad Walk, once home to Rod Stewart and popular with showbiz types and wealthy executives. We drove along in stealth mode (sidelights only at fifteen miles per hour) and noticed a youth dart into a driveway. We drove past and Dick got out on foot to backtrack and find our prey. Dick spotted him walking along the street again and we thought he could be a burglar.

Dick gave a radio commentary, and I drove in a loop so that I was back on the other side of him again. We were now walking toward the suspect from different directions. Neither of us could quite make out what the suspicious character was up to as he darted behind cars in driveways and reappeared in another driveway further away on the same street. We decided to stop and challenge him to find that he had a bag full of car badges that he'd been prising off the boot lids and bonnets of Mercedes and BMWs along the street. We retraced his steps and found most of the parked cars denuded of their emblems. We arrested him for theft and criminal damage. Back at the station, like hunters showing their catch, we laid out all the badges on the charge room table. There were dozens of car badges of relatively little value, in terms of property, but quite costly to fix the bodywork of the cars they came from. I blame the Beastie Boys!

We were back in uniform the following night and were called to a noisy party in a nice apartment block. I'm no killjoy—live and let live, I say—but this selfish individual lived in a short-term rental in a block otherwise occupied by people who want a quiet life. It was now 3:00 a.m. on a weekday and he was pushing his luck. He greeted me at the door with that 'What the hell do you want?' kind of attitude. Despite my sage words of advice, he was having none of it and partied on. A call to the noise abatement team at the council was all I could do, except I was on night duty all week and he didn't strike me as an early riser. A couple of days later, just before returning to the station to book off duty in the very early hours, I visited his front door again, ringing the bell repeatedly until he answered. 'Just checking everything's OK and that there haven't been any problems since the other night,' I asked, knowing I'd disturbed his sleep as just a little taste of his own medicine. He grunted his disapproval and closed the door. It was a little petty of me, I know, but his attitude that night deserved a response, and we were never called back to that address again.

When I was back on day duty, I received a rather important-looking letter in the internal despatch. It was from our deputy commissioner. Gary and I were awarded commendations for bravery following the 'mad dog' incident. I feel I don't deserve it as I was more of a hindrance to Gary than I was brave, but I'm quietly pleased to have it on my record though.

I'd been dating a girlfriend for a while, and it was serious enough for us to consider moving in together. We had a small deposit and would easily qualify for a mortgage on an apartment in Enfield. I'd grown out of the section house and looked forward to domestic bliss, which turned out to be a good move. Within a couple of years, we'd moved again into a semidetached Victorian-style house a few streets away, which was to be my home for another ten years. It had original marble fireplaces, wooden shutters, and a fantastic community. It felt like a very lucky find.

At work, I yearned for change and decided to look for a transfer away from Edmonton Division to somewhere a bit livelier. Edmonton had given me so much in my first years in the job, but I wanted a bit more action. I tried to go to the bright lights of the West End but there was no one willing to swap postings. That was the basis on which a transfer would be possible across area boundaries. I asked where was the furthest I could go into London without relying on a swap. 'That would be King's Cross,' said the area chief inspector, 'but no one willingly transfers into King's Cross from Y district. They'd snap your arm off to get a five-year PC, with panda and van driver authorisation.' And so, my transfer was duly arranged.

CHAPTER 4

King's Cross

EVERYONE AT KING'S CROSS ASSUMED I'D BEEN TRANSFERRED AS A 'defaulter'—the term used for someone sent to a division like King's Cross under a dark cloud. My new colleagues researched and found out about an incident at Arsenal where I'd been sent back to division in disgrace and decided it must've been for that. No one transfers into King's Cross from an outer division voluntarily. I let them believe what they wanted, and it made me sound much edgier than I was.

King's Cross Road Division, as it was formally known, was in N district. The station was the first purpose-built police station in the country, commissioned in 1870. Other stations had been adapted from buildings used for other purposes. The building had character but was badly out of date. We would bring prisoners in through the main corridor from the back of the building, with civilian staff having to scurry back into their offices when a lively one was being bundled in. The charge room was antiquated, and the cells included a drunk tank, which was an oversized cell with a sloping floor and grid in the middle so that all manner of bodily fluids would drain away. Behind the station was a stable block in use by the mounted branch. The proximity of an active stable would perfume the air inside the building every day. When the farrier came, the smell of burning hooves would add another unique aroma to the working day. It was often said that all forms of life could be found at Kings Cross. The character of the place had an edgy feel to it, but there was a camaraderie among the officers and staff that made it great to be a part of.

I retained my divisional number, PC123, at my new division. I worked day duties my first few days, off the usual shift rota with Carl, a fantastic character from my new team who'd been assigned to work with me until I found my feet. He was to show me around the King's Cross and Islington divisions so that I knew where our ground ended and the bordering divisions started. He'd also show me the trouble spots, the council estates and the millionaire's squares, the prisons, the street markets, and the business districts. It was like a history tour of the life and crimes of King's Cross and Islington. I felt I'd arrived properly in working London.

I was young, but with five years' service, I was among the more experienced officers on shift at King's Cross, which had a much younger demographic than Edmonton. I was as enthusiastic as ever, and there was a friendly competition between me and Andy, a PC with similar service who had transferred from equally suburban Barnet. We were both pro-active and quickly learned that arrests were like shooting fish in a barrel compared to an outer division. We were falling over them almost every day and quickly earned reputations as 'thief takers,' a flattering term for coppers with an instinct for catching criminals. We were enjoying the

Figure 4.1. PC O'Leary in callsign November 1, King's Cross Road Police Station, 1990. Photo courtesy of author.

time on shift, and our new team said that our enthusiasm was infectious and had lifted everyone's game. That was great to hear.

I was the team van driver most days and would push a rather tired Leyland Sherpa van around the streets of King's Cross, responding to calls, picking up prisoners, and being proactive when time allowed. It was a tough patch for vehicles in busy London stop-start traffic, so the fleet managers would assign some rough vehicles to us. My Sherpa van usually ran on three cylinders, instead of four, despite being sent back to the workshop several times, so we just accepted it and would chug around the streets with an occasional loud backfire to startle everyone nearby. Police vans and unmarked cars, up until the mid-1990s, were fitted with bells instead of sirens (which were still the preserve of area cars) and were comical when used. We figured that everyone knew they were useless but were fitted to newly commissioned vehicles right up to this period because that was in the police fleet manual, which no one had ever thought to question. The policy wonks missed that one.

A switch on the dashboard labeled 'GONG' would sound the bell and take us straight back to the 1940s and invoke our best BBC/Pathé news accents as we drove along. We only ever used the bell in fun.

Back then, King's Cross was a well-known beat for street-level sex workers, which brought all kinds of associated problems with it: drug use and street dealing, pimps, who would beat the girls into compliance, and all manner of unattractive individuals who would be drawn there to score, one way or another. It was a run-down area, often violent, dirty, and crimeridden. I loved it!

After a very long run of shifts in which I'd done nothing else but push the dilapidated Sherpa around the streets, I was given a day off from driving. They sent me out on the beat—foot patrol—tall hat and everything. Fabulous! It was the late shift, and I was headed for Kings Cross, when a well-known local sex worker emerged from a squat in one of the backstreets and made a beeline for me, screaming, crying, and pointing to the squat. Her man, Michael (also well-known to us), had beaten her up and taken her money. I knew this was going to be weary and that, as soon as she'd got her money and had calmed down, she wouldn't want to press charges. However, there was a recently introduced positive arrest policy that meant my lovely walk was over and that I'd be spending the next few hours sorting this out.

I pushed open the door of the squat, a once beautiful Georgian house, now boarded up and way past its glory. At some point, someone had been able to force their way in and it was clear that it been a squat for quite a while. I took a moment to let my eyes adjust to the dark interior of the house and then made my way down the hallway toward a door. I opened it and entered a room that had naked flames burning, which could've been candles, but as my eyes adjusted to the darkness, it all came into focus and I could see they were lighters. I had just crashed a rather large crack cocaine party. There I was, in full beat uniform, standing in the middle of a drug den, on my own, apart from about twenty crackheads with no stake in society and pretty much nothing to lose. I hadn't radioed in where I was and so my sudden awareness of being in real danger kicked in. It was like I was in one of those spaghetti westerns where the sheriff walks into a bar, the piano music stops playing, and everyone looks around and waits to see who's going to make the next move. What the hell had I done?

I scanned the room, eyes locking with its inhabitants, as I searched for where the danger was going to come from. Then, I saw Michael, my intended target for investigation, standing at the back of the room. 'Michael, can I have a word with you, outside please?' at which he complied and walked toward the door. Everyone stopped what they were doing, mouths agape in equal astonishment at what they were witnessing.

You could sense the palpable relief in the room that the deadlock was broken. I was going to leave with Michael and no one else. This was a 'discretion the better part of courage' opportunity. I took Michael outside and radioed in where I was and what was happening. At the same time, I could hear the partygoers escape out the back, evading capture from the backup that would reach me within moments and raid the place. It was a silly move to have entered that building and I breathed a sigh of relief that it had turned out the way it had. I survived to manage the arrest and the paperwork that took me the rest of the shift to complete.

It was 1990 and the year of the poll tax riots in Central London. At the time, I was on an aid serial, not a shield serial. I was in normal beat duty uniform when the serial was sent into the north side of Trafalgar Square, and it all kicked off. This was a demonstration that was well anticipated and televised as thousands descended on Central London to show their displeasure at the introduction of a new tax based on each adult paying a contribution rather than just per household. It would be introduced and later replaced by a system of household tax by a different name.

Huge crowds, turning angrier by the minute, filled Whitehall and Trafalgar Square. The situation descended into a riot. I saw mounted branch officers from Kings Cross on crowd control duty, their sergeant's face bloodied from being hit by a missile thrown at him. It was like Broadwater Farm all over again in the sense of noise and atmosphere, except this was taking place during the day.

It was a hugely violent riot. Thankfully, I was with another officer when we arrested someone for throwing missiles at police. Suddenly, we were cut off from the rest of the police line and were walking toward Leicester Square with our prisoner when we became surrounded by protestors who tried to snatch him from us, when, luckily, a random passing prisoner transport van pulled up. We threw ourselves and our prisoner in the back and sped off toward the charge room at a designated station away from the area. Even the prisoner seemed to breathe a sigh of relief.

That was the end of my day. The rest of my day was spent waiting with the inevitable paperwork and lots of waiting for the attention of the custody sergeant. It would be my last time at the sharp end of a riot.

Things had drifted apart at home. My then girlfriend and I decided, amicably, to go our separate ways. I took on the house, got a lodger, and went on a holiday with some of the boys from station. We had an absolute belly laugh for a couple of weeks in the sun. It was an absolute tonic. Those lads remain among my very best friends to this day.

Back at work, I went out on patrol in a panda with a new sergeant who was part of the accelerated promotion scheme. We referred to people on the scheme as 'flyers,' as they were selected to fly up the ranks quickly. She would later become one of the most senior officers in the country, but on this day she was on patrol with little old me. As we drove past

Pentonville prison, I noticed a car parked on a side road alongside the prison wall with a single occupant in the driver's seat; something that would always catch the attention of an inquisitive copper. I pulled up alongside the driver and engaged him in conversation to find out what he was up to. He was evasive and nervous, so I knew I was on to something, but I just couldn't get any satisfactory information from him. I searched him and the car. Nothing. It was time to be completely honest and ask him what he was up to, but he insisted that nothing was going on. I wasn't buying it and suspected he was giving me a false name as well.

There were a few reportable defects on his car, so I told him I was nicking him for these minor things and, as I suspected, the details he was giving me were false, I was going to arrest him. If he turned out to be innocent, I'd let him go with just a warning. My sergeant sidekick observed with interest but otherwise kept quiet as my prisoner protested his innocence all the way back to the station and through the booking in procedure with the custody sergeant. I looked him in the eye and promised that I'd find out who he was and told him that he wasn't going anywhere until I was completely satisfied with his identity. He then paused and said, 'OK, I suppose you'll find out anyway. I used to run a very busy pub. I let the takings build up and I ran off with about thirty grand. I've been wanted ever since.' And so, with his real name, a quick check on police records revealed the details of the warrant for his arrest. He'd been trying to look up an old friend who lived near the prison and made the mistake of being noticed. My sergeant ride along was very impressed with my copper's instinct, so it seemed. But she did correct me on my grammar in my report notes. Bloody flyers!

I earned the opportunity to take a highly sought-after advanced driving course and was sent to Hendon for six weeks of training. I had the best fun driving at very fast speeds, legally, up and down the countryside. I passed and returned to King's Cross as an area car driver.

My first day driving 'November 1,' the call sign for the King's Cross area car, was to be in an MG Maestro EFI rather than the standard Ford Sierra or Rover SD1 stock of the period. The Maestro was being evaluated and was a nimble little rocket around the streets of Kings Cross, compared to the usual fleet. Andy, my one-time competitor for arrests, was my radio operator. It had rained lightly, and the roads were a little greasy, I noted mentally. We took a call, and for the first time as an area car driver on went the blue light and siren. I made rapid progress toward King's Cross along Goodsway, an ancient road that ran alongside the train station where the delivery of goods was made, as the name suggests. The broken road surface revealed patches of the old, cobbled street below, which was as slippery as oil in the rain.

I approached a one-way section where the road turned to the left and applied the brakes, but the car went into a skid, and wasn't slowing down. I tried again. Same response. In a rapid moment of evaluation, I started plotting where to point the car, so I'd crash with the least damage and risk to anyone. Not there, I thought, noticing an elderly couple. Not there either, looking toward the metal railings that might impale us.

At that moment, my training kicked in and I started cadence braking. Before the days of ABS (antilock braking system), cadence braking mimicked the effect of passing the most efficient point of braking just before wheel lockup by repeated pumping of the brake pedal. This method was more effective than an uninterrupted skid. Plus, as the wheels rotated after each pump of the brakes, the car was able to steer as the wheels would regain traction.

We approached the point of no return and as I released the brake pedal from cadence one last time, the wheels gripped, and I turned into the corner. I made it out the other side of the turn perfectly and accelerated away from the would-be witnesses and the shame that could've seen me crashing the area car on the first call of my first day behind the wheel. Andy broke out of his moment of silent terror, 'Bloody hell Kev, that was brilliant. Is that what they teach you on the advanced course?' 'Oh, cadence braking? Yeah, that's part of it,' I replied, matter of fact, saving face and snatching credit from a near miss. I took it a little easier, noting my overeager start to the day and ended the shift in one piece.

I'd been approached to take several new probationers out for their first few weeks on the street duties course. With six years under my belt, I was considered eligible to teach new recruits and was to become a street duties instructor, temporarily. In a typical cliché of a work romance, I met a pretty probationer, and we started dating. She'd become my wife a few years later.

I was driving in for a late shift teaching the street duties course, which meant that I was going into town against traffic as all the day commuters were driving out. There was a line of traffic at the front of which was a single motorist who'd stopped when all was clear ahead. As I drew nearer, I could see all was not right—the driver had collapsed at the wheel. I stopped because I knew I had to get him out of the car to give him CPR. Other members of the public helped me pull him out of the car. One I knew as an off-duty colleague. It was going to be down to us to revive him. We began to work on him together until the ambulance arrived. When it did, the paramedics were able to register a pulse and within seconds had him in the back of the ambulance and on the way to hospital. I decided to move his car, pending the arrival of local officers who would take over contacting next of kin and getting the car towed away. I hadn't quite appreciated the consequences of a sudden collapse, including relaxing of bladder muscles, until moving the car and that sense of getting a wet backside. Oh, the glory of being a lifesaver!

I learned that he lived for eleven days after the accident, which was enough time for his family to gather and say goodbye. Not the outcome I'd hoped for, but I'll take it as a consolation for the family.

As a street cop, I had developed various ways of dealing with conflict, which sometimes worked to a greater or lesser extent. It comes as part of the job that people sometimes react badly to being stopped by the police, whether they're driving badly, behaving badly, or acting suspiciously. When younger in service sometimes, there's a multiplier effect of people not appreciating being spoken to by someone younger with authority and your own lack of experience trying to manage situations using a spectrum of techniques from calm, patient persuasion to rolling around on the floor with them when you've miscalculated. It's a learning curve, often accelerated by being on the receiving end of a punch in the face or two.

I used to let them rant at me in various, somewhat predictable, ways: I should be catching real criminals; they pay my wages; I'm only picking on them because I'm a bully, was bullied at school, have a problem with people who are richer/better/classier than me; a racist, and I should be warned that they know the chief of police/home secretary/prime minister/God, and so on. During their rant, I'd tilt my head backward and look up into the sky until they would look in the same direction and ask what I was looking at. To which I'd reply that I was looking at them, one hundred feet up and was waiting for them to come back down so that we could have a chat about whatever I'd stopped them for. They would either pause and then appreciate that they were being a bit of an idiot and be amused by it, or it would be mentioned in the official complaint they were going to file.

I remember one particularly angry driver I'd pulled over for driving like an idiot. It turned out that he was to continue being an idiot in our initial discussion and was not willing to listen. It felt like things were escalating, so I said, 'Look mate, if we're going to have a fight about this, let's get on with it. Otherwise, let's sort this out reasonably so we can both move on, shall we?' He stopped ranting, looked me straight in the eye, and burst out laughing, appreciating how ridiculous he was being. I'm not sure that would work in every situation, but the calculated risk seemed worth it that day and it paid off.

I heard on the radio that colleagues had stopped a man in Kings Cross and the situation was going downhill. As I arrived in response to the call for assistance, I saw two of my colleagues wrestling on the pavement with an angry giant in a nice suit. An equally smartly dressed woman was standing calmly nearby and, I assumed, was his companion. They looked like they were going out for the evening, but my colleagues decided to spoil their fun. It turned out that they'd identified him as someone who was wanted on an arrest warrant and had chosen poor timing (for him) to take him in.

I decided a different tack to joining the wrestling match, as it seemed to be marginally in hand. I kneeled down so he could hear me, and I suggested that, if he stopped resisting arrest, he wouldn't ruin his suit and he could walk the fifty yards to the police station with a little dignity. That would mean we could assist his companion and make sure she got a taxi home, which we would arrange for her. To everyone's complete surprise, including mine, he said, 'Okay then' and stopped struggling. He walked across the road with the two, not particularly short, arresting officers, but he was still head and shoulders taller than them, so it looked like he was helping them to cross. I flagged down a passing taxi for the woman and she went on her way. Upon reflection, I thought that he'd probably kicked off in the way he did because he was being challenged in the presence of his companion. I'd given him a face-saving way out, as I'd mentioned ensuring she would be helped to get a taxi home and he could latch on to the potential gallantry, on his part, if he did what was best for her. That was fine by me.

Another day on aid I was assigned, to my delight, as the driver of a battle bus supporting a confidential operation to execute multiple warrants. I'd had some instruction on these curiosities of the fleet during the advanced driving course, as it was expected that all advanced drivers would be able to drive a serial, almost regardless of the type of van, minibus, or personnel carrier available. I had to pick up some colleagues from Kings Cross and then Holloway on our way to Hendon Police College for a briefing. The bus chugged its way up Highgate Hill and almost came to a halt as it didn't quite have the puff to make it. It was like driving a small house.

When we got to the briefing, all was revealed. We were going after street robbers and burglars in Tottenham. There were dozens of warrants to execute. Scotland Yard's covert operations unit had set up a sting shop in Tottenham called Stardust Jewellers and, in a groundbreaking operation, had captured evidence of criminals selling stolen property to undercover officers there. It was an amazing investigation, and I was delighted to be part of something that would put these merciless, and often violent, street robbers and burglars behind bars. I remember being quite proud of what the Met had achieved as so often, as a divisional officer, I'd seen the effect on victims. Now, the criminals would get their comeuppance. We raided multiple addresses simultaneously and suspects were arrested in droves and taken to a custody office for processing. It had been a great day at work, and I'd even enjoyed the novelty of driving a battle bus for the day. Little did I know it wouldn't be my last experience of covert policing.

A few days later and back at Kings Cross, I was driving the area car 'November 1' again. I noticed a clean Peugeot 205GTI parked in Pentonville Road with a for sale sign in its window. These were among the most desirable (and stolen) hot hatch cars of the 1990s and I couldn't help but take a closer look. I could see that all wasn't right, with multiple holes in the number plates that suggested they'd been fitted previously to another car. I noted the phone number on the advert and went back to the station to call the seller, pretending to be a potential buyer. He agreed to meet me by the car and show it to me, completely unaware, during the call, that I was a police officer.

I waited for the agreed-upon time and pulled up in the area car in full uniform, making no reference to having called him and making out that it was a chance encounter. As soon as I checked the vehicle identification (or chassis number), it was confirmed it was a stolen car and the seller was duly arrested. The car, someone's pride and joy, had been stolen a few days earlier in the Thames Valley area. My 'seller' explained that he had bought it from a man called John in the pub, who had yet to come forward. The seller was charged and convicted in court.

One early shift, the cells were empty. The custody sergeant complained that he'd had to navigate a disorderly street drinker's 'cheese and wine party' on his walk to work from Kings Cross Railway station and I was to take the van out and round them up. I took a couple of PCs with me, and we filled the van with a few partygoers who were drunk, smelly, and making a nuisance of themselves. They knew they'd get a breakfast out of it, so didn't complain too much. We filled the drunk tank, and in the confines of a cell, the stink was concentrated. Within a few minutes, it wafted along the corridor in a perfectly putrid perfume. The custody sergeant then announced that he was off to court and was to be relieved by a fellow sergeant who would inherit a cell full of smelly drunks. Quite innocently, we'd been duped into facilitating a prank between the custody sergeants. I was quite impressed.

I remember when the same cells were being refurbished and the radiators that were closely built into the cell walls were removed. Behind those metal panels they found a history of contraband: both real and fake notes, knives, credit cards, drugs, and incriminating documents. It just goes to show that searching the arrested doesn't always find the stuff we might've found to make a case stick.

One day when I was driving the area car, we attended a call where a sex worker had been assaulted by a customer. I was searching the alleyway where she'd been attacked for any blood or potential forensic opportunities, when I trod in dog crap. It was relatively fresh and stunk to high heaven. There was no way I could get back in the car in that state, so the wiping of the shoe dance commenced, like a frantic Michael Jackson-esque moonwalk. Probably everyone has trodden in dog crap at some stage in their lives, but this was something different. Then, my colleague commented that, judging by the crumpled and well used paper nearby, unless someone had trained their dog to wipe afterward it was actually human crap, which made it much worse! *Arrrggghhh!* What the hell? What's wrong with people? I decided, there and then, that the shoes were to be retired, immediately. I put them in a bin and trod carefully to the area car and drove in my socks back to the nick where I had a spare pair in my locker. Of course, within minutes of the incident, everyone on the shift knew about it and the comments over the radio were relentless. The funniest was from the person who sung the line from 'Love is all Around,' 'I feel it in my fingers, I feel it in my toes.'

I'd always read the daily intelligence reports before going out on shift. They were a mine of information about where things were happening and more importantly, who was at it. One day, the pages featured someone I remembered—an old face from Edmonton who'd escaped from a stolen car I'd stopped a couple of years back. At the time, there were three to arrest, but there was just me and another cop. As we struggled with the driver and one of the occupants the third seized on the opportunity to escape. When things like this happen, to console ourselves in the moment, we like to say that 'they'll come again,' Now, a couple of years later, I was looking at his mugshot as he was now wanted on warrant for other crimes.

It was about two weeks later, on night duty near Kings Cross railway station, when I saw the man from the mugshot loitering. I didn't remember immediately what his name was or what he was wanted for as it had been a couple of weeks since I'd read the intelligence briefing, so I radioed in and asked someone to flick back through the pages of the daily bulletins to find the entry I'd described. They checked and confirmed he was still wanted, to which I replied I'd arrested him after spotting him in the street. Everyone assumed I had amazing powers of memory and were impressed with my coppering. It wasn't that. It was just proof of the old idiom 'they'll come again,' and he did. You can imagine his delight when I reminded him where we'd last met. Some call it 'the long arm of the law,' meaning that we'll get you, no matter how long it takes.

ARMED ROBBERY

Back in the 1980s and early 1990s, armed robbers were hero worshipped by a small but significant section in society who romantically saw them as 'proper criminals,' and Islington had its fair share of both robbers and worshippers. I was driving the area car and took a call to an armed robbery at a bank in Chapel Market, Islington, and by the time we arrived the robbers were long gone. We did our best to get descriptions and directions of escape to circulate over the radio to no avail. We then turned our attention to the shaken members of the staff who were just doing ordinary jobs and had been threatened at gunpoint. I could see how frightened and upset they were. A few locals gathered outside making comments that were clearly in admiration of the daring bank robbery and making fun of the situation. It was very irritating. I was approached by a man wearing a crash helmet who seemed very interested in what was going on and being nosier than was acceptable. In an unguarded lapse in professionalism, I suggested the best thing he could do right now was to bugger off. And with that, he walked back toward his motorcycle and did indeed bugger off.

As detectives arrived on the scene to take over, I'd got all that was needed to file an initial crime report and went back to the CID office at the station to write it up. Crime reports were pen and paper forms back then and as I went to put it into the binder, a detective approached and asked if that was the report for the bank robbery. I confirmed that it was. He introduced himself as Mick, a newly posted detective sergeant, and added, 'You don't remember me without my crash helmet, do you?' At that moment, I wanted the floor to open beneath my feet. I offered a very fast apology. Thankfully, he laughed and said that he should've shown his ID and approached it differently too, perhaps. He was really decent about it, and we had a bit of a laugh before parting and getting back to work. Our paths would cross again later in our careers. The events of that day became a frequently recalled funny story—always at my expense.

Back on day shift, Carl was out and about in Kings Cross on a motorcycle, having transferred to traffic. We stopped for a chat, and he told me there was a talk of a stolen vehicle squad being established at his base. It would be a mix of detectives and stolen vehicle examiners, a qualification I held. He said that he'd keep me posted and I said I'd think it over, but it sounded right up my street.

One sunny afternoon on patrol in the area car in Pentonville Road, a car made an illegal turn in front of my marked police car. It was as good an excuse as any to give it a pull. The driver emerged apologetically for 'taking liberties,' in the language of the affable geezer that stood before us. I wasn't aware of who he was, but he was quick to introduce himself. As a former henchman of the notorious London gangsters the Kray twins, Tony Lambrianou was now a reformed character and was just taking a cheeky shortcut, for which he politely expressed remorse again. His appearance was straight out of central casting, presenting himself in the persona of a lovable East End villain from the days when you could leave your door unlocked. I didn't buy into those nostalgic lies and wondered about the violence he'd been part of or willingly witnessed. Still, he wasn't much of a threat that day and his minor infringement was as deserving of a warning as it would be for any other motorist.

With nine years in the job, I wondered what to do next. I liked being proactive and was a street copper with a good instinct for catching criminals. The sergeant's exam was an option, but I didn't fancy being tied down with a custody sergeant's job just yet.

CHAPTER 5

Squads

I APPLIED FOR A NEW JOB, AND WITHIN A THANKFULLY SHORT TIME, I was posted to the North East area stolen vehicle squad, based at a traffic garage. Later in my detective career, I'd take some ribbing for working in the Traffic division, but I tried to take it well, knowing that it was an unorthodox pathway to being in a dedicated crime squad role. This was a plainclothes unit, established to deal with a surge of vehicles being stolen and sold on false identities by organized crime gangs. It was led by an inspirational detective sergeant who was one of the most hardworking cops I'd ever met. He had been part of the central stolen vehicle unit at Scotland Yard and had won a bid to set up a trial unit in this part of London. Assisted by one of his vehicle examiners as office manager, also a veteran of the central car squad, along with a couple of local detectives on attachment, I'd work with Jason as investigators and vehicle examiners, sniffing out the stolen cars and places where they were being cloned. In this posting, I'd learn about surveillance, informant handling, case building, investigative techniques using partner agencies, vehicle manufacturers, and forensic scientists. It was an excellent pathway to detective work.

During the 1990s, it was possible to buy a written-off salvage car and then steal an identical model and swap their identification numbers. Criminals would clone the stolen car using the salvage identity and sell it to an unsuspecting buyer. However, when the new owner applied for their registration documents from the Driver & Vehicle Licencing Agency, a notification was sent to the police to inquire whether it was a legitimate vehicle. We had piles and piles of these notifications. Sometimes, the car was a legitimate rebuild. Sometimes it was a stolen car bought innocently by someone who'd been duped. Sometimes it was a criminal, chancing it to see if they could get a document to sell the car with. They'd always claim to have bought it from the ubiquitous 'man down the pub,' an elusive John Doe character of many an attempt to explain their innocence, always of average height, build, and appearance and always completely untraceable, mainly because he didn't exist.

It was often the thieves' undoing to have left evidence all over the place. These enquiries kept us busy, but often with small-scale operators. Before long, intelligence would lead us to the higher tier criminals who were doing this on a more professional scale.

One of the more memorable cases involved a couple of entrepreneurial brothers from North London who'd set up a distribution warehouse trading in stolen parts. They had credit card facilities and racks of parts carefully indexed from dismantled stolen cars, with adverts in the trade newspapers and magazines presenting themselves as an outwardly legitimate business. You could buy anything from a wheel to a whole bodyshell from them. The cars were stolen to order and 'slaughtered' (broken up for parts) at other premises before the components were brought to the warehouse for sale. When we raided them (with a search warrant), we had to take the property away in several lorries to a storage facility.

Among the parts seized as evidence were several panels and a complete interior from a new Ford Mondeo, a model that had only been launched that year. It was obviously a complete dismantled car, minus the bodyshell. When its engine was found, the serial numbers had been ground off. I arranged as many of the parts as I could find and laid them out in the yard outside the warehouse for the forensic team to photograph. It looked like a model kit, or a workshop manual image where all the parts are shown in exploded view. There was one stolen car on the police national computer that matched, but I would have to prove it was the same one. I contacted the owner and he said he'd only had it for about a week before it was stolen, and he'd covered about four hundred miles in it. Other than that, he wouldn't be able to describe anything unique about the vehicle from any other car of the same model and specification. I'd recovered the speedometer from the stolen parts, and it showed 410 miles.

Proving that this car was stolen would be an uphill struggle, but I decided I'd give it a go as it would make great evidence at court if I could prove the true nature of their criminal enterprise in trading stolen and dismantled cars. I started with the exact, model, engine, and specification. The paint code was helpful as it was salmon red, somewhat rare and that would narrow the search a bit. Then I found the date codes on all the plastic parts and glass, so I knew the earliest and latest dates of when it might have been built. Ford provided me with a list of cars that matched, which got the list down to a few hundred. Then, I checked to see which of those cars had been taxed since the date of the theft and contacted the owners to verify the cars were still in their ownership. There were fourteen salmon red, two-litre, four-door Ford Mondeos left on my shortlist. I managed to contact the owners of thirteen of them who provided statements to confirm they still owned the cars and could account for them. Only one car was left untraced—it was the stolen car. My statement was served on the defendants, and they decided it was a fair cop and pleaded guilty at court. One of the brothers approached me as I waited outside the courtroom and confessed that he was amazed that I'd managed to identify the stolen car, not by the remains I'd discovered, but by proving it wasn't possible that it could be any other car. He said that he had to plead guilty out of respect for the impressive detective work. That, and the fact that his lawyer told him he stood no chance and would get a longer sentence if he didn't throw in the towel. As you can imagine, I quite enjoyed that job.

My next case emerged from an intelligence unit in north London. A person they were interested in was driving, on false plates, a BMW that had been given to him as part of a debt. A couple of days later, we waited in Palmers Green, the area where he lived so that we could stop him when he was in the driving seat. That way, he wouldn't be able to claim he had nothing to do with the car. We found him driving around in the car and pulled him over. One look under the bonnet confirmed a rather amateurish job of replacing the identification numbers, so we arrested him and seized the car.

A search of his home for documents relating to the vehicle also resulted in the recovery of tens of thousands in cash. He was 'at it' alright, but this was before the law changed to allow us to seize the cash as unexplained wealth. It was galling, but we'd have to give it back to him and took some consolation in charging him with theft of the car. We had a good idea where his money came from but couldn't prove it.

He used the old 'I bought it in cash from a man called John down the pub' excuse as an explanation of how he'd acquired the BMW and planned on giving it a run at court. Some months later, during the court case, it emerged that one of the jurors had been compromised and the trial was brought to a halt. There would be a retrial in another court and the jurors would be given protection to prevent 'jury knobbling.' This meant that every juror would be given police protection 24/7, whether at home or at court and everywhere in between, until the trial was over.

As it turned out, our defendant was found not guilty, and the jury passed a note to the judge asking why they had to be protected from a guy who seemed perfectly decent. I can't blame the jury for that. They did their bit and didn't know what we knew. Sometimes, criminals can be charming bastards.

I had three fantastic years on the stolen car squad, but the budget was being withdrawn and the squad disbanded. It was a shame as we were so productive, but all good things must come to an end. We were all to find new jobs or if we didn't find any, be posted randomly to vacancies. One of the reasons why we were being disbanded was to fund a new area level crime command to tackle organized crime in North and East London. I decided to apply for the organized crime intelligence unit within the command. I had heard from other applicants that the bosses wanted to make it a smoke-free working environment, so I was prepared when I was asked, 'Tell me, do you smoke?' 'No sir, but I'm willing to learn,' I replied. Forget anything about what I'd done—my skills and experience; that cheeky answer got me the job.

I spent the best part of two years in hiding places, watching criminals in static and mobile surveillance operations. It was a very forward-thinking command. In order to develop into a fully-fledged detective, they posted me out for six months to the local burglary squad to build up my investigation experience at a divisional level and to the child protection team in Hackney to work with vulnerable victims and partner agencies, such as social services.

Child Protection Team

There were many difficult and upsetting situations that I encountered during my career. I would tell myself that the victims needed someone who would do their professional best to help them and to bring offenders to justice. It wouldn't do much good if the police officer they relied on was emotionally wobbly, so that's how I managed to keep a distance and not take the sad stuff home. Child protection work was to pressure test that philosophy and those that continue to serve in this line of work, regardless of the agency, have my respect and admiration.

I was part of the Hackney and City child protection team. The caseload was astonishingly heavy, with many examples of 'failure to thrive' cases, as they were then called, in which children were neglected through indifferent, incapable, or incompetent parents. I don't mean to be judgmental. Not every situation was caused by bad people, and there were certainly some cases meant for supportive intervention by social services. It was easy to imagine better circumstances for these children, and, often, their lives were improved with a little help.

Then there were other cases where children were targeted by predatory men in single-parent families, and it was both heartbreaking and anger-inducing in equal measure. A regular modus operandi for these men was to begin a relationship with a single mother, sometimes years before the children would reach the age where the predator would be attracted to them. By then, the mother would be emotionally and, often financially, dependent on their partner and would either not understand that their children were being abused or would be in denial. It would be a personal double disaster for them to lose their partner and discover their children were victims of such an awful crime.

These men were cunning and manipulative. I can recall meeting more than one in such outwardly cozy family situations. Knowing what they were there for and that, in some cases, they'd done it before was a challenging scenario for a police officer. Proof was almost always elusive, and the poor mothers were more likely to take their partners side than listen to police or social services. Thankfully, the law, police and agency procedures, joint working protocols, and campaign groups have emerged to provide better interventions, but I'm sure it still happens to some extent.

I'd managed to arrest one such man and wanted to interview him. The case wasn't strong, but I was willing to build it and an early arrest might make him think carefully about his intentions. There was nothing to lose and everything to gain by questioning him.

He was entitled to (and was provided with) access to a legal adviser before the interview. We were required to provide some disclosure about the circumstances so that the adviser and suspect could consult privately. I remember the hostile attitude of the young legal representative who we met, and I could tell she was not a great fan of the police; she was bristling with attitude.

I disclosed the facts that had led to his arrest and the solicitor said, 'Ha. Is that all you've got?' And then looked at her client and said, 'This won't take long.' Unfortunately, she was right. We wouldn't have enough to charge him, and he was released, but I wasn't going to let an opportunity to arrest him pass. You never know what it might lead to and if it stopped his activity for a while, then it was worth it.

The solicitor's attitude stuck with me for a while. I know that everyone is entitled to a legal representation and that people are innocent until proven guilty. I have no problem with that. And I accept that we all deal with our professional challenges in ways that allow us to leave it behind when we go home. However, this type of case makes you think more deeply about victims, and I doubt whether such thoughts ever entered her mind. She seemed to relish her win a little too gladly for my liking. These adversarial experiences with legal representatives reinforced beliefs, among many officers, that we were on different sides of the legal system.

BURGLARY SQUAD

My time on the burglary squad at Barkingside was not quite as challenging as being on the child protection team. I was already experienced in most of the routines of investigation that this posting had to offer, but it was a change, and I liked the people I worked with, which made it enjoyable.

I picked up a series of burglaries where shops and petrol stations were being attacked. The criminals smashed the plate glass windows and swept the cigarette displays clean of all the stock before carrying them away in plastic dustbins. Cigarettes are an expensive, untraceable, and readily saleable commodity.

The damage these offenders caused was the biggest problem for the shop keepers and while some were owned by big corporations, most were small businesses owned and run by a family. I did feel sorry for them, but I was glad no one had been hurt or attacked by the burglars.

CCTV wasn't as widespread as it is now and forensic evidence was elusive, until we had a breakthrough in the form of an intelligence report suggesting it was two juveniles working for a Fagin-type character who was behind the criminal enterprise.

Night-time surveillance wasn't an option, so we waited for the next incident and watched the addresses we had for them, but they didn't show. This would continue night after night until we saw them come home empty-handed late one morning, presumably after they'd got rid of their haul. We arrested them on suspicion of burglary and searched the address, finding a few incriminating items, but it wouldn't be enough to prove their conspiracy to burgle. Our fatherly Fagin character thought of himself as a hard man and he was certainly aggressive and angry toward us. He had a criminal record and had served time for armed robbery, so we weren't dealing with a shrinking violet.

Agitated, he stood guarding a sleeping baby in the living room. Something didn't feel right and a colleague I was with decided to search the baby's pram. I expected Fagin to kick off, but his whole attitude changed into something far humbler as my colleague pulled a loaded handgun from beneath the mattress. He knew he was going to be charged with illegal possession of a firearm and, because he was out on license, he was headed back to prison, which he seemed to accept.

Back at the station, I conducted my first-ever forensic glass recovery. I combed the hair of one of the suspects onto a clean sheet of paper and submitted it to the lab for comparison with samples taken from the scene of the latest overnight shop break-in. If two pieces of glass have the same refractive index, the forensic scientist can conclude that they originated from the same source. Bingo! Our results confirmed exactly that, and he was charged.

CHAPTER 6

Enfield CID

I COMPLETED MY DETECTIVE ACCREDITATION AND WAS POSTED TO THE criminal investigation department (CID) at Enfield Division, along with a handful of others that had been through the same accreditation path. There was a good atmosphere, and I liked my new team. We had a reasonable and varied case load, and I was working closer to home than I had since my section house days.

I got married in a traditional ceremony in a beautiful English village church. The weather was kind, and everything went smoothly, but the marriage would last just fourteen short months before we'd go our separate ways. I'm a statistic. My then detective inspector consoled me: 'Ah well, you're not a real detective until you've got at least one divorce behind you!' He then poured me a scotch in a symbolic ritual of welcoming me to the club.

At the time, Enfield took in part of the Hertfordshire Borough of Broxbourne. There was a Metropolitan Police station at Cheshunt, a suburban town where the local council complained that there was no detective presence. As I'd passed my sergeant's exams by then, the bosses decided that they would send me there to supervise the volume crimes team. And so, I became the only detective in town and would lead a team of uniform constables, working in plainclothes and investigating whatever came our way. Assaults and thefts were our mainstay, with a good number of harassment and criminal damage cases too. This was a great experience, and I really liked my team. They called me the Sheriff of Cheshunt (which I quite liked).

After my year away, I returned to the CID office at Enfield and picked up where I'd left off.

MARGINAL GAINS

From these early days as a brand-new detective, a wise, old detective sergeant gave me some feedback about interviewing suspects in custody, which transformed my approach. Imagine an experienced detective who's been there, seen it all before, and is an exemplar of wisdom. That guy. He said that, while I was technically good and covered all the requirements of process and procedure in my interviews, he did all of that too, but approached the whole situation differently by making it more relational.

It's sometimes difficult to have empathy for some of the characters we'd have to deal with, but his approach was to keep it professional, park his feelings and treat each situation as a human interaction. Now that might sound obvious to you, but there are some bad people out there and, I don't know, maybe it was about self-preservation and keeping a distance so as not to erode one's own values and acceptance of society's wrongs by seeing oneself solidly opposed to the actions that had led to their arrest.

That's not to say we had a closed mind to potential innocence or mitigating circumstances when they were evident. However, it was the experience of many police officers that we'd either see the same faces repeatedly or we'd be dealing with something abhorrent that was unlikely to draw out our best rapport-building skills.

My sergeant's approach was to take a holistic view from the first moment he met the suspect in custody, to the discussion he'd have with the solicitor attending the station to represent them, and throughout the whole encounter. His view was that, if you could make small changes throughout the interaction, there was nothing to lose and the possibility of a better outcome for the investigation, the suspect, and the victims.

He explained that it was about small gestures, such as an offer of a newspaper to read while they were languishing in the cell, or a drink, or allowing them to make phone calls. Small gestures that didn't cost much if anything at all. When lawyers turned up to represent them, he'd be hospitable rather than treat them as the opposition, as some cops would. If they needed somewhere to work, he'd offer them a quiet waiting room and make the same offer of a drink and would spend some time explaining the circumstances of the case, the purpose of the interview, the questions and gaps he would ask about that only the person in custody could answer.

He described how, prior to the interview, rather than leaving it to the detention staff, he would personally collect the suspect from the cell and fetch the lawyer from the station lobby and bring them together. He called it 'rescuing the prisoner' as he would be seen as the person removing them from isolation and connecting them with their support. Just another opportunity for a positive micro encounter.

By removing some of the tension, reducing the adversarial confrontation, and showing respect, compassion, and making a few small gestures to ease the conditions for those involved, he achieved better outcomes. Suspects were always entitled to remain silent and there was no obligation to answer questions, which they would often be advised not to.

More cases were resolved quickly as suspects were more likely to give an account of themselves rather than the frequent 'no comment' response. This led to more of his investigations being resolved because he had answers from suspects that he was able to investigate. That is not to say he got every suspect to talk, but more so than other detectives without his charm and skill. Over a long career as a detective, that makes a very real difference.

In today's language, this is known as the doctrine of marginal gains, which we saw in the 2012 Olympics as a strategy for athletes to make fractional improvements across a range of inputs that would aggregate as an increase in total output. Athletes would take their own bedding when touring for competitions, every component of equipment, every piece of clothing was customised to perfection for the individual and when the difference between gold and silver can be a few milliseconds, everything counts.

My sergeant's approach to investigative interviewing made him something of a legend and those of us who worked with him took his advice and transformed our ways of working. It extended beyond the interview into all interactions—making small changes here and there to be more relational than just transactionally correct in our work. For example, going to see victims, witnesses, or making routine inquiries I'd regard as low conflict, low stress situations. For me, that might be the case, but there are many people who've never had any contact with the police and have only seen detectives on TV. By appreciating that every encounter held the potential for a slight increase in stress for others and thinking about the situation from their perspective changed the way I worked.

You make allowances for ways of behaving you might think are unusual by accepting that the encounter is unusual for the people you're meeting. You must accept that you don't always see people at their best, which is a particular marvel of British understatement if you ask me.

Where possible, I'd avoid rushing to the solution, as I might perceive it and allow a little more time for a conversation so that we could get past the initial nervous reaction.

WEEKEND CID

It was my turn to cover weekend duty. One Sunday morning, I arrived at work to a collection of cases awaiting CID attention, including a suspect being held in the cells who'd been arrested overnight on an allegation of rape. All the initial forensic procedures had been completed, and the victim was with a specialist officer trained in the investigation of sexual crimes. The name of this specialist role has changed over the years from SOIT (Sexual Offences Investigation Trained) to RASSO (Rape & Serious Sexual Offences) and, of course, the processes have evolved along with the precision of the forensic evidence now available. What remains a constant is the challenge that this vital role presents to those officers who volunteer for it. Victims are often, understandably, distressed, and it can be difficult and time-consuming to get an accurate account of what happened. Long hours, disrupted personal lives, and working with people in distress is stressful, but essential work. Those officers who do it are unsung heroes.

I reviewed the investigation and needed to get an account from the suspect as soon as possible while I still had the scene being held and ready access to the victim, who lived at the other end of the country. Rape cases often hinge on the issue of consent, and anything that might prove or disprove that would be essential to preserve in the golden hour of the investigation, if such evidence was available.

The suspect had asked for the duty lawyer, and I went to the cell to inform him of what was being arranged. He wasn't or didn't seem like he'd been drunk or hungover. Of course, using my newfound wisdom, I got him a hot drink and agreed he could make a phone call. To my surprise, he called his girlfriend and gave her a full and frank account of what he'd been arrested for and assured her it was a misunderstanding. His girlfriend, who lived a couple of hours away, decided to come to the station in a gesture of support, though there would be nothing she could do but wait.

Mark, a solicitor I knew from a local firm, answered the call out on this Sunday morning. I knew Mark, but only professionally from our shared encounters with suspects in custody. This was an example of how the different approach I mentioned earlier had a positive effect on ways of working. There was an acknowledgment of our different roles and a mutual respect and, I dare say, trust, to keep to our boundaries but be professionally cooperative where possible. I could have a conversation with Mark, and I explained where we were in the investigation and what I needed from the interview to safely manage the scene, some witnesses to the events of the evening, and the victim, who wanted to go home after she'd spent most of the night being medically examined and answering questions.

After the solicitor and suspect had been able to have a private consultation, we were ready for the interview. The suspect gave his account of the events that took place the previous night.

Along with other prospective students, he'd been invited to visit a university in London. Those who might occupy residential halls were allowed to stay for the weekend to see what it would be like. There were about a dozen who accepted the weekend accommodation.

That evening, some of them went to a local pub and afterward went for something to eat. The party continued back at the halls of residence and someone in the group suggested they try the outdoor pool. It was a clear summer night, after all. The suspect described a group of eight or ten of them using the pool. It was probably 2:30 or 3:00 a.m., when he and a fellow prospective female student found themselves in an unexpected romantic clinch, as he described it. He said that it was no more than a kiss and that he had certainly not raped her or anything of the sort. By way of further evidence to support his account of the events, he said that, although it was summer, the unheated pool had been freezing and, even if he'd wanted to, he couldn't have raised a smile, let alone an erection. I made a note to have the temperature of the pool water measured the following night. After some further questioning to complete his account of the events, I ended the interview to review the statement from the victim and to consult the specialist officer who'd spoken with her.

The victim's account was vague in her description of the physical act of rape she'd alleged, and so I tasked the specialist officer to explore this further with the victim.

By now, our suspect's girlfriend had arrived at the station, and all I could do was offer her the hospitality of the police canteen as the most comfortable place to wait. It was Sunday, so the catering facilities amounted to a vending machine, but I was able to supply endless cups of tea courtesy of the CID office kettle.

My specialist colleague returned with a dramatic turn of events in the investigation. Our victim had a long-term boyfriend and felt an enormous sense of guilt for kissing someone else and had reacted in the most extreme way by claiming that it had all happened against her will. She claimed to have misunderstood what rape meant and wanted to withdraw her allegation and go home with her parents. She could have been charged with perverting the course of justice and wasting police time, but after looking at all the circumstances in the following days, it was decided that lessons had been learned, and both victim and suspect were content to move on.

I shared the news with Mark and his client, and the now-exonerated suspect was reunited with his loyal girlfriend who was still waiting in the canteen. They seemed to need a private moment and would do no harm in the deserted canteen, so I left them to it for a while. When I returned, I was greeted by two tearful but smiling people who looked like they needed to go home. So did I.

About a year later, I received a personal letter from the couple. They wrote about how the experience had changed their lives for the better. They both accepted and understood they were meant to be with each other and planned to marry. He went on to study at another university, and they were both very happy to have put the experience behind them and moved on with their lives. I've still got the letter.

Central London Crime Squad

HAVING PASSED THE WRITTEN EXAMS, I WAS A CANDIDATE IN THE SER-geant's promotion process and had some good examples for the final assessment process from my recent experiences. To my utter astonishment, out of about eight hundred applicants, I was at the top of the list of successful candidates, which meant that I could apply for the accelerated promotion scheme and have an early posting to a number of advertised vacancies for detective sergeant.

I decided that the 'aggravated promotion scheme,' as I called it, wasn't for me. If I'd wanted a vertical career, I could've taken promotion far earlier and was happy to take things at my own pace and enjoy whatever I was doing from one posting to another. I was accepted for a post at West End Central, a station I'd had my eye on when I transferred from my first posting in Edmonton but ended up at Kings Cross. Now, I'd get to work in the West End of London after all. Or so I thought.

My transfer was intercepted by a detective inspector I'd worked with previously and who'd seen my name on the promotion list. Now I was going to work as a detective sergeant on the Central London crime squad and my daily commute from North London would take me to the squad base in Notting Hill. I went from the most local posting to the furthest, but my home circumstances were different now, so it was a trade-off that wasn't too problematic. I decided to use the time on my commute to study for the inspector's exam. It wasn't too bad in the morning as I had a fresh brain but reading the dry legislation on the homeward journey was sleep-inducing and I missed my stop on more than one occasion.

Notting Hill was probably at its peak of cool in the late 1990s. Millionaire celebrities lived there in Georgian houses, cheek by jowl with the less well-off residents in their council and housing association homes.

My role on the crime squad would involve intelligence gathering and operations to tackle the growing problem of street drug dealers who would often barely conceal their activity and brought an atmosphere of intimidation and lawlessness to the area. They were a huge source of both community intelligence and public concern, but catching someone with drugs and money doesn't always prove they're dealing, so the Crown prosecutors would say. Often, people who were persistently dealing would be charged with personal possession and return to business quickly, which was frustrating for both police and the public. We needed evidence that they were dealing. I would lead covert operations to catch them in the act and provide evidence to the courts of the true nature of their criminal activity by deploying undercover officers acting as drug users to buy from them. By securing evidence that they were readily open to selling hard drugs, undercover operations would ensure that the courts could convict on the facts, often presented with corroboration in the form of video and/ or audio recordings of what was said and done.

The other teams in the squad dealt with violent street robbers, criminal gangs, and other persistent crime problems that needed a dedicated effort above that which could be achieved at the local divisional level.

There were some impressive officers, both detective and uniform in this command. Long hours and hard work were the norm. My sidekick on the squad was Rob, a proactive PC who shared my view that, in some quarters on the squad, there was a sense of it being something of a boy's club, with a strong 'in group' who'd worked together before. We were both definitely outsiders looking in, but we persevered and let our work and results do the talking.

SO10 – FIRST IMPRESSIONS

The type of covert operations I was leading had to be signed off by a senior officer at Scotland Yard. All paperwork would go through the undercover unit there, known by its departmental designation SO10. Specialist Operations, or SO, was, at that time, the part of Scotland Yard that covered all detective departments. SO10 was in the part of the command that covered surveillance, confidential informants, witness protection, and undercover operations.

A visit to SO10 was not a particularly pleasant experience. The fifth-floor office was found along a beige walled, linoleum floored corridor. Visitors entered through a rather anonymous looking door that led them to a Formica counter, beyond which was for SO10 personnel only. It felt quite hostile to outsiders who weren't made to feel welcome by some of the hard-nosed detectives, men and women, who seemed to reluctantly deal with inquiries from visiting officers.

The detectives there would read through applications line by line, with serious expressions on their faces and no offers of reassurance or help. If any information was wrong, you'd feel their displeasure. They were the experts and gatekeepers of this department and made you feel like you didn't belong there. I didn't enjoy going there and resented the lack of professional support I thought they should be providing.

Back on the ground, our tactics were proving successful, time and time again. We were taking out drug dealers and robbers, restoring peace to areas once plagued by crime. The West End of London was a hotspot for street dealers at the time, mingling with crowds in Theatreland, around the streets of Chinatown, and the bustle of Charing Cross Road. Dealers were prevalent and often transient, so it wasn't always easy to identify them through a careful intelligence phase.

We worked with the local divisional crime squad to take out dealers with a single evidential buy, followed by a rapid arrest team taking them out on the spot, or 'buy-bust' as it was called.

Sentences were not as lengthy, and sometimes not even custodial, but it was an effective way of keeping a lid on it. Some in the team uncharitably referred to it as 'pest control.'

Before too long, our work was being noticed by managers at SO10 who heard of our results and the efficient operations we conducted. I was invited by them to lecture on the undercover courses run by SO10. One or two or the more difficult members of staff had moved on. Attitude toward me changed and was far friendlier from the hard-nosed coppers at Scotland Yard who turned out to be quite a good bunch after all. The audience consisted of both undercover officers in training and operational managers who would use the tactics in their investigations. During my lectures, I would explain how I would run operations with officer safety as the number one priority. I explained the preparation, briefing process, and how we'd protect undercover operatives when they were deployed. It felt like quite an achievement to be invited to do this, and a privilege too.

BRIEF ENCOUNTER

One morning as I was walking through a park in Notting Hill, which was a shortcut from our base to the tube station, a rather attractive lady caught my eye as we approached each other from opposite directions. Could this be my lucky day, I thought through sustained eye contact as she began to smile? Then it clicked. She had been on the jury that convicted the two brothers I mentioned in Operation Zebra. We had a brief chat, and she told me that the jury had seen through the excuses and were glad to find the brothers guilty, especially when they heard about their previous convictions after the verdict. After an exchange of pleasantries, we continued our separate ways. Not a romantic episode, after all, merely a brief encounter.

STEPHEN LAWRENCE

At around 10:30 p.m. on April 22, 1993, Stephen Lawrence and his friend Duwayne Brooks were waiting for a bus when a group of white youths set upon Stephen, who was separated from his friend as Duwayne went to see if the bus was coming. In those few moments, Stephen was fatally stabbed, and the subsequent investigations were unsuccessful in bringing his attackers to justice. It isn't possible to capture all dimensions of this awful crime and its consequences, but the government appointed inquiry produced the Stephen Lawrence inquiry report, which was published and is readily available to read online.[1]

I was not involved in the investigation but felt the impact of the report and a shared sense of professional shame in an institution I was proud to be part of that was now described institutionally racist. The inquiry report defined this as:

The collective failure of an organisation to provide an appropriate and professional service to people because of their colour, culture, or ethnic origin. It can be seen or detected in processes, attitudes and behaviour which amount to discrimination through unwitting prejudice, ignorance, thoughtlessness and racist stereotyping which disadvantage minority ethnic people.[2]

The then-commissioner of the Metropolitan Police Service (MPS), Sir Paul (now Lord) Condon is quoted in the same report:

If this Inquiry labels my Service as institutionally racist the average police officer, the average member of the public will assume the normal meaning of those words. They will assume a finding of conscious, wilful or deliberate action or inaction to the detriment of ethnic minority Londoners. They will assume the majority of good men and women who come into policing . . . go about their daily lives with racism in their minds and in their endeavour. I actually think that use of those two words in a way that would take on a new meaning to most people in society would actually undermine many of the endeavours to identify and respond to the issues of racism which challenge all institutions and particularly the police because of their privileged and powerful position.[3]

The inquiry report noted,

We hope and believe that the average police officer and average member of the public will accept that we do not suggest that all police officers are racist and will both understand and accept the distinction we draw between overt individual racism and the pernicious and persistent institutional racism which we have described.

Nor do we say that in its policies the MPS is racist. Nor do we share the fear of those who say that in our finding of institutional racism, in the manner in which we have used that concept, there may be a risk that the moral authority of the MPS may be undermined.[4]

This was a blow to the professional confidence of the MPS and the officers who did indeed feel marked by it, but what happened to policing after this event was a major change in the way we worked and how we treated each other and the public, though there remains a way to go. Investigations were transformed so that everything, from the initial response to the end of the trial, was improved. These were changes for the good and made investigators accountable for every action, every decision, where progress in cases was reviewed by a structured process of checks and balances that leveraged the experience of others.

It made you wonder how senior detectives managed before these changes were introduced. There was a mystique attached to Scotland Yard detectives, especially those involved in murder investigations, that assumed that their experience and skill would weigh more in the outcome than any structure, process, or procedure. Don't get me wrong, there were indeed some amazingly talented detectives out there and still are, but no one can doubt that the changes had a significant impact on the success of investigations and higher detection rates.

The change in approach began from the very start of an investigation and would be determined by the frontline officers responding to emergency calls.

The newly implemented definition of a critical incident would trigger a response to situations that required scene management and the callout of supporting services. The definition was deliberately broad so it would provide an effective response. If it had been narrowly defined it would have limited resource allocation. The new definition is as follows:

> A Critical Incident is any incident where the effectiveness of the police response is likely to have a significant impact on the confidence of the victim(s), their family, and/or the community.[5]

In most critical incidents, the scene would be a physical location and subject of the 'golden hour' principle, which is a phrase borrowed from the medical field that acknowledges the period of time immediately after a serious injury when there is the highest likelihood that prompt medical and surgical treatment will prevent death. Likewise, in an investigation there is a period between the commission of the crime and a successful investigation in which the scene is saturated with opportunity in the form of witnesses, physical material, and digital evidence all of which needs to be captured before it decays with time, fading memories, clean-ups, and recording loops that wipe it all away.

Positive action in the period immediately after the report of a crime reduces the amount of material that could be lost to the investigation and increases the chance of securing the evidence that will be admissible in court. This became a vital part of response policing in which those arriving at the scene would secure and preserve evidence by holding a wide area within a taped off cordon until those responsible for the investigation could attend and assess the crime scene. This practice alone would ensure better evidence gathering, securing forensic opportunities that might otherwise be lost and unrecoverable later.

Scene management was further enhanced by documenting everything that needed to be evidentially captured in the moment, including the use of scene logs to record what happened, when and which officers, forensic scientists, and photographers came and went from the scene. Decision logs captured the prevailing circumstances in which decisions were made from the initial response throughout the investigation. They were used to record notes about the situation, options, and why one was chosen over others. This detail would be almost impossible to recall later and ensured that supervisors and senior leaders could account for their decision-making processes every step of the way.

The creation of homicide awareness teams, that were sent to serious assaults that might be life threatening or life changing, would ensure expertise was available to local officers as early as possible to support the golden hour. Roles and responsibilities including supervision and leadership improved the way investigations were managed, resourced, and reviewed.

There were difficult times for the police service following the Stephen Lawrence inquiry, but if any good came of the tragedy it was the professionalization of training, responses to critical incidents, and investigations into murder and other serious crimes.

NAIL BOMBER

While most sensible people were winding down one late Friday afternoon and starting their weekend, I sat in an unmarked car with three colleagues in London's West End. We were helping another unit on the crime squad with a surveillance operation that was expected to end with arrests, and we all knew that would be just the beginning of a very long shift and likely to intrude further into our weekend. Arrests mean the clock starts ticking, counting down the amount of time someone can be detained before they must be charged or released. Fewer legal representatives will be as readily available to come to a police station out of hours and the inevitable home searches, suspect interviews, and endless paperwork burns through time. We were all resigned to it and accepted that it was a price worth paying if we could catch a group of violent criminals. It was a beautiful spring day in late April and people were in shirt sleeves soaking up the sunshine, thankful for the warm weather.

We were parked in a side street in Soho, four to a car, waiting for the 'off'—that sudden urgent call to action when a surveillance target makes a move. Police work often involves waiting: long stakeouts surveilling a location in anticipation of something happening, waiting for someone to come to board up a burgled shop or tow away an accident damaged car, or sitting in a personnel carrier waiting for crowd trouble. It is often typical in police work that hours or boredom can be punctuated by moments of frantic action and sheer terror.

Cops with a preference for action aren't very good at sitting on their hands for very long. Boredom can set in quickly and lead to conversations that you wouldn't want HR to hear: dirty jokes, slagging off people not there to defend themselves, and forbidden subjects including religion, politics, and football, sparking controversy just for something to talk about to pass the time.

The long afternoon was slowly giving way to early evening when we heard a call on the local channel for urgent assistance from officers who mentioned an explosion at the Admiral Duncan Pub on Old Compton Street. We were nearby and quickly changed priorities to get there and help our colleagues. We didn't know what we were heading toward and whether it was a gas explosion, a terrorist bombing, or something else, but there wasn't time for fear to set in; if some of our colleagues were there, they were in more danger than us and we might change the odds if we could add to their numbers. The main concern was the potential for secondary devices, designed to explode when the scene was attended by emergency responders to increase casualties. Even so, in this situation no one would seriously think of standing back while that risk was considered.

There had been two recent bomb explosions in Brixton and Brick Lane in the East End that were targeted at black and Asian communities, but this was Soho in the West End, and it didn't immediately register that this event was a continuation of that activity.

We arrived soon after the explosion to support two uniform officers who were first on scene. We were in plainclothes and had only our ID cards and badges to wave around to show we were police officers, but one of the uniformed colleagues was the local duty officer, a young inspector I knew. In a moment of humility, she said she wasn't exactly sure what to do or where to start, and I could see the horror of the scene etched into her face, likely reflected on my own. I think it was more of a verbalization of the sheer enormity of the situation and a moment of taking it all in before deciding where to start, rather than an inability to act. There are well established major incident procedures[6] that are trained for, practiced, and published in a manual designed between the emergency services, but real life is always more overwhelming than any exercise can prepare you for. Should the street be cordoned off to prevent more people moving toward danger? What if it was a bomb and there's a secondary device? Should we start moving bystanders away from the area? Should we evacuate nearby shops and offices? Should we tend to the injured? Should we coordinate the arriving emergency services so they can access the location and provide help? Should we send radio communication providing updates on the situation? The answer to all those questions is yes, of course. The challenge is prioritizing what to do first. I worked with the duty officer, supporting her, and going through the initial steps, making our priority getting help for the injured and preventing other members of the public from walking toward the danger. Without thought for their own safety, to start helping with the casualties, three officers from my team ran toward the Admiral Duncan pub.

The duty inspector began coordinating the response by standing at the road intersection so that she could communicate with and organise those arriving.

As more help arrived, she found her stride and sent some officers to manage cordons and keep the public away from the danger, while others self-tasked toward the injured with other blue light services, who now began to arrive in numbers very quickly. In that moment of commanding the response, the inspector led at the scene impressively, her confidence at odds with the surrounding chaos and debris. She was now surrounded by uniformed colleagues so I stepped away to find my team, approaching the locus of the bombsite.

The injured were leaning on the walls and against the shopfronts on the opposite side of the road from the pub, which looked like it was frozen in time from the blast with its main doors blown out and the remains of the arms from the awning jutting forward at an odd angle. It became clear that a bomb had exploded rather than a gas explosion or anything else. There was a crunch of glass underfoot and the smell of smoke and explosive material in the air. However, the blast radius was limited in that it didn't cause widespread damage beyond the front of the pub itself, with nearby properties appearing largely untouched.

More emergency services were arriving and pouring into the pub to attend the worst of the casualties. I announced to one of the survivors sitting directly opposite the pub and bleeding from cuts to the head that I was a police officer. His hair was singed and seemed to be still sizzling. His eyebrows and eyelashes were gone, and his face was pockmarked with debris and blackened with soot.

I did what I could to assess him and, from the first aid kit that I'd grabbed from our unmarked police car, offered him a bandage to press against his wound, which was less serious than his bloody face had suggested once I'd traced it back to the cut. I was sure he'd be OK. I asked his name, to which he replied 'Cinders.' His scorched hair and face made me think how darkly ironic that name was, but of course, I didn't say it.

He was in shock and clearly distraught. Just at that moment, an angel in a green paramedic uniform stepped in to take over.

An advantage of being in such a central location was that all emergency services were in good supply and the situation was rapidly coming under control. One member of my team had taken the initiative to go to the hospital where casualties were being taken and establish a liaison point to gather information on the names, severity, and number of dead and injured. Those injuries were made more severe by more than a thousand four-inch nails that had been packed into the explosive device, which was confirmation that the so-called nail bomber had made his third attack within two weeks, this time targeting the gay community as part of an ongoing hate campaign.

Three people were killed by the bomb. Andrea Dykes, twenty-seven, was four months pregnant and was killed instantly along with her unborn child. Her husband, Julian, was seriously injured. Their friend, Nik Moore, thirty-one, was also killed, and the best man at their wedding, John Light, thirty-two, died of his wounds later in hospital. More than seventy people were injured, with four suffering loss of limbs.

Two weeks earlier, on Saturday, April 17, 1999, a bomb exploded among the shoppers and traders of Brixton Market on Electric Avenue, an area of South London with a large black population. The bomb was made using explosives from fireworks taped inside a sports bag, which was primed and left at the side of a market stall. Traders became suspicious of the unattended bag and moved it to a less crowded area near Iceland supermarket. At one point, a trader opened the bag to see the crude device, complete with a clock as the timer. The police were called and arrived at the scene just as the bomb detonated at 5:25 p.m. Forty-eight people were injured, many of them seriously because of the four-inch nails that were packed around the bomb.

The antiterrorist branch would begin its investigation to find those responsible and considered that it was more likely to be a neofascist group rather than Irish republican terrorists because of the location and community targeted. Witnesses described seeing a suspicious man around the area at the time who was then located on CCTV footage. Although Brixton had a good number of public and private CCTV cameras, technology was not as advanced as it is today and the quality of video was poor, providing grainy images of the white, male suspect in a white baseball cap and dark jacket. Investigators had to visit and collect tapes rather than receive footage digitally. All this work to locate, collect, and view CCTV took a lot of time and resources.

The following Saturday, April 24, another nail bomb was detonated on Brick Lane in the East End of London. A vibrant area, also known as Banglatown for its significant Bangladeshi community, was considered a destination for the best curry houses in London. There is also a street market on Sundays, which the bomber didn't know about and had turned up on the wrong day. This meant that the street was much quieter than it would've been on market day. The bomb was placed in a holdall and left in the street until it was spotted by a passerby who picked it up, thinking it was lost property and took it to a police station further along Brick Lane, which was closed. Not quite sure what to, he put it in the boot of his car and closed the lid moments before the explosion, which destroyed the vehicle and caused severe damage to nearby buildings. Thirteen people were injured, but the casualties were far fewer than might've been.

The investigation continued at pace and, among the mountain of CCTV footage from Brixton, a clearer image of the suspect emerged from the Iceland supermarket internal camera looking outward toward the entrance. On Thursday, April 29, the best eight images were released in an appeal for information. Hundreds of calls came flooding in from the public trying to help identify the man in the images, which required investigators to triage the information, giving more weight to those who could say more than it was just their hunch and give something more specific or where there were multiple repetitions of a name already offered.

The following day, the bomber's identity was revealed by a coworker who was able to identify him in the published images. The bomber was David Copeland, a twenty-two-year-old engineer's assistant that he worked with at the London Underground. The coworker who called in mentioned Copeland's far-right leanings, which added credibility to the tip.

Copeland had attacked the Admiral Duncan on Friday rather than the next day because of the publicity and the likelihood of being discovered, but the information from his coworker reached the investigation team too late—only an hour before the deadly explosion and too late to stop him. The following day when police found an address for him in Hampshire, he was there waiting for them and freely admitted he was the nail bomber. 'Yeah, they were all down to me. I did them on my own,' he told the officers. On the walls of the small bedsit were Nazi flags and newspaper cuttings about the bombings.

David Copeland was an insignificant loner who had no achievements to speak of and who drifted in his young life, until he became an active member of a far-right group. His motive was hatred of difference, be it racial, sexual orientation, or faith, and his mission was to spread fear and resentment throughout the country. He gave full answers when interviewed by detectives and had no remorse for his actions. At one stage, between interviews, he asked his legal representative at the police station, 'Am I a serial killer, now?' 'No,' she replied, not giving him the satisfaction of his idea of warped glory. 'You're just another murderer.'

The following year, Copeland was convicted for his crimes and given six life sentences with a minimum term of fifty years before he would be eligible for parole, placing him well into his seventies.

'Cinders,' nicknamed by his friends for liking to dress up in flamboyant outfits, was the injured man I'd met and tended to that day in Soho. Otherwise known as David Morley, he would visit those in the hospital after the bombing for weeks afterward, being generous with his time, his warm company, and sympathy for those still recovering from their wounds. Cinders continued as the bar manager of the Admiral Duncan and, after it was reopened, he received an unexpected visit from representatives of the Bangladeshi community of Brick Lane in a gesture of solidarity and support, which inevitably moved him to tears. Over time, running the Admiral Duncan became a bit too much for him as he suffered from flashbacks and panic attacks, so he was reassigned to another bar in West London, owned by the same company.

One warm night in 2004, Cinders and a friend were sitting on a bench by the side of the south bank of the Thames chatting. They had been there for hours. It was shortly after 3:00 a.m. when a group of teenagers approached them and lured them into conversation before attacking them both and knocking them to the ground. When the brutal attack ended and the teenagers left, Cinders and his friend were found by passersby and rushed to the nearby St Thomas' Hospital. Cinders suffered forty blows, fractured ribs, and a ruptured spleen. He died from his injuries that night. The teenagers were later caught and convicted of their senseless crimes.

For a man who was the epitome of kindness to have been met with so much hate in his thirty-seven years of life is an affront to humanity.

Indeed, indeed, I cannot tell,
Though I ponder on it well,
Which were easier to state,
All my love or all my hate.

—Henry David Thoreau, c. 1840

OPERATION STRONGBOX

Our ever-evolving squad was to form a new initiative called Operation Strongbox in which we would be deployed to support territorial police divisions, or borough operational command units (BCU) as they were then known, to address acute, local crime problems. My team would carry out our well-established street drug operations to tackle the visible signs of dealing and to disrupt the activity that went with it.

In our first Strongbox deployment we worked Brixton Station Road Market, Atlantic Avenue, Electric Avenue, and Coldharbour Lane, leading to a haul of evidence against a bunch of dealers who'd been ruling the roost for a while. Their time was up. Our team was feeling like we were running a well-oiled machine and our first Strongbox posting passed without too much drama.

I was in the police canteen at Brixton when I received the phone call I'd been waiting some time for. I'd passed the inspectors exam and would be eligible to apply for promotion at the next opportunity.

Back then, most of the senior officer's separate canteen areas had been merged with the main rooms and the use of senior officer's crockery, which had a green floral band rather than a single blue line, had become a rarity, along with brown uniform gloves for inspectors and higher. My team knew I'd been waiting for the news and seemed genuinely pleased for me, until that is, when I pulled from my rucksack a perfectly preserved senior officer's cup and saucer, along with a pair of brown gloves. It had the desired effect of making me a target for piss taking. Subsequently, I was served a cup of the Met's finest brew in my own guvnor's cup while they thought of as many derogatory comments they could come up with. I loved this team.

After Brixton, we went to Hackney and worked with a great bunch of people in the local crime squad to reclaim a junction on the main road through Dalston toward the city. The area had become a scary place to be after dark due to the usual territorial dominance of a local drug market and associated acquisitive crime including street robbery.

I've heard the debates about legalizing drugs, and I don't want to rehearse the arguments for and against it. Regardless, I do know from experience that street level drug dealing is a problem for the communities that suffer it. The public is not blind to lawlessness and experiences intimidation as they navigate dealers and users loitering around. It doesn't take long before seeing hand to hand exchanges and the comings and goings of an obvious drugs trade. Property crime tends to increase near open drug markets because of opportunistic thieves taking anything they can sell to fund their next fix. People increasingly feel that they don't live in a nice area.

Dominating the busy junction of Amhurst Road and Dalston Lane, near Hackney Downs station, is Downs Court. It's a wide, seven-story 1930s building in the art moderne style that provides homes on the six floors above street level. The ground floor is formed of separate retail shops, one of them a betting shop.

The betting shop, part of a national chain, was heading for closure as it wasn't trading as well as it has been a year or so earlier. Staff were going to lose their jobs and another shopfront would be boarded up, in another visible sign of decline. At the turn of this century, this was a high crime area, and it was no secret that the betting shop had been overrun with drug dealers. It was an ideal spot that provided cover from the streets. Staff had complained to their management, who then passed it on to the head office. Local police gave some attention, though it was difficult to do much more than disrupt the dealers temporarily, from time to time. Staff became resigned to the shop being occupied by dealers most days and saw their regular customers gradually withdraw rather than run the gauntlet of intimidation as young men sat around the shop staring down anyone who wasn't there to score a deal.

Operation Strongbox provided an opportunity to put a stop to the mischief and reclaim the shop for its owners, customers, and staff. With the help of the head office security team, and concealed even to the staff in the shop, we managed to install a hidden camera during the night, which would capture every deal, provide evidence of the level of the illegal enterprise, and who was involved. We deployed undercover officers, acting as drug users, and before long we had enough evidence to move into the arrest phase.

We could've just walked in and detained them, but it's always useful to get them with our money in their pockets and drugs in their possession to sell, so we introduced a few more covert buys on the day of the arrests.

We wanted to surprise the dealers and ensure they were all caught in one go, so I asked the territorial support group to help with the arrest phase. More than a dozen officers in riot gear jumped into the back of a box lorry in the car park behind Stoke Newington police station to carry out the raid. My team kept observation on the shop, waiting until all the players were there before calling in the hit. The lorry made its way to the front of the shop before coming to a halt. It looked like an ordinary delivery, until the back rolled up and its cargo emerged, causing everyone in the street to stop and look in amazement as the riot kit-clad officers poured into the betting shop and dominated those inside in a show of shock and awe. They were all detained and found in possession of drugs and cash, some of which we'd marked, ensuring we could provide further evidence of its origins.

The local grapevine spread word of what had happened, and it made a world of difference to the area, ridding it of the dealers and reducing acquisitive crime, which had been generated by the need to buy drugs. The betting shop survived and still trades at the time of this writing.

After Hackney, Operation Strongbox shifted to the two next boroughs to the west, Islington and Camden. For this posting, it was decided that I would oversee the intelligence unit rather than tackle yet another covert drugs operation. I would be based in an office at my old station in King's Cross. It was nice to return to my old stomping ground, although King's Cross Road Police station had, by then, become a police office where various units were housed rather than an operational response station. All that activity was now run from a purpose-built station opened in 1992 in Tolpuddle Street, a little way up the road.

The work was a little more deskbound than I'd been used to in recent years, but the hours were kinder and I got to work with an old pal from the last time I'd served here, and we were both now sergeants. There were more meetings to attend than I would have liked, but I'd get to work with the Borough superintendent and detective chief inspector who were very good to be around.

Someone on the borough made their own version of the in-house staff newspaper *The Job*, in which some of us were parodied using references from old TV cop shows. I was referred to as a geezer in a shiny suit from the Yard who spoke out of the corner of his mouth. How dare they! (I've still got my copy.)

The commissioner, a detective through the ranks, was concerned about a shortage of detective inspectors (DIs) and created a process to temporarily promote detective sergeants to DI if they'd passed the exam. The process required applicants to submit evidence in the competencies for the target rank and would be considered along with their superintendent's recommendation by a promotion panel. Around seventy candidates applied, and I was among forty that were successful. Luckily, Islington had a vacancy for a DI, and I was invited to stay on after Strongbox as a DI in the CID main office, which I accepted.

In a further development, shortly afterward, the commissioner decided that, as we'd been through a selection process, albeit an ad hoc one, it would be up to local management to confirm our promotion to the rank without further assessment. Result! I'd start in the new year on the first of January 'on call,' though most staff would be on leave until the fourth.

CHAPTER 8

Islington

Detective Inspector

I WAS IN DORSET STAYING WITH FRIENDS AFTER A NEW YEAR'S EVE party. It was the morning after when the phone rang. 'Guv'nor. I understand you're on call,' said my new Islington CID colleague. I was indeed on call, but I was a couple of hours away and hadn't really expected to hear from anyone on the morning of my first day, but here it was in the form of an unexplained death. I was thankfully sober having taken it easy the night before, just in case. And so, with a hasty goodbye to my hosts I made my way to the scene—a low-rise block of council flats in Highbury, which is home to both wealthy and poor. Grand houses in Georgian squares on tree-lined streets give way to local authority housing built in the 1960s and 1970s in spaces left blank after bombing from enemy aircraft during World War II. These blocks tend to be three or four floors high with communal spaces adorned with killjoy signs such as 'No Ball Games.' Nevertheless, some were immaculately kept homes and I envied them living in an inner London area where everything was a short tube ride away. In others, your feet would stick to the floor if ever you had reason to visit, and I was glad to live on the outskirts of town where I could escape from it all.

'Hello guv'nor,' the smiling detective sergeant on scene greeted me. He was at King's Cross when I last served there as a PC. This was a very experienced and respected detective sergeant and I wanted to make a good impression.

I would decide what happened next. Was it suspicious or a tragedy that was otherwise a natural end to someone's life? There was no sign of a fight or a break-in, but there were all the hallmarks of someone in later life living in diminished circumstances and with booze as a close companion. The main concern was that the flat was insecure as there was a disused coal hatch between the front of the house and the hallway that was just about big enough for someone to crawl through, and it was open. As the flat was quite untidy it was difficult to tell whether anything had been turned over or was missing.

As he lived alone, I decided to secure the scene and request a fast-track postmortem. The alternative was to call out forensic services and post a uniform officer to guard the scene 24/7 until we could be more certain about the cause and circumstances of death. That's what an arse covering guv'nor would do—transfer the risk to others so that you could go home while others would have to manage your inability to make a practical decision.

A better way would be to use a boarding up service to secure the hatch and get a patrol to drive past a couple of times per shift to keep an eye on the place. Everyone involved in the call would get to go home and eek out the last couple of days before everyone started the new year at work. It felt like I'd made a good decision, and the experienced DS nodded his approval.

Being a new boss, everyone was watching me, and I had a station full of judges trying to work out whether I was going to be a pain in the arse to work for or a decent guv'nor, as the rank now entitled me to be informally referred to. Dealing with an unexplained death, in a pragmatic way, during the holiday season when everything is just a little harder to manage made for a good start in my reputation bank. As it turned out, the postmortem revealed no suspicious circumstances and confirmed death from natural causes.

As I'd been called out on New Year's Day, I'd already been to the office and started sorting myself out in my new surroundings so it wouldn't feel like I was the new boy starting at big school when everyone came back from leave. I'd also spent some time on the computer, looking through the crime reports and the progress of investigations. I'd left comments on some of them. Nothing too critical, but just putting my marker down that I was interested in what people were doing, to show support and take responsibility for their workload. Naturally, it caused a bit of a buzz. Some liked the idea of their work being seen and noted, others felt over supervised. I didn't mind either perspective and was not seeking approval for showing my presence.

I was one of two new DIs and I'd work with an old friend, Mark, who was also a PC on the borough when I was there before. What a fortunate coincidence that we'd both be back, now with brown gloves, as it were! Mark and I got on very well and we had some laughs, but always making sure the work was done. We called a meeting with the detective sergeants, some of whom knew us both, and we set out our expectations in a way I know I'd want to hear from a new boss. Detective sergeants are the backbone of the CID and when I met our team, I was so pleased to have such an experienced and highly competent office to work with.

Our clear message to them was one of support and a commitment to keep them in the loop with everything. We'd have regular meetings to manage workloads and pool efforts across the various CID teams when a job needed it, rather than let someone shoulder the burden of a challenging case. Every investigation would be classified into its crime type, but each was unique and couldn't be assessed in terms of complexity by the quantity and classification alone. We were a team and would manage together. This seemed to work well and any initial suspicions about the new guv'nors in town were soon allayed by keeping our word and, of course, by sharing a swift half in the local after work from time to time. We soon dubbed our local 'The Clinic,' as our safe space to decompress from what was sometimes a frantic and demanding job.

The CID office at Islington was a long, wide room and each CID team was formed around a cluster of desks and led by a detective sergeant. At the other end of the office was the crime reporting team who would classify, sift, and allocate crimes for investigation. In the middle of all this was what we referred to as the 'goldfish bowl,' which was the DIs office made of panelled walls, the upper part of which was double glazed with built-in venetian blinds that could be closed for privacy when there was a confidential conversation, or for when someone was getting a bollocking.

From time to time, Mark would suggest closing the blinds to wind up the troops and make them think that something was going down. He'd time how long it took before someone was either brave enough or lost the toss-up and was sent to knock on the door. 'Come in' would be the reply and a politely inquisitive colleague would peer in and ask, 'Is everything OK, guv?' Mark's face would crack into a broad smile and our caller would back off with an 'Ah, you bastard guv'nor' and the blinds would be opened to reveal both of us smiling back at the gathered audience. Provided we didn't do it too often, we'd usually get a bite.

Among the differences I noticed in the years I'd been away was the high level of violence taking place in Islington. Once upon a time, a fight would result in a fat lip, a black eye, and wounded pride, but now stabbings were frequent and often resulted in life-changing or life-ending injuries.

Responding to critical incidents was routine, not a rarity, and the way my uniformed colleagues secured and held crime scenes, following 'golden hour' principles was impressive.

Sadly, there were too many examples, and they would often happen at night. It would involve one of the DIs responding, 'on call,' which would usually include being woken in the middle of the night.

Caledonian Road stretches from near Kings Cross station in the south, to Holloway in the north. Beautiful houses stand on one side and there are many small shops, takeaways, and a couple of pubs you wouldn't want to go into if you weren't a local. Pentonville prison adds a touch of local character.

After a night out in Islington, a small group of friends went in search of something to eat and found themselves in a kebab shop on Caledonian Road. As young black men they were not in the most welcoming of areas at the time. An argument started between them and some of the locals of similar age. In the fight, one from the visiting group was stabbed and he lay dying as his assailants disappeared into the night. The victim died in the resuscitation room of Whittington hospital, and I had the unenviable duty of meeting his father and introducing myself as the detective in charge of the initial investigation that would now be taken over by the murder squad. What struck me was how dignified he was. He was courteous and remained composed as he listened to my explanation and asked a few questions about what would happen next.

I have met too many loved ones in tragic circumstances and always admire their dignity. This was yet another senseless killing with lives ruined.

My fellow DI, Mark, asked one afternoon if I could cover his on call for the night as he had a social event he wanted to attend. It's quite common to swap duties and if someone is available it's not a problem.

Mark left the office just as a call came in about an unexplained death at Holloway women's prison, which was just about to land on my shoulders as the now DI on call.

Holloway Prison had been rebuilt in the 1970s, replacing Victorian-era buildings arranged in a hub and spoke design that enabled a single warder to monitor multiple wings from a central position. The prevailing view in modern times was that its women prisoners tended to be less troublesome and violent than their male counterparts and didn't need the same levels of surveillance. The new design consisted of multiple separate buildings to promote the concept of smaller family groups of prisoners providing support for each other. Still a high security prison and the largest women's facility in Europe, these red brick buildings were arranged more like a campus, with shared facilities such as a gym, sports hall, and swimming pool all separate from the residential accommodations.

I attended along with a young female detective. We slowly made our way through the various checkpoints and gateways to reach the cell block and what we would treat as our crime scene. The cell was specially designated for close observation by staff and was intentionally minimally furnished. The deceased prisoner, Emily, was in her late twenties and had been in and out of detention facilities over the years. She cut a very sad figure, slumped as she was against the bedframe from which she'd hanged herself from the modified bra that she'd fashioned into a noose. Emily suffered from addictions, depression, and suicidal tendencies. Because of this she was on enhanced monitoring with frequent checks and was kept from being able to access anything that could lead to self-harm. Even so, this surveillance did not cover every minute of her daily life and, in a moment of solitude in her cell, she took her own life.

Staff at the prison seemed to be quite matter-of-fact about it and set about the routine procedures for a prisoner death. That's not to say I thought they didn't care, but I expect they deal with death in a way that lets them cope with it as a professional reality, just as other professions do, including mine.

Even so, there is a procedure to follow to ensure there are no suspicious circumstances, including photography, evidential examination of the scene, and recovery of the body. Another important feature of suicide by hanging is to preserve the knot so that it can be examined to work out whether it was tied by the deceased or someone else. When a homicide is made to look like a suicide by hanging, the knot can betray the killer when experts are able to demonstrate that the victim couldn't have tied it.

Also, in the postmortem, the pathologist will look for discoid bruises, which are those caused by fingertips and an indication of strangulation rather than suicide.

In ligature strangulation and in hanging, another significant finding can be the mark left by ligature itself. This would leave either a straight line across the neck in a ligature strangulation, or in a hanging case as a mark that rises to a point because of the suspension. There could also be defensive marks and material below the fingernails, indicating a fight, or a frantic attempt by the deceased to remove a ligature from around their neck.

My role at the scene is to look for any obvious signs of foul play and to preserve the body with the ligature in place for the forensic examination that will take place during the postmortem. One must look at the scene with curiosity and an investigative mindset that gathers detail and context at the same time.

To complete this assessment, I sat going through a stack of documents with a senior prison officer, which had been copied ready for me to take away as exhibits. The documents were immaculate and provided a record going back over time of every incident, response, and decision concerning the care, interventions, and ongoing monitoring of Emily while in detention. These notes were handwritten by different authors, through many changes of shifts and personnel, which added to their verification and authenticity. I spoke with a cellmate who knew Emily well and had spent a lot of time with her. Though upset about Emily's death, she was able to provide an account of Emily's life in recent months and her repeated references to taking her own life.

Tragic as it was, there were no suspicious circumstances evident from the scene, which the subsequent postmortem the following day confirmed. What a sad way for a life to end. I went back to the station and made enough notes to be able to pick up on things in the morning and made my way home after a sixteen-hour day.

I eventually pulled up outside my house at around midnight and had just put the key in the door when my mobile phone rang with a call from the night duty CID. There had been a stabbing in Essex Road, Islington, with a single victim in hospital, and it looked like he wasn't going to make it. As a result, members of his family and some of his friends were on the rampage looking for suspects and some of them were headed for the hospital in a furious mood.

Essex Road is about a mile long and runs northeast from the trendier parts of Islington toward Stoke Newington and mainly consists of Victorian-era townhouse style properties, some with shopfronts containing independent businesses, restaurants, takeaways, and pubs. Residential properties are either those at the more expensive end of older period homes or social and local authority housing. Nearby, toward the north end of Essex Road is the Marquess Estate. Built between the mid-1960s and 1970s, it gave priority to pedestrians rather than vehicles, with a series of streets built too narrow for cars, and with family homes around green spaces. It was hailed as a showpiece of design of the time. However, it wasn't long before the estate acquired a fearsome reputation for crime and vandalism, with its tight and intricate layout being perfect for criminals to escape into its depths. The victim of the stabbing was from the estate and those involved in seeking retribution were his friends and family.

As I ended the call with my night duty team, I wondered if I could just pop into my place and change my shirt, but I decided it wasn't going to make any difference. It was pouring rain and it wasn't going to be the moment for looking one's sharpest. I'd given my team directions to preserve the scene and protect any evidence from being washed away by the weather, improvising by using anything they could find to cover it. I also decided they should close Essex Road to traffic, and I sent uniformed officers to the hospital to head off any trouble there.

Meanwhile, local officers were responding to reports of suspects from the stabbing being in addresses on the Marquess estate and, in their eagerness to apprehend them, were kicking in doors to find they weren't there after all. This was draining resources to clear up the aftermath when I needed any spare units to support the investigation, so I gave the order not to force entry to any premises without my express permission. I needed everything to calm the hell down! I'd given enough directions to hold the line until I could get there, which would take about forty-five minutes.

I took charge at the scene. There, I was met by my night duty detectives who gathered with me in a huddle to discuss the situation, so far. I sent one of them back to the station to be the intelligence point of contact—someone who would find out who the victim was, the alleged suspects, and the network of people involved. This would help us to focus on where we might find the suspects, as they would be likely to seek shelter with someone who would give them sanctuary for the night. There was no point in kicking down every door in town.

In the street, I called together a huddle of a handful of officers and supervisors from the uniformed night shift and shared my plan with them. We stood in the middle of the road in heavy rain for a town hall-style meeting to share situational awareness and an action plan. I could feel cold rain running down the back of my collar and down my neck. I was making notes as they took turns to share their updates with me, but my notebook was soaked, and my cheap pen was making my writing barely legible as it struggled to mark the wet paper. One of the officers said that they'd been getting pressure to reopen the road, which was a main route into Islington as well as a bus route. It was now around 1:00 a.m., a weekday, and pouring rain. The buses would have to wait or go around—this was a potential murder scene.

In fairness, the police response had been pretty good, so far. The rain brought pros and cons. The scene was in danger of being washed away unless we worked hard to preserve it: the site of the stabbing, discarded clothing, and the weapon and blood on the ground. And it was miserable to work in torrential rain. On the upside, rain is a brilliant copper as it tends to get everyone off the streets and would usually provide for a quiet night. As this was the biggest thing going on across the division, I had plenty of people to help.

This incident was another example of senseless violence in which an individual was stabbed to death in the street over an argument that shouldn't have escalated. As this was now a murder investigation, it would be taken over by the homicide team, who would arrive early the next morning for the handover. I would be there to provide them with it.

My boss came in early and saw me at my desk, exactly where he saw me at the end of the previous working day and in the same clothes. He gave me a knowing look and a put his hand on my shoulder. 'I'm so glad we had a competent pair of hands dealing with everything that's happened overnight, but fuck me Kev, you must be the unluckiest bloke I've met in a long while!'

I was sent home, and Mark came in full of smiles, having narrowly swerved what should've been his night on call. I was the butt of jokes from him and my boss for the next few minutes until they got it out of their system, and I was able to hand the reins over to them. I got home around lunchtime and crawled into bed after pulling a brutally long shift. The murder was solved, with the suspect being caught soon after.

Weak Signals

For good reason, depictions of detectives in TV dramas tend not to reflect all the realities and workloads that go with the job, as some of it isn't very exciting. There's a huge administrative part to the job, which increases with rank along with the responsibilities of leadership. Monitoring and supervising caseloads so everyone keeps on top of things, approving applications for forensic submissions or accessing phone records, checking warrants, attending management meetings, and keeping up with appraisals and budgets are not the stuff of a Netflix drama.

It's true of all areas of policing that increasing demand outpaces the capacity to respond to and resolve society's need for protection and safety. I remember from the early days of my career when calls were assigned with a message number starting with 01 on the stroke of midnight and ending in the thousands one second before the following midnight. Before widespread ownership of mobile phones in the early 1990s, a call to the police would come from a landline or a call box on a street corner, but gradually the calls increased and message numbers routinely exceeded ten thousand, daily. Having the ability to call the police immediately from the device in your hand made it easy to report incidents, accidents, and call for help. It removed the friction and delay in finding a phone and increased demand for which the service wasn't configured for back then and grapples with to this day.

Crimes reported by the public were triaged by a crime management team that allocated those of a serious nature or with potential leads to investigators. There were some property-related crimes, which were often reported for the purpose of an insurance claim and offered no realistic hope of being solved and so were classified as 'screened out,' leaving our investigative capacity for those crimes that really needed it.

It was the early days of the new year, and I was sitting at my desk in the CID office in Islington facing a mountain of work. One of my responsibilities was to review missing persons if they hadn't been found within twenty-four hours of being reported or for higher risk cases, as assessed by the reporting officer. There are many reasons why a missing person will be considered higher risk, including having an illness; being a vulnerable child or young person; having a history of anxiety, substance abuse, self-harm, or any other reason that heightens concern for the safety and well-being of someone.

A missing person report, in and of itself, means that someone is concerned for another. Sometimes, those making the report don't want to overreact or trouble the police, leaving it until later to make a report in case the missing person shows up later or in circumstances they hadn't anticipated. Those concerned will usually have taken the initial steps to find the missing person themselves, calling friends and family members, maybe even calling hospitals to check whether they've been involved in an accident. In most cases, when someone reports a missing person, they have run out of ideas, are worried, and need help from the police.

Around 180,000 people are reported missing every year in the United Kingdom and not all are found. Mental health, domestic abuse, relationship breakdown, dementia, and child exploitation are among the common reasons for people to go missing. The law assumes an adult person is entitled to their privacy, which includes leaving a life behind, ending of a relationship, or even separating from their family if they choose to. This happens. People fall out with others or have a desire to start a new life afresh and the police can't violate that right to privacy if that's what the person wants. Sometimes, people are reported missing, then found and, although they may be reassured that the missing person is safe and well, their whereabouts are not shared with the person who filed the report. Other cases involving vulnerable people at risk need to be carefully assessed and someone to pull the right levers to escalate the response when necessary.

There was (and probably still is) a tension between officers on front line response duties who, understandably, want to manage their workload and the investigating teams that, similarly, want to manage their case-loads to take on only those that need their attention. Many investigations and incidents, including reported crime, domestic violence calls, disputes, child protection, cases of stalking and harassment, and missing persons carry the risk of suddenly escalating into a more serious problem. Any officer holding such a case, or who was the last to deal with the situation, can find their actions and decision-making under intense scrutiny. It is easy to find examples of officers being subject to internal investigations, sometimes taking months or even years before being resolved, because of these ticking time bombs that lie dormant in the ever-growing caseloads and calls from the public. It can be career limiting, morale sapping, and depression inducing for those under internal investigation. Following the report into the Clapham rail disaster in 1988, the senior lawyer, Anthony Hidden QC said, 'There is almost no human action or decision that cannot be made to look flawed and less sensible in the misleading light of hindsight.'

The essential skill was in distinguishing weak signals within the noise of daily tasks and to notice and react to something that needed closer inspection.

Sometimes, I noticed a tendency by reporting and supervising officers to write up missing person reports so that they met the higher levels of risk in the assessment. This would tend to kick the case up the road for someone else to take responsibility, that someone being me, but I understood the tensions and usually forgave them for their creativity.

We had several children's care homes on our patch. Any child or young person who was late home would be reported missing in what I was told was an ass-covering exercise by its staff, who would pass the buck to us and create an enormous and unnecessary workload. Sometimes these children were described as 'runaways,' a term that tended to downplay the risk as a feature of their own petulance or bad conduct over which they had agency.

These were children who had often faced challenges in their young lives and were more inclined to take risks than other children of a similar age, so they were doubly vulnerable. We had years of data that demonstrated that nearly all reports resulted in the young person turning up safe, but later than their curfew and beyond an arbitrary threshold that triggered a call to the police.

I tasked a personable and efficient officer with finding ways to manage the demand. She came back with some interesting feedback from the care homes. It seems that they were only reporting these cases because they thought that's what the police required them to do. The staff at the homes followed a rules-based approach because that's how it had always been done, and for a long time had been part of the training for everyone who came into this line of work. Digging a little deeper, we came to learn that this procedure was a clear example of a policy created during a time of much lower demands on police time. The police told the care homes what they should do, and they willingly adopted it as policy. I remember seeing a TV news clip from the early 1980s in which the commander for Hackney district, in response to an issue raised by a journalist, said that it was for him to decide how Hackney is policed, and no one else. It sounds odd to hear this from the modern perspective of partnership, collaboration, and community involvement in deciding the priorities for policing, but this posture was from a time when police were more authoritative in approach and others more compliant. Many years prior, the police created the missing person reporting rules for children in care homes, a policy that had been followed ever since. It was time to take another look. We came up with several scenarios for these homes to consider before calling on us for help: A child or young person is one hour late. So what? How old are they? Are they usually punctual? Have initial actions raised concerns? Were they out with others who have returned? Did they go off with others who didn't return? Can the staff take some initial steps before contacting the police? Has this raised or increased concerns? We reached a conclusion that acknowledged that context would be more important than an arbitrary time-based threshold.

Care home staff said that they would be content to wait a reasonable amount of time in most circumstances where there wasn't any reason to be concerned. We agreed on a protocol that cut down the number of reports overnight, saving their time and ours, while managing risk rather than following a one-rule-fits-all policy. I made sure the officer was suitably commended for developing the protocol and given the deserved credit.

I had fewer reports to read through after these changes were implemented, but there were still plenty to assess. One in particular caught my eye.

Paula Fields was a thirty-four-year-old mother of three boys who were in care. She had acquired a drug habit that changed her life dramatically, turning to sex work to fund her addiction.

Did the fact that Paula was an addict and sex worker mean that her life was in disorder to the point of being chaotic and less deserving of being considered vulnerable? Should the threshold have been higher for her to be in the high-risk category? Did her life matter less because of her lifestyle? I ask these questions knowing that some factions of society might think so—a view I didn't share.

Paula loved her children, of that there is no doubt. Despite the challenges in her life, she would see them regularly and keep in touch with her sister. Paula would keep doctor's appointments and collect her prescriptions. She maintained her 'pay as you go' mobile phone and used her debit card to make payments and withdraw what cash she had in her account. There was routine to her life that gave it a pattern and, since going missing, that pattern had stopped completely. Paula would not leave money in her account untouched as she needed this to survive in a hand-to-mouth subsistence lifestyle. It was a simple exercise to draw a line down the last day or two she was probably alive, as all her routines ended suddenly.

I began an investigation, raising the classification to high-risk and appointed a dedicated officer to work on several lines of enquiry. The first thing that needed to be done was to have her home in Finsbury Park searched for any signs of life, establish whether there was a crime scene, or see if she left it in a hurry, but little was evident so I sealed it off so that we could go back there when more became known. Our investigation continued with family, friends, other residents, and those agencies that had been part of her life, with some information about her movements and friendships but nothing to propel us forward significantly. It was going to be a matter of searching everything methodically, one step at a time. How could she live without money, her phone, and medication? We checked hospitals, prisons, and a swathe of public services, hostels, and rehab facilities, all to no avail.

Unless I could show that there was evidence that Paula had come to harm, her case remained a missing person report and wouldn't have any further resources allocated to it. I was lucky to have an officer I could dedicate to the investigation, and she did a great job in just a few days uncovering the recent history of Paula's life. Paula had moved to London some years prior to better her life, but it didn't work out well for her. Drugs, depression, and removal of her children into the care system because of her lifestyle took a toll, and eventually she turned to sex work to pay for her addiction. One of Paula's sisters had last spoken with her around the middle of December and said that she hadn't shown up for Christmas, which was out of character. When they hadn't heard from Paula or been able to reach her on her phone, their concerns grew and by mid-January they made a formal missing person report, which I had picked up.

A couple of weeks went by, and I was enjoying a rare weekend off with tickets to a rugby match at Twickenham. Barely above the noise of the stadium I heard my mobile phone, or probably felt its vibration it in my pocket. It was the senior investigating officer from the homicide team on call.

The Regent's Canal was a popular urban fishing spot, and two friends were angling from the towpath on a section in Camden, bordering Islington, where Paula lived. One of their lines caught on something under the water and after struggling to land it, they pulled it out and examined their discovery. It was a sports holdall that contained some bricks and broken tiles, below which were some plastic bags that, to their horror, contained human remains. A walker, passing by and witnessing their distress, went to help them and called the police.

The resulting crime scene led to a section of the canal being drained. Five more bags, weighed down with bricks, were recovered and held ten separate body parts. The torso was in two pieces and each of the arms and legs were cut in two. However, to thwart identification, the head, hands, and feet were missing. Initially, all that was known was that it was the body of a woman within an estimated age range. Without the other body parts, facial recognition and fingerprints were not an option for identification and there were no tattoos or marks to check against missing persons records. There were few forensic opportunities at the scene as the remains had been in the canal for at least a month, so, at that stage, detectives didn't know who she was, when she died, or where she died.

Of course, DNA would provide a good identification, but it needed to be compared with ante mortem samples known to be from the person when they were alive, such as a used toothbrush that would have cells from inside the mouth, a hairbrush that would have DNA from a stray hair, or a sample that could be matched with a known family member, none of which were options in this case as her identity was unknown. The only other way to match DNA from a scene was against the national database, meaning that the person had a criminal record and had their DNA sample taken when charged. Blood was taken from the remains and a match with Paula Fields was confirmed, as she had a record for a few minor convictions. The homicide team had found our missing person marker on the same database, which led to the phone call I was now answering. I headed into the office and did what I could to help and handover what we had discovered in our investigation. It was a small comfort knowing that our missing person investigation had given the homicide team a head start, along with access to Paula's flat, which was still preserved and secured as a crime scene.

Paula's family were informed, and it devastated them to learn not only of her death, but that she had been brutally murdered and how her body had been disposed of. I also broke the news to the officer who'd been carrying out the investigation under my supervision. I don't know if it was because I'm a thoughtless idiot or had just become hardened to violence and death in my professional life, but I hadn't anticipated how upset she'd be. Of course, she'd got to know some of Paula's family and friends, but also had grown attached to Paula even though she'd never met her. She felt sorry for Paula's circumstances and had learned during her part of the investigation of the love Paula had for her family, which shone through in conversations with people who knew her. I was clumsy and hadn't appreciated she'd become so attached. That would leave a somatic marker on my memory and remind me that the role of a leader isn't so much about what you do, but how you make people feel.

Now a confirmed murder, the investigation was supported by a full team of homicide detectives who discovered that Paula had been seeing a man called Joe Johnson. He had been staying occasionally with the resident of another flat on her block, a man called Tony. What they found out was that Joe was an alias. His real name was John Sweeney and that he was Tony's brother, who had been covering for him. Joe Johnson and John Sweeney were the same person. The reason he used an alias was because he was wanted for attempted murder of his then girlfriend Delia Balmer a few years earlier in 1994.

In common with Paula, he too was from Liverpool and had moved to London in the mid-1980s. Back then, people said he reminded them of John Lennon in appearance, accent, and because of his apparent bohemian lifestyle. He worked as a carpenter, which enabled him to pick up work where and when he chose as there was always a building site somewhere in London that needed his skills.

It was at one such Central London building site where detectives tracked down Sweeney, which resulted in his arrest, but not without a fight. He had nothing to lose by resisting. He was fit and strong, but officers overpowered and arrested him for the attempted murder of his former girlfriend, Delia.

Delia's story was harrowing. She and Sweeney met in 1991 in a London pub, where she was alone and noticed him staring at her. He approached her and struck up a conversation and seemed rather charming and charismatic. They seemed to hit it off. Before long, they were seeing so much of each other that they decided he should move in with her.

However, over time, the relationship deteriorated as Sweeney became jealous of any associations she had with others and demanded to know where she was at all times. He became controlling, possessive, and aggressive to the extent that Delia wanted him to leave. She confided in Rosie, a friend at the hospital where she worked, about the problems she was having in her relationship. She wanted out and had repeatedly asked him to leave, but he prevaricated, saying he would do so, making promises that weren't kept. One holiday weekend in May, after yet another argument, she went to see Martine, a friend who lived in Hackney, and was invited to stay over for some respite from him, enjoying the evening and the next day wandering the local markets and visiting a couple of pubs. Delia returned to her own flat on Monday evening as she had work on Tuesday. Sweeney was there waiting for her.

He questioned her aggressively about her appearance, where she'd been, and with whom. She tried tactical avoidance by going to bed in an attempt to stop the argument. Within seconds of reaching the bedroom he pounced on her, tied her up, produced a gun and a kitchen knife, and threatened to cut her tongue out if she screamed. He tied her hands and feet to the bedframe and continued to question her angrily about mementos of male friends from her past that he'd found in a search through her possessions while she was out.

Then, he untied her legs and raped her in her own bed. She lay there all night, hands tied, fearing for her life, and wetting the bed for fear of asking if he would let her use the bathroom.

Late the following morning, the phone rang, and he answered it. It was the hospital asking where Delia was as she was expected at work. Sweeney calmly explained that she'd had to leave for an emergency and would be back the next week and ended the call. Within a few minutes, the phone rang again and, this time, there was an angry exchange between Sweeney and Delia's colleague, Rosie. He slammed the receiver down, rattled by the second call. He told Delia that Rosie was threatening to call the police if she didn't hear from Delia by midday, so he decided he would untie her and let her make that call, closely watched by him so he could hear everything she said. Rosie accepted Delia's explanation and the call ended. Sweeney didn't tie her up again. They spent the day talking as he shared with Delia accounts of his harsh upbringing, seeking sympathy from her.

She managed his temperamental mood carefully and spent another night under his control, where she convinced him to agree that they would go to counselling the next day. In the morning, Delia gathered up the soiled bedding and said she needed to go to the launderette, but he was having none of it and, at gunpoint, told her he was going to have to kill her along with any of her friends if they came looking for her. She talked him out of killing her in that moment and he put the gun down, vacillating between being angry with her and being nice. On the fourth day they ventured out together to a café, Delia still very much under his control. They returned to the flat, Delia mulling over the lost opportunity for a potential escape and Sweeney reassured that she hadn't tried to. Probably feeling that she wasn't going to have him arrested, he decided to leave the following morning. With bags packed, he handed Delia the keys and he took a minicab to stay with a friend in Holloway. Initially, Delia was relieved that it was over, but this proved to be short-lived. He came back the next day, letting himself in using a spare set of keys he'd had made. He told Delia that he'd changed his mind.

Delia returned to work the following Monday and shared her experience with her friends, not knowing what to do. The obvious answer was to go to the police, but she was scared that they wouldn't be able to protect her and that he would come back for revenge and likely kill her.

After many months of seemingly interminable coercive control, he left for contractor work in Germany. Delia changed the locks. She had peace at last, or so she thought, but once again her nightmare wasn't over. One evening she came home from work to find him inside her flat waiting for her. He entered by using a ladder to reach the bathroom window, which was slightly open. She screamed and he thrust his fingers down her throat, injuring her in the process in what he later said was an attempt to pull her tongue out. He kept her prisoner in her own home again. Delia knew it was pointless to attempt an escape. She was terrified of him. He spoke about killing himself and taking her with him. His volatile mood swings from anger to being nice were unpredictable. He later suggested that they both leave the flat and go for a drink, which Delia initially refused, but then accepted it was the only way to get him out of her flat, so they went to the pub down the road and sat at a table outside and had a drink. At the end of the evening, Delia took the opportunity to go into the pub on the pretence of needing the toilet. Once inside, she pleaded for help from the bar staff. Sweeney gathered that she wasn't willingly going to let him go back to the flat with her and that being in a public place with witnesses there wasn't much he could do, so he disappeared into the night. Delia went to the police who escorted her back to the flat. He didn't come back that night. Delia spoke with her friend Martine the next morning, arranging to meet her for a drink at two o'clock that afternoon, telling her what had happened and how desperately frightened she was of him.

Delia got ready to leave, bracing herself that Sweeney may be waiting for her. As she opened the front door he barged in and immediately attacked her, again forcing his fingers down her throat, telling her to be quiet, and that he just wanted to speak to her after which he'd leave. He revealed that he had been hiding on the roof at the back of the flat when the police brought her home the previous night and that he'd heard her speaking with Martine on the phone. A short time later, when the phone rang, they both knew it would be Martine, but they didn't answer. Martine came by and knocked on the front door. She could tell someone was home and so persisted in knocking and calling out Delia's name, but still there was no answer. Thankfully, she didn't let it go and called the police, suspecting there was something wrong. The police arrived quickly and aware of Delia's recent history with Sweeney, they demanded the door be opened. Delia cracked open the door slightly to see two police officers then ran past them into the street to be consoled by Martine. Sweeney was arrested, charged with assault, and remanded into custody until a later hearing in which he was granted bail. Was it finally over?

Delia, deeply troubled by her ordeal, tried to go about her daily routines and then, one evening as she arrived home from work on her bicycle, Sweeney appeared menacingly behind her on the steps to her flat. He attacked her with the wooden handle of an axe, raining blows on her as she screamed for him to leave her alone. Then, he lashed out with the blade, striking the bike's metal frame as Delia tried to protect herself with it. He dropped the axe and pulled out a long knife and plunged it into her chest, puncturing her lung. He then stabbed her in the thigh, before swapping back to the axe, chopping off the top of one of her fingers, right there on her doorstep. At that moment, the twenty-one-year-old son from the family next door appeared and having heard the commotion, had armed himself with a baseball bat and struck Sweeney hard on his back after which he fled along the street, still carrying the axe. Police and an ambulance crew arrived, and she was taken to the hospital where she'd remain to make a slow recovery from her serious injuries.

On examining Delia's flat as a crime scene, officers found what can only be described as a body disposal kit that included a groundsheet, a handsaw, masking tape, scouring pads, a sponge, and a change of clothing—everything needed to dismember and dispose of a dead body.

Detectives investigating Paula's murder learned that during her imprisonment by Sweeney, he'd told Delia about a girlfriend Melissa, an American model he'd lived with in Amsterdam, and when he found her in their apartment with two other men, he shot all three of them and sat with the bodies for three days before dismembering them and disposing of them by dumping their remains in canals in Amsterdam. He'd retracted this the following day, telling Delia that he'd made the story up to frighten her. However, detectives were struck by the similarities to the way Paula's remains had been discovered.

Forensic examination of the soil from bricks found in the bags recovered from the canal Paula was found in revealed that they were a good match with soil from the garden of the house where Sweeney was living at the time of Paula's disappearance. It wasn't enough to charge him, let alone convict him. He denied knowing Paula and there was no solid proof that he did.

Firearms, demonic and macabre artwork, poetry, and notes were found in the search of Sweeney's home some six years after the attempted murder of Delia and the new investigation into Paula's murder. They included anti-establishment and misogynistic drawings and writing, with graphic violent images of women being hurt. There were also notes including an account of his relationship with Melissa, which mentioned that because she was overstaying her visa in the United Kingdom, they first went to Vienna and that he hoped to be with her again when he dies, implying that she was already dead.

In one of the handwritten poems, it said:
Poor old Melissa,
Chopped her up in bits,
Food to feed the fish,
Amsterdam was the pits.

Detectives contacted Dutch police, but they had no record of the murders of two men and a woman, but they did have an outstanding missing person report on file for Melissa Halstead, a US national who'd been reported missing by her family back in 1990. Detectives learned that Melissa had been living in Amsterdam with a British boyfriend called John Sweeney. They were renting an apartment together. When the landlord called round to pick up overdue rent, he found it empty. Because Melissa had suggested to her family that she might go touring around Europe, there were no immediate concerns for her, but as time went on those concerns grew, and she had formally been reported as missing. There was no evidence at the time to connect Sweeney with Melissa's disappearance.

Sweeney appeared in court on the allegations relating to Delia and other matters including firearms charges. In 2002, Sweeney was found guilty of the attempted murder of Delia Balmer, false imprisonment, actual bodily harm, and unlawful possession of firearms. He was sent to prison on a life sentence, though would be eligible for parole in nine years.

There was insufficient evidence to charge him with the murder of Paula Fields so it became a cold case, until 2007 when the Rotterdam police contacted the London homicide team and reported that they had reopened an investigation into the recovered, dismembered remains of a female body found in the Westersingel canal in 1990. Mirroring Paula's body, Melissa's too was missing her head, hands, and feet but modern DNA procedures had now resulted in a positive identification. Rotterdam detectives had then been able to link the missing person report from Amsterdam with the grim discovery. The dots were connected to the Paula Fields case with the high suspicion that Sweeney had murdered both Melissa and Paula.

Sweeney had met Melissa in the mid-1980s. They journeyed to Milan, Vienna, and Amsterdam. Sweeney was known to be violent with her as there are friends and family accounts of him hitting her with a chair on one occasion and a piece of wood on another. Melissa had confided in her sister that if she ever went missing, it would be Sweeney that killed her, and he would make sure her body was never found. After one particularly violent episode, he was charged with assaulting her with a hammer and detained in custody pending trial. Despite this, he pleaded with her to drop the charges and promised to leave her alone forever. She relented and he was released, shortly after which they both disappeared. Eighteen years later, the remains found in Rotterdam were confirmed as Melissa's.

By the time the cold case was reopened, Sweeney was just a few months away from being eligible for parole and both police forces began a joint investigation. Each case was identical in the way the remains were found, identical patterns of violent relationships, and the reported conversation Sweeney had with Delia about killing Melissa. Each case was providing supporting evidence for the other.

Forensic examination revealed that of a piece of Sweeney's artwork had correction fluid covering a repainted section and special lighting showed the depiction of a gravestone with Melissa's name, date of birth, and death date with three question marks after it, which leave open the date she died.

In Gartree prison where Sweeney was serving his sentence for the attempted murder of Delia, he was arrested and later charged with two counts of murder and, in the first case of its kind, was prosecuted for both murders through the courts in England. Although there had been other serious crime cases from different jurisdictions jointly prosecuted in the UK, this was the first murder case.

Sweeney's own paintings and poems were damning when presented to the jury. In these documents he incriminated himself, including a drawing that carried the title 'The Scalp Hunter' that depicted an axe and a female skull hanging from a belt. Another, found in his cell at Gartree, was the outline of a headless, dismembered body identical to the way Paula's body had been mutilated. As the jury was told, time had failed to dim Sweeney's fascination and preoccupation with dismemberment.

He was found guilty and sent to prison for life. Only one hundred prisoners in UK prisons are serving a whole life tariff, such is the relative rarity of those serving with the expectation of never being released.

I started this chapter by pointing out the statistics relating to missing persons, whose numbers are far higher than most might expect. I appreciate my good fortune in living a safe and relatively comfortable life when I say that I don't know anyone in my extended family or circle of friends who has been reported missing and remains among the long-term unfound. Neither can I think of anyone who knows anyone beyond my circle in these circumstances. It must be a nightmare for those who do, hanging on in limbo without being able to grieve with certainty and holding out hope that they might be alive, in whatever circumstances.

In her book *Living with a serial killer*,[1] Delia said that Sweeney had several girlfriends or associates that have disappeared. They include Sue, a trainee nurse from Derbyshire, who frequented the North London area before she went missing; Irani, a Brazilian national who worked and mixed in the same social circles in North London; and Maria, a

Colombian national whom Sweeney knew that went missing from High-bury in 1998.

Sweeney's artwork discovered during the investigation is said to have depicted some of these girls. Whether they came to harm has not been proven.

The international criminal police organization, or Interpol as it is better known, issued a 'black notice,' which is an alert shared with police worldwide to seek information about unidentified bodies. The notice announced an investigation by the name 'Operation Identify Me,' which is a public appeal to identify twenty-two women believed to have been murdered in Belgium, Germany, and The Netherlands, but whose identity has never been found. Most are cold cases—women who died ten, twenty, thirty, or even forty years ago.

Among the cases are some that could not have involved Sweeney as he was in prison and others that were dissimilar in method. However, some dismembered remains were found in circumstances with similarities to the way Paula and Melissa were found, having been discovered in waterways.

In 1992, a passerby found two hands in a canal in Amsterdam. A search by police discovered two lower legs and a suitcase containing the torso of a female. Some days later, more body parts were found at Prinsengracht and forensic evidence established that all body parts belonged to the same person. Her head was never found. This person's identity has not yet been established.

In January 1995, in a creek in Amstelveen, a suburb of Amsterdam, a passerby saw a plastic package floating in the water and called the police. It contained part of the body of a woman wrapped in a sheet. Her head, lower legs, and one arm were not found. The police investigated the case but have not been able to establish the woman's identity.

I should add that these facts do not mean that Sweeney is responsible for any of these crimes, but the violent death of all twenty-two women and the concealment of their remains in the circumstances described in Operation Identify Me are equally as tragic to those of Paula and Melissa. I hope their identities and deaths are successfully investigated.

Knowing as we now do about Delia and Melissa's life with Sweeney, Paula's final moments would have been horrific.

From a routine day in the CID office studying missing person reports, the ripple effects of this case would reveal a long history of brutal crimes. The investigation would've begun anyway, but I'm thankful that I reacted to the weak signals and took the time to dig deeper, taking the disappearance of someone in unfortunate circumstances as seriously as we did.

Commissioner's Focus Group

By random good fortune, I was given a place on the Commissioner's focus group. Then Commissioner Sir John Stevens formed a reference group of one hundred officers and staff from across the service as a sounding board for ideas and to keep him informed about what was going on. He'd bring us together in the briefing room at Scotland Yard and ask for feedback about our work and life in the Met. He was refreshingly candid, curious about us, and had an authenticity that was uniquely impressive. In answer to one question about officers being concerned about the force being sued if they got things wrong, he said, 'Do your job. If you've acted in good faith, I'll back you all the way. And as for being sued, we get sued anyway.'

He was such a clever operator and knew that such stories would become legendary, amplified throughout the workforce. One of his other tricks was to 'arrest' plainclothed officers in the lobby areas or elevators of Scotland Yard if they weren't wearing their ID. I think his real concern, rather than a terrorist infiltration, was that an investigative journalist would embarrass the Met by walking freely around the building. Their arrest would result in the officer being taken to his office and having a cup of tea with the commissioner, who would want to know all about their work and how he might be able to support them. Most arrestees spoke of him highly and about the amazing conversation they'd had with him. Their detention would end when the officer's supervisor or senior officer was summoned and, arriving in a sweaty panic, was praised for having such a good officer and for doing great work. In a very skillful marketing exercise, everyone began to wear their passes, without fail, for fear of a similar encounter and thus we learned about his unique leadership style.

I was one of a handful of people from the focus group invited to lunch with the commissioner, deputy commissioner, and the journalist, Sir Max Hastings. We dined in the commissioner's dining room, which, as far as I could tell, was a rather large, if otherwise ordinary meeting room where the table had been set with a tablecloth, silver service, and a waitress to serve the same canteen food from the other side of the kitchen. I wasn't complaining and I wasn't really there for the food. The conversation was a little formal, but Sir Max seemed genuinely interested in what life was like in the Met. We were given carte blanche to tell it 'warts and all.'

I genuinely loved my job at that time and told him so. My biggest disappointment was the label of institutional racism, which was hard to take, but the Lawrence enquiry had led to real change that you could see every day in our response to every critical incident. I was acutely aware at this moment that I was being presented as the acceptable face of the Met and knew some of my old colleagues would enjoy taking the piss out of me if they could see me now!

The focus group led to an opportunity to join the commissioner's leadership course and go on a week-long leadership event in the beautiful and historic town of Arundel, Sussex. We were a group of about fifty from different departments, institutions, and businesses, split into smaller teams to spend time together in breakout rooms and join shared events such as presentations from leaders in policing and beyond. I was in a group with an architect from Property Services in the Met, a senior Crown prosecutor, a senior manager from the communications giant BT, and a facilitator from a consultancy known as the Industrial Society.

We had deep and meaningful discussions, and I poured everything into it that I could. In the whole group sessions, we went through a leadership exercise based on the story of Henry V, which was led by Richard Olivier, son of the famous actor Laurence. It was, without doubt, the most beneficial and inspirational leadership training experience I'd ever been through while in the police, and I remember it fondly. By chance, I've met Richard since in another context and shared my thoughts with him.

An architect in our breakout group had been thinking about leaving the Met. I was flattered to learn that I'd changed her mind by sharing some of my experiences with the group. She said it reminded her of the reason why she'd chosen to work in the Met in the first place, rather than in a private practice. She felt she'd lost her purpose before connecting with it again during this leadership course and was reminded about differences she could make to the front line.

I'd learned a lot in that short, but intense week. For the most part, I'd learned about myself, my leadership style, and to stop beating myself up about things. Also, it was clear that I was trying to do everything and should stop trying to 'boil the ocean.'

Among the worst nightmares for hardworking cops is the guvnor who returns from a course and tries to change the world in their first few days back, using everything they've learned. I decided it was best to do nothing for a while and just reflect. To my former colleagues—you're welcome!

I was at the age where most of my friends were in successful long-term relationships, some were married with children to whom I was a godparent. I'd decided I was a poor effort of a godparent if I didn't see the kids from one year to the next, so I committed to going to a children's birthday party to show my face and make amends. I even helped by taking the sausage rolls out of the oven and testing several of them.

I stood with the parents of other kids attending the party while we watched the entertainment, and I was getting along rather well with one of the ladies who was way out of my league. Besides, she probably had a husband and so I thought I'd better behave. After the party, I stayed behind and helped to clear up some more sausage rolls and anything else I could shove in my face to save me the effort of making my own dinner that evening. My godchild's father had taken notice of how well I'd been getting on with Jane, the mother of three- and five-year-old girls at the party who went to the same school as my godchild. It was suggested we'd make a nice couple, now that she was a single parent, and how would I feel about an instant family?

Well, the rest is history. Those little girls are now in their twenties, and Jane and I have been together for over twenty years. I'm still a work in progress as a godparent, but I think I've done an OK job of helping to raise Jane's girls along with another girl and a boy Jane and I had together. Yes, four kids. At least I'll never be lonely.

Islington continued to serve up its share of the Met's critical incidents and I was thankful for the teams in uniform and detectives that responded like a well-oiled machine. Regardless of the time of day or night, I was consistently impressed with the unwavering commitment of everyone. On one occasion, off duty after a full day's shift in the office, a few of us decided to retire to 'The Clinic' for a couple of drinks on the way home. No sooner had our very charming host filled a row of glasses and put them on the bar than a call came in about a stabbing in Holloway, which the uniform response team had declared a critical incident.

I broke the news to my CID colleagues that I'd have to go, and they should carry on without me. They all refused to hear it and having paid for the drinks, asked the landlord to keep them cold until they could get back. They all tipped out of the pub before a drop had passed their lips and came with me to the incident to help investigate and coordinate everything that needed to be done. They might call me guv'nor, but this was a team with a real shared sense of purpose and esprit de corps. They were totally reliable, dependable, and effective at what they did. It was one of those moments in my thirty-year career when I felt I was totally in step with the team I was working with. They were a special bunch, and this was one of the best periods of my service.

I picked up the phone to Matt, the detective chief inspector (DCI) and head of the undercover unit at Scotland Yard. In a very flattering call, he invited me to apply for a DI vacancy on his team. I'd been keeping up with my appearances on the undercover training courses, presenting as often as my workload permitted, hence me coming to mind when the vacancy arose. I suspected I was there to fill the shortlist and imagined there would be a long list of more experienced squad hoppers, one of whom was already earmarked for the job.

Yet I was being invited to apply, so I filled out the forms and went along with it. A week later the DCI said he'd received my application and would like to talk it through with me. He invited me to the Yard for an informal chat where he would explain the next steps. And so, a few days later, I went to the meeting as planned and, much to my surprise, walked into a full interview board consisting of the DCI, HR manager for the specialist crime department, and a detective superintendent. I was ambushed!

They fired a few questions at me, which I answered as best as I could, referencing my experience here and there to demonstrate that I'd faced some of the situations and scenarios they were asking me to hypothetically respond to. I went back to Islington half angry at the sneaky ambush and half smiling at the cheek of it. I resigned myself to thinking I wouldn't hear from SO10 again and was certain that my theory of a preferred candidate was spot-on.

Back down to earth and the reality of my job on division. Another critical incident occurred, this time during the day. There were plenty of us on duty to pour out onto the streets. Both Mark and I attended as a DI double act, along with half of the CID office. A man had been stabbed in the chest on his own doorstep and was dying. By the time we arrived, the air ambulance was just landing. The medics began working on him straight away.

The suspects had escaped along an alleyway leaving a three hundred-to-four-hundred-yard blood trail toward the road where a getaway car had been waiting. This had been a targeted and planned attack, so I ordered the alleyway to be cordoned off as part of a huge crime scene, while I figured out what this was about.

The doctor and paramedic from the air ambulance had opened the victim's chest and were desperately trying to keep him alive with a defibrillator. In one coordinated movement, they both seemed to understand they had reached the right moment to get him into the helicopter, and off they went. I anticipated we were dealing with a murder and continued the investigation working with the Homicide Awareness Team and forensics to manage the scene while Mark dealt with the who and why of the victim and potential suspects.

One day passed and then another. Before we knew it, two weeks had gone by, and our victim not only survived but was being discharged from hospital to continue recovery at home. Some might think these helicopters are just big expensive ambulances, but they're actually a flying accident and emergency hospital and make a huge difference in the chances of whether someone lives or dies. One day they have someone's chest open using a defibrillator directly on the heart, and two weeks later he's at home. Bloody amazing!

SO10 Covert Operations

Part I

THOUGH I HADN'T APPRECIATED IT AT THE TIME, I'D MADE A GOOD impression on the detective superintendent in my ambush interview. He thought I'd bring a fresh perspective to SO10 and selected me for the role. Considering the way I'd been approached, I considered turning the job down, but it was too tempting. I took advice from a friend and colleague who was closer to understanding the world within SO10 than I was. It was described as something of a club within which there were rival cliques and factions all vying to be top dog. I'd probably be OK as I would be seen as an impartial, independent newcomer, but I was warned to expect some strong characters with equally strong egos who would be tricky to manage. However, there were others who were described as quiet heroes who were easier to work with. My confidante advised me that if I could get over my unorthodox route to selection, it was a career opportunity of a lifetime. I'd be involved in some of the most interesting and challenging investigations, including serious crime cases that made the headlines. I was told I'd be an idiot to turn it down and so I decided to play the hand I was dealt and took the job. Whatever happened, I'd make the best of it, I thought, and give it couple of years before I'd move on.

The tactics used by SO10 were courageous and groundbreaking and some of the undercover officers were the most impressive officers you could meet. But the office was a hot mess, stuck in a bygone era. The walls were adorned with notices, calendars, and assorted trash held up by sticky tape, curling at the edges and drying out through age. The furniture was typical of most detective offices—mismatched, begged, borrowed, and stolen from other offices when someone had moved out. The walls were made from metal partitions, which was how individual offices were constructed within the building at Scotland Yard. They were covered with standard issue wallpaper that tended to yellow or may have yellowed over time when smoking in offices wasn't objectionable or against the rules. Either way, there was a beige blandness to the place that belied some of the outstanding work that was planned in its rooms.

Everything was managed by paperwork, whether an approval for an operation, the case files, register of operations or training documents. I thought this was risky in such a confidential environment and suggested we acquire a standalone computer to make everything more efficient, but everyone moaned that logging onto a system was a pain and thumbing through an index in a hardbound book was quick and easy and that we should stick with that. I decided to pick my battles and get the funding for a standalone, secure system before I'd bring it up again.

I started to read through some of the current case files to understand the operations currently underway or being proposed by the various units in the Met. There was some amazing work going on to tackle drug trafficking, gun running, organized crime, fraud, child abuse, contract killers, and more. There were cases where criminals had become untouchable or unsolved murders where an infiltration might be possible.

Every week, a meeting was held to discuss operations, their progress, and to share ideas about new cases and how evidence might be secured using covert tactics. These were a clever, cunning bunch of detectives and were a constant source of creativity about how they might bring serious criminals within reach. Twelve years prior, I was a uniformed PC driving a battlebus to arrest some of these untouchables who'd escaped justice until caught in an operation devised in this very room. Now, here I was, a guv'nor in the unit where the magic happened. Everyone was on first name terms, firstly because there was an informality in squads like this and secondly because you need to get out of some of the habits of the job when operating in a covert environment. You don't want to refer to someone as 'Guv'nor' in public if you're pretending not to be cops!

Within my first two weeks I learned that there had been an allegation of misuse of covert assets that hadn't been proved in the end, but at the time it led to an investigation involving a colleague at the Yard. As he'd had some operational contact with SO10 it was highly likely to include our department within its scope. Matt thought we might be inspected and find all wasn't as shipshape in the office as it could be. Regardless of the other matters under investigation, I needed to sort things out quickly so that we didn't come out of it too badly.

I set about the office, getting everyone to sort the place out, rolling up my sleeves to clear the walls and feed the shredder. I knew the team thought I was a shiny shoe do-gooder of a guv'nor, focusing on the wrong things, but I didn't care too much about that. They didn't know what I knew, and the office needed sorting out anyway. A couple of days later, when the anticipated inspection arrived and passed without incident, I came out of it quite well now that the team understood what had motivated the tidy-up.

Still, I saw a department that was doing amazing work, but desperately needed to be brought up to date and in step with the rest of policing and developments in technology. I'd have a battle on my hands as elite operational departments like this live on action, achievements, and results. To action-oriented cops, talking about change is management speak, which is why things stay the same and the mentality is that if it works, don't fix it. However, eventually, change catches up and effectiveness tails off. SO10 was born of change and new ideas once in the past and I wanted to make a difference and provide the fresh perspective I was hired for. Matt wasn't one for change and would block most of my ideas, for now, learning of objections through his loyal detective sergeants who would go around me to get him to veto any suggestions I made. When you train people to operate this way, an absence of transparency should come as no surprise. Not for the first time in my career, I felt like an outsider. It was uncomfortable, but I signed up for this, so I persevered.

As I passed the office of the superintendent from the ambush interview, I was ambushed yet again. He told me that I was to be on-call the following week for kidnap response and was directed to an operations room where a kidnap operation was running right at that moment. I sat with a colleague using a dedicated phone line between the operations room and the negotiator, which would be the role I'd be on call for. It seemed straightforward and a new experience and another string to my bow.

Back in the office, one of the detective sergeants ended a phone call and turned to me. 'Kev, we've got to find some black and Asian operatives. I've got loads of work and more white geezers than I can shake a stick at, but if we want someone who doesn't look like a shaven headed London gangster, we're screwed.' He was right, and it was something I'd make a priority.

I looked into the recruitment, selection, and training process. The problem was clear. Undercover officers (UCs) were selected through contact with existing UCs, either in operations or because they knew them from other postings where their paths had crossed. Invariably, the UC or the prospective recruit had been a police officer for more than ten years, and often nearer fifteen by the time they had reached a squad where exposure to undercover operations would be possible. Most of the officers in these positions were white and male—not all, but most. It shouldn't have come as a surprise that UCs were recruiting in their own image and the lack of diversity was a direct outcome from the 'tap on the shoulder' approach to acquiring talent. Although the police service was now making great efforts to recruit from London's diverse communities, it would take a long time for those changes to shift the profile of the elite squads.

I proposed an open day to invite officers to a presentation at Scotland Yard to help them understand what the role had to offer, what the recruitment and training process entailed, and to present some case studies showing video clips of covert operations that had already been dealt with at court. The ink was barely dry on the proposal before it had been vetoed as too high in the risk it presented in exposing covert operations. This was a department shooting itself in the foot!

I had it out with my boss, Matt, and explained the rationale for a more open recruitment process. I told him that I would manage the risk by banning the use of mobile phones in the auditorium and would have the technical support unit there to detect any phones in use. Reluctantly, on his part, the event went ahead in the fifth-floor briefing room at

Scotland Yard, which was a conventional auditorium for an audience of around one hundred.

At the front of stage was a box with a blinking red light on top. I explained to the audience that the box would detect anyone recording or transmitting on a mobile phone. Throughout the presentation, I could see everyone was complying with the order to not use their phones. Of course, the box was empty apart from a tiny battery connected to the blinking red light, but it did the job! The event was well attended, and a good number stayed for a chat with a few UCs afterward. It was a small change, but a huge step for a unit with a preference for staying in the shadows.

MAKING LAW

It was summer, and most civilized people were on holiday somewhere. News of a decision in the House of Lords was emerging about a ruling emanating from a court case that had been referred to the Lords on appeal. Two men were shot and killed at a party, allegedly by the defendant, Ian Davis, who was extradited from the United States and tried at the Old Bailey (Central Criminal Court) for two counts of murder. He was convicted by the jury and appealed on the basis that evidence had been given by witnesses who were granted anonymity, which was argued as being against the common law right to know your accuser.

The case was heard by five law Lords who unanimously held that Davis had not had a fair trial since his counsel had been unable to adequately challenge the prosecution evidence or test the reliability of the anonymous witnesses. Davis's case had been that his ex-girlfriend had told lies about him to the police or had persuaded other people to tell such lies on her behalf. Without being allowed to know if the anonymous witnesses knew Davis or his ex-girlfriend and had been forbidden to ask any questions that might reveal who they were, his counsel had been so hindered in his attempts to probe their evidence that Davis had not received a fair trial.

The law Lords were of the view that witness anonymity had grown incrementally and that it was time that it was ratified in legislation, should the government wish to do so.

For the time being, undercover officers would be affected as they had always been allowed to give evidence using their covert names, provided that the trial judge knew their true identities. This new ruling in the case of Davis was a disaster. Undercover officers couldn't give their true identities as it would put them in grave danger. If they couldn't have anonymity, current cases would be dropped, and future deployments would have to be for intelligence only and all those criminals who thought they were beyond the risk of detection would find life a whole lot easier as there would be no undercover officers to give evidence against them.

It looked like I was left holding the baby on this one as everyone else was either away on leave or looking the other way so they wouldn't get caught up in it. I contacted the Home Office and found the team who were drafting an urgent piece of legislation and I provided a briefing on behalf of undercover policing and how our work would be impacted by this ruling. We worked on a few different scenarios, and they shared various drafts of the wording of the proposed legislation, which we picked apart and put back together again several times. They had to make sure the legislation covered a wide range of witness anonymity requirements, so my needs weren't their only concern. I became the de facto national representative for covert policing and spread word to national units to share scenarios and drafts of proposed changes in law to inform the development of a new law and I followed the progress of it through Parliament until it achieved royal assent. Not a bad 'What I did this summer' story.

DATA LOSS MINI CRISIS

One afternoon, we turned the office upside down looking for a binder that held the details of every UC. It contained highly confidential information that was said to have been 'here a minute ago.' This was serious, and I decreed that no one was leaving until it was found. I was thinking about calling the Covert Operations Support Unit (COSU), a department that would deal with a data loss and any breaches of standard operating procedures, like an air crash investigation team for covert policing.

Just then, a team member walked into the office, and in answer to the obvious question, said that he'd hidden the missing binder on top of his deskside drawers. He reached underneath and produced it. The relief was palpable. 'We're getting a secure computer,' I announced, grumpily, wishing I'd had the courage of my convictions when I first raised it. On the upside, its introduction was accepted without further objection by anyone.

I consulted COSU anyway as I wanted their advice on introducing a secure, standalone computer and was pleasantly surprised to meet an old friend. Mick was the detective sergeant I'd spoken with at the bank robbery in Islington a few years back and he was now a detective inspector in COSU. He wasted no time in telling everyone about our Islington 'bugger off' encounter. He'd become a close friend and, later, we'd set up a business together and travel the world astonished at our good fortune and that anyone would pay to listen to us. For now, it was helpful to have someone to run things past without having to initiate a formal referral.

Promotion to DCI

The DCI announced that he was going in for the superintendent's promotion process. Shortly afterward, there would be a chief inspector's promotion process and I said that if he was going for promotion, so would I. Perhaps I could step into his shoes as I'd only been there a short while.

As it turned out, he made the rank and was invited to stay in the covert command, retaining responsibility for several operational units, including undercover. I went for my interview and presented to a uniformed chief inspector and a superintendent. I knew the superintendent had served at Islington earlier in his career, but I didn't know him personally. I gave examples across the competency-based interview, mostly referring to the challenges I'd managed at Islington, a context that the superintendent understood, of course.

I passed the promotion process and was invited to step up as DCI and head of the undercover unit at Scotland Yard, albeit with the previous incumbent keeping his hand in. Nonetheless, head of Scotland Yard's undercover unit? Me?

My department had responsibility for the officers who were deployed to street level drug operations, known as test purchase officers, many of whom I'd deployed during my time on Operation Strongbox. Here I saw a more diverse group of officers with a proven track record in undercover work, but who were trained differently and kept at arm's length by the elite SO10 undercover officers. I saw the test purchase officers as a natural recruitment pool for SO10, but I knew many had been put off by the air of perceived hostility toward them. Higher-level undercover officers were concerned that test purchase officers were not as highly trained and lacked the ability to infiltrate more hardened criminal groups and be able to withstand scrutiny, which was a fair assessment. That doesn't mean they shouldn't be encouraged to apply for the training and be supported as close allies. I thought I could change that, now that I led the unit. I proposed a training process that would bring them closer to us and created a development pathway to train them at the higher level and create a more diverse pool of UCs.

I was summoned to the superintendent's office. He had a copy of my paper before it had been submitted to the national working group. He asked whose idea it was. I claimed it as mine. It was vetoed and doomed to the shredder. His words were, 'It's a lovely dream and against everything we've ever fought for.' This is elitism above pragmatism, I thought, resigned to the understanding that getting the department to adapt to changes wouldn't be easy and that I'd have to find a different moment to take things forward.

CHAPTER 10

Negotiation

I WAS OFFERED A PLACE ON THE NATIONAL HOSTAGE NEGOTIATOR training course, which, conveniently for me, was held at Hendon Police College. It was a great course where you learn new things and, at the same time, unlearn old habits that are less useful in this role. Police officers are problem solvers. They are trained to respond to calls and keep the peace, investigate, and discover quickly and effectively, but that doesn't work as well in a hostage scenario or where a person in crisis is threatening to take their own life. Patiently allowing them to talk and, by doing so, vent their problems, anxieties, and frustrations, takes as long as it takes. A common misconception is that negotiators talk them down from a situation, whereas the reality is that they 'listen' them down, and those that can't get their heads around this don't make it as negotiators.

I went on a few calls with other experienced negotiators to ease myself into the role before going on call alone, which was always in addition to my day job running the undercover unit. One involved an early morning visit to a school where a burglary in progress had been reported. The lone suspect escaped onto the roof and was refusing to come down, threatening to jump if the police rushed him. Local officers had contained the scene and called for negotiators. I joined one of my experienced colleagues on a fire escape, which gave us a view across the rooftop to where our subject was. We could see him sitting with his back to a low wall that ran around the roofline. My fellow negotiator had already been talking with him for a few minutes and had assessed that he might be either drunk or otherwise intoxicated, as he was quite erratic and slurring. Negotiators are always alert to the possibility of mental health issues, drug abuse, or drunkenness in these situations, as they are common to people in crisis and need to be managed as part of the negotiation strategy. Someone who is physically unsteady and on a rooftop might unintentionally stumble to their death, so we were keen to encourage him to stay put until we could work things out.

I stepped forward to take the lead negotiator role, trying to engage him in conversation to generate dialogue about anything at all, except getting him to surrender. It was the early hours of the morning, shortly before dawn and so it was quite chilly. Asking whether he was cold, hungry, or thirsty might demonstrate that our priority was his welfare rather than his immediate detention. It didn't matter that he declined any gestures of good will; the fact that he was responding was useful in helping us to assess whether he was rational and what his mood was. The next hour or so involved patient probing to understand how he'd got himself into the situation he was in, and his explanation was surprisingly logical, once the effects of what he'd consumed began to wear off.

He admitted he had a long history of addiction and needed something to sell to raise some money. He didn't like the thought of breaking into someone's home because of the distress that would cause the home-owners and he might get caught if someone was in, or saw or heard him. Commercial properties were usually better fortified with good security in the form of proper locks, alarms, and CCTV, so he thought an older school would be easier to burgle and find something of value he could find and sell on. School buildings were more isolated so he could take his time without fear of being detected, but he was clumsy, making enough noise to attract the attention of a passerby who called the police. He panicked and wasn't thinking clearly when he found a way onto the roof and that's where the standoff with police began. By now, he was tired but clearheaded and agreed to come down peacefully, where he was detained by local officers.

I was on the rota for overt negotiation and called out one afternoon to King's Cross. There was a report of a man holding his family hostage with a knife. He had, apparently, walked out of a mental health ward where he was being treated for addiction and was having a cannabis-induced psychotic episode. I was partnered with a fellow negotiator, Steve. We tag-teamed the task of trying to keep a distracting conversation going with him while the fire brigade worked outside to get a ladder up to the second-floor window of the flat, where the family huddled as far away from him as possible.

It was quite a squeeze as we talked on the staircase just outside the door, while behind us was a serial of public order officers kitted up and ready to break down the door and mount a rescue by force if there was an immediate threat to life. The public order teams, known as the Territorial Support Group, or TSG, are usually never far away from a siege. It's their job to step in if negotiations fail. They are very effective at dominating a violent situation not only by their sheer numbers, but primarily because that is what they train for. The TSG dreaded the negotiators being called out as they knew that we would patiently listen, gently probe the conversation, and try to end it with the subject deciding to surrender peacefully, which took a long time and was quite boring for people who were action-oriented. The TSG just wanted to get in there and sort it out, and I sometimes had more than a little sympathy with that school of thought.

I remember a call out one Saturday afternoon to a hostage barricade in Kingston on the London-Surrey border. I was at home in North London, which might as well have been the other side of the world at that time of day. A man with mental health problems hadn't taken his medication and was holding a visitor to his flat hostage and shouting aggressively from the first-floor balcony toward the local officers who'd responded.

I had an unmarked car and dashed around the M25 motorway, eventually reaching the scene just when the TSG decided to zap the subject with a taser and brought the situation under control. It was all over in a moment, and although I'd made rapid work of the journey on the way there, I couldn't drive in emergency response mode on the way back and so it took forever. You win this time, TSG.

Back to the cannabis-induced psychotic siege. After we'd exhausted all of our small talk, neither Steve nor I could get any response from him. We were concerned about what he might do next, as he wasn't engaging with us any longer. We gave the TSG officers the nod, and they crept toward the door and used the hand-held battering ram and almost took it off its hinges. There, in the hallway, on the floor was our man, fast asleep like a baby, off his head on cannabis.

Everyone on the negotiator's rota had become familiar with a campaign group known as Fathers for Justice (F4J), who had taken to pulling stunts to draw attention to their cause, which was about fathers getting the rough end of the deal in child custody cases. Protestors from the group would dress up in superhero costumes and climb buildings, bridges, rooftops, and construction sites to disrupt London as roads would have to be closed beneath any site they chose to occupy.

One afternoon, I was on-call, and I found myself on the roof of the Royal Courts of Justice in London, speaking with two F4J protestors dressed as Batman and Robin. The court buildings are home to the High Court and the Court of Appeal and it is a grand Victorian gothic structure in the Strand. I went there straight from the office, meeting another negotiator, and we climbed the stairs to the nearest access point to where the protest was taking place. Both characters were a bit stroppy on initial contact, fearing we were going to force them to come down. In fact, at the start they declared that they would only speak with us if we addressed them as Mr. Batman and Mr. Robin, which was silly but indicated that they weren't taking themselves too seriously. I couldn't help thinking about the ridiculous situation I was in. There I was, a senior Scotland Yard detective, dressed in a suit and tie, speaking with two blokes in fancy dress on the roof of the High Court. It was one of those 'How the hell did I get myself in this situation?' moments.

It took us about an hour to get them to discuss and agree to terms. I was fairly relaxed about it as I knew they just wanted a moment in front of the TV cameras to get some publicity from their stunt. We knew they weren't intent on jumping, so we could dismiss the unrealistic possibility that they were contemplating ending it all. We also got their assurances that they wouldn't cause any damage to the building or throw anything off the roof endangering the people below. All they wanted was to unfurl a banner, which they'd already hung from the front of the building and stay there until the TV news cameras had given them some attention. As negotiations go, I'd had far worse options to deal with and this was a fairly low-risk prospect. We agreed not to try to rush them and pull them back from the roof if they kept their part of the bargain to come down after the TV cameras had been there for half an hour. With that, we were able to withdraw and let local officers deal with them and, true to their word, they came down as they said they would.

In the early hours one morning, my phone rang, awakening me from a deep sleep. There was a man threatening to jump from a bridge, currently in conversation with local officers doing their best to contain the situation but needing help.

Archway Bridge, built in 1897, traverses the affluent North London suburb of Highgate above the busy A1 highway, which links North and Central London. It's a listed historic structure with low and easily climbed sides that make it attractive to those thinking about ending it all. This man wasn't the first and wouldn't be the last to stand on the parapet looking at the dual carriageway fifty feet below and now closed in both directions.

Well-rehearsed plans were invoked by the local police team responding to another suicide intervention at the bridge. They isolated the scene, unrolling reels of blue and white tape bearing the familiar caption 'POLICE LINE—DO NOT CROSS.' Both ends of the bridge were cordoned off to the public and diversions set up to reroute traffic.

I crept downstairs, muttering the full range of British profanities at the prospect of another sleepless night, got dressed, quietly left my home, and got into my unmarked police car. I managed a call with another negotiator with whom I was planning to meet at the scene to discuss the negotiation strategy. My twenty-minute drive allowed some thinking time and contemplation about what I might be facing for the next few hours. How does someone reach this point in their life that they decide to end it, and in such a horrific way by jumping off a bridge? In my tired mind, I wondered whether this could be more of a cry for help than someone intent on jumping? Does that make any difference to my role? I thought not as it would be a huge error of judgment if I approached this cynically and was wrong. I drove with the window open, the fresh air waking me up and shaking off my mild grumpiness.

I arrived at the scene to a palpable sense of relief as the local officers beat a hasty retreat from direct engagement with the man on the bridge, waving me forward. I'd intended to wait for my fellow negotiator to join me, but the officers were desperate to hand over and I found myself too close to the situation with the person I could now see, hear, and tell was quite drunk. It was dark, with some street lighting providing pools of light here and there, but the bridge was undergoing maintenance with scaffolding erected on both sides, part covered in plastic sheeting making it difficult to get a good view. The scaffolding provided a platform that was above head height from where I stood on the pedestrian walkway and from where I now tried to engage him. He was white, with a London accent, early forties, and wearing only a T-shirt and jeans. He was highly emotional and energized as he climbed along the platform, holding on to the crisscrossing scaffold pipes and traversing above and in front of me one moment to walking twenty or thirty feet along the platform toward the other end of the bridge a moment later. I began to walk in his direction, tracking him as he moved back and forth mirroring his energy, so I decided to stay in one place in the hope that he would follow suit. I wanted him to hear me, but I didn't want to shout so I spoke loudly enough to ask him to come over to me, which he did.

He was tearful and sounded desperate, sometimes making it difficult to understand what he was saying as he cried out his words in half-spoken and half-shouted frustration at what was troubling him. I spent a few minutes trying to lower his energy, offering reassurance that I was there to listen and doing my best to encourage him to stay away from the edge of the scaffolding and the fifty-foot drop on the other side.

I followed my training and let him get things off his chest. He told me of his deteriorating home life, which had reached a new low that day when his partner kicked him out of the family home. Booze was the cause of all his woes and coming in late and drunk (again) was the final straw for his long-suffering wife. He was suddenly homeless and feeling sorry for himself, sobbing and wobbling perilously close to solving it once and for all. He spoke about his children and how his wife wouldn't allow him to say goodbye to them.

At that moment, his mobile phone rang. It was his wife. His emotional state suddenly became highly charged again as he sobbed and told her where he was and what his intentions were. I intervened, offering to speak with her. He handed his phone to me, allowing me to calmly explain to his wife what was happening. Having access to his phone and the potential for ongoing dialogue with his wife was creating a potentially more volatile situation, so I talked through that moment, distracting his attention from the phone and reassuring him that we were talking to her. I needed him to know he had my full attention, so I handed the phone to my fellow negotiator who had arrived a few minutes earlier and let him handle the fallout from that end of the family crisis we had become involved in.

I continued to focus my attention on doing everything I could to keep the man calm, inviting him to focus on me and our conversation. He explained to me how desperately sad he felt about the possibility that he wouldn't be able to see his children, and I explored whether this might be an overly pessimistic view, given that many separated couples have access arrangements even in quite challenging circumstances. We discussed his relationships and how things had deteriorated. He accepted his drinking had been to blame for his wife reaching the decision that he needed to leave. He started crying again, talking about his children. I took the opportunity to ask him, 'When do you think you'll be able to see them again?' His reply provided the pivotal moment in the conversation: 'I suppose, she'll let me see them when I stop drinking.'

This was a telling response. It indicated his vision of a future when he would be able see his children and the recognition that there was something he could do about it, although it would be a tough journey for someone with alcohol addiction. The conversation shifted to exploring new possibilities and optimistic outcomes. It was a complete turnaround from what he had contemplated when he climbed over the edge of the bridge. I suggested he could come down. There would be help to get him where he wanted to be if he was willing to give it a try and, within minutes, he was down from the ledge. He hugged me, crying on my shoulder and thanking me for helping him. It was quite a moment, but I'd done all I could for him at that stage and left him in the hands of support services who'd take it from here. He was taken to the nearby Whittington Hospital where they would check him over and assess him for suicide risk, given the situation he'd been in that night. He was about to start a long path to recovery, should he wish to go in that direction, with the help of health services and addiction support groups.

Local officers began to withdraw and answer other calls, go about their patrols and the business as usual of a mid-week night duty shift that was coming to an end. Cordon tape was removed from the lampposts and road signs that had supported the makeshift barriers, opening the bridge and roads above and below to traffic, that quickly resumed as if nothing had happened. As is often the case during night duty, by morning there would be no signs of what had taken place. The residents of Highgate had enjoyed a peaceful slumber unaware of the crisis.

My involvement in his life was to end there. After a quick debrief with my fellow negotiator and the first responders at the local station I was on my way home. I crawled back into a warm bed not long before my usual morning alarm, trying unsuccessfully not to wake Jane. She'd been sleeping lightly unsure of when I'd return. 'What did you do, bore him down?' she said in her inimitable way of keeping me grounded.

I attended several suicide intervention calls as a negotiator and, thankfully, managed to 'listen them all down.' According to figures from The Samaritans, the UK's main suicide prevention charity, there are over six thousand suicides in the UK each year of which men remain almost three times more likely to die by suicide than women.

Traditional male roles through the generations can be characterized by the societal expectation of being the breadwinner, to keep a 'stiff upper lip' in the face of adversity, and to 'man up' rather than show emotion, which might be viewed as weakness. The perceived stigma attached to showing emotions can discourage men from speaking up, with excessive drinking or substance abuse used as a coping mechanism when depressed or anxious rather than seeking professional help.

In his philosophical essay *The Myth of Sisyphus*, Albert Camus examines the absurdity of man's need to attribute meaning to life and the unreasonable silence of the universe in response. According to Camus, this is the only question in philosophy that matters. Does the understanding of the meaninglessness absurdity of life necessarily require suicide? He describes the absurd condition: 'We build our life on the hope for tomorrow, yet tomorrow brings us closer to death and is the ultimate enemy; people live their lives as if they were not aware of the certainty of death.'[1]

For Camus, taking the absurdity of life seriously means acknowledging the contradiction between the desire of human reason and the unreasonable world. Suicide, then, also must be rejected: without man, the absurd cannot exist. The contradiction must be lived; reason and its limits must be acknowledged, without false hope. However, the absurd can never be permanently accepted: it requires constant confrontation and constant revolt. He argues that happiness is about living one's life while being aware of its absurdity because consciousness allows us to better control our existence.

I saw a post on social media that caught my eye recently by a subscriber who had asked one of his male friends to stop using the phrase 'man up' in recognition of its negative connotations. His friend agreed and instead started using 'fortify.' The subscriber said it was just a little thing, but it had made a difference. He said, 'To be honest, it's really quite funny when I'm starting to deflate in the library and he leans over and says "FORTIFY!"' The post had over 135,000 likes and many supportive comments.

I thought about 'fortify,' considering whether it amounted to the same thing, requiring the man to respond as if from a position of exposed weakness. I don't think it does. Whereas 'man up' is a pejorative, like 'pull yourself together,' 'fortify' is an encouragement to draw on one's strengths; to resolve to care for oneself. If to fortify is to revolt against the realities of our absurd existence, I'm for it.

KIDNAPS

Although I'd take my turn on the rota for crisis negotiation, the reason for being trained as a negotiator in the covert policing command was for kidnap cases, which required a covert response, working quietly in the background to find the hostage and get them out safely.

The kidnap investigation team was part of the serious crime command, a separate team to covert policing. When a kidnap broke, a temporary team formed to support the crisis response around the negotiation. The negotiator would usually come from the covert policing command. Intelligence officers and analysts on call from other parts of the serious crime command would form an intelligence cell to work on rapid discovery of the background of the hostage and piece together anything that could be found about those suspected as being behind the kidnap. An operations room at the end of the building at Scotland Yard was the focal point of the response, where all the component parts of the team assembled to work on the case until the hostage was safely recovered. This was a well-rehearsed system and even though the individual team members might not have worked together before, each knew their role and could jump into their seat to make the whole perform effectively. It was impressive to behold. Scotland Yard's kidnap team had a 100 percent success rate.

In all kidnap cases, the number one priority is the safe return of the hostage. This would be announced by the senior investigating officer (SIO) and repeated regularly in the operations room briefings and typed in block capitals hourly on the database used for documenting directions, actions, and decisions. If anything went wrong, it would be clear that the focus was not about evidence and convictions, but a concern for preserving life. This was our commander's intent—the North Star we followed to enable decision-making and empower every moving part of the response to the safe recovery of the hostage.

The SIO would set the strategy. The negotiator worked at arm's length with a single point of contact to ensure there was always only one version of events shared between negotiator and the operations room and ensured strict discipline around managing information. This meant that the negotiator and their assistant, usually a detective sergeant, worked in isolation with autonomy to decide how to manage the negotiation. Without a doubt, my experience in the undercover world helped me to be creative as I'd absorbed some of the techniques UCs and cover officers used to innovate and come up with negotiation plans and responses to the kidnappers that enabled plausible deniability; explanations that satisfied their demand that they were being taken seriously while buying time.

Back in the first decade of the 2000s, kidnaps were more frequent than you'd imagine. There would always be a kidnap when I was on call. Often, there would be three or four, and in my worst week, there were nine. I managed three of them and got stuck with the fourth, as it was complicated and dragged on for a few days, so they called in other negotiators to deal with the other five. I'd signed up to life as a negotiator, but it was exhausting to do this as an additional role to an already demanding job as head of the undercover unit. Family life was strained by this workload, and it seemed that the on-call rota was being shared by fewer negotiators than were needed to maintain what I mockingly referred to as my 'work/work balance.'

Many kidnaps are criminal against criminal, with a typical scenario being a drug debt they couldn't resolve, so they are kept hostage to enforce payment, usually calling someone close to the hostage to initiate the demand for ransom. By the time police are involved, the person receiving the demand for ransom has probably exhausted all options and so we're the last resort. I worked with quite a few people I knew were ordinarily not on our side and it was an added complication to negotiate knowing that they were potentially being educated at the same time, learning how a kidnap response works from one side of the operation.

We had our fair share of scams too. Rich kids, stepchildren, or grandkids were sometimes behind their own kidnappings in collusion with criminal friends who'd watched too many Hollywood movies and thought they'd get away with ripping off family members for a big payday. They didn't. We could always tell the difference and would usually resolve them quickly.

In one of my early kidnap cases as a negotiator, I was called to a family home in West London, not very far from Heathrow Airport. I met my on-call detective sergeant nearby, traveling the last mile or so together. We presented ourselves at the front door of a semidetached suburban house to be met by the parents of an eighteen-year-old lad who'd had been kidnapped and they'd received some threatening calls demanding money. It seemed an unusual case as the young man involved, an only child, still lived with his mum and dad in suburbia. They were in their mid-thirties and appeared to be Mr. and Mrs. Average, with a neatly kept home, which was warm, well decorated, and nicely furnished. Sometimes, your copper's hunch triggers your instinctive assessment that someone you are speaking with isn't being entirely straight with you: microexpressions of nervousness, delays in giving answers to straightforward questions, holding back rather than leaning into the discussion with a desperate eagerness to help. Of course, the situation was stressful for them, but even making the usual allowances for this, something didn't feel quite right about them. I knew the intelligence team back at the operations room would be digging into the history of the hostage and the family and I wanted to do my part to learn more about them.

I needed to find out why someone would've taken their son. The parents couldn't come up with any logical reason and were mystified. I asked the mother if I could search her son's room to see if I could find anything that might provide a clue about any connections or signs of trouble—she refused. She was quite within her rights to do so, and I couldn't search it without the parent's consent or a warrant, and I certainly wasn't going down that route.

I couldn't help thinking that if my child had been kidnapped, I'd give the police anything they wanted if it would help. I'd be invading their privacy, but this was a serious emergency and was clearly justifiable in the circumstances, but I didn't want to present that argument as I thought it was better to be patient and supress my irritation with this unhelpful obstruction. I needed a moment to think about a different approach.

I suggested that there might be a diary, notebook, something in his room that would tell a story about something in his life that Mum and Dad weren't aware of and might be picked up by fresh eyes. I topped off my speech by telling them that, whether we like it or not, children keep secrets and lie to their parents. As anticipated, Mum did all the talking, refuting the very suggestion that her son would lie to her, as she chain-smoked nervously throughout our conversation. Spotting an opportunity, I asked her when her parents found out she smoked, and she looked thoughtfully at her cigarette and then back at me. 'They still don't know,' she said. 'I did it, you did it, and your son is doing it. Kids keep secrets from their parents,' I said, trying not to look too clever about the trap she'd walked herself into.

I considered the possibility that they might be worried I'd find something incriminating, so I explained that our priority was his rescue and that was all. That didn't mean I was going to give immunity for anything we did find, but it wasn't my focus.

She let out a sigh of resignation and gave her permission to search the room. I think they knew he wasn't completely innocent, and I was surprised they didn't follow me to his room, leaving me to go through his drawers and cupboards. It wasn't long before I'd found the unpaid court fine notices, the notebook containing deals, prices, and names of those he was in business with. The parents made a show of being astonished, which didn't convince me, but I wasn't concerned with appearances. My detective sergeant called the operations room explaining what we'd found, which was already being discovered from that side of the response as a familiar pattern of small-time dealer not paying his debts to his supplier.

It was around 3:00 a.m. when I told the parents that they should go to bed and grab a couple of hours' rest. We could've taken them to a safe house to continue the negotiations, but nothing would be happening until the morning and it was safe to stay put until then.

The parents went to their bedroom, though I don't know if they managed to get any sleep. Downstairs, I took one sofa and my sergeant the other and we nodded off for a light snooze for what seemed a few minutes. I'd closed my eyes but wasn't asleep. My brain was still awake and alert to the possibility of a call from the hostage takers or the operations room with an update. I sat quietly for a while until I heard an almighty roar and suddenly got to my feet, startled at the noise that rattled the windows. I rushed outside to find out whether it was an earthquake or an explosion to see a British Airways 747, the first of the day to land at Heathrow and on a low pass over the street. I wondered how anyone could suffer living here and wandered back inside. It was dawn and I was now fully alert, thanks to my flying alarm clock. Mum and Dad came downstairs and offered us breakfast. I accepted a coffee and decided this was not the time or place to ask if they had any crunchy nut cornflakes.

We checked in with the operations room and, before long, intelligence work had identified an address they were preparing to raid where they suspected our hostage was being held. I wondered how the hostage takers, who were probably not the most sophisticated criminals, would react to a dozen armed bastards giving them a wakeup call, which is how the kidnap operation ended, midmorning. Detectives from the kidnap team arrived at the parents' house and took over. I made my way back to Scotland Yard to hand in my notes and evidence. I expected it would be deserted as it had felt very quiet at our end of things. As I entered the room, it was full of people who'd been working on the investigation through the night. I was impressed with how well attended it had been. In isolation, out in the field, it feels much different, and it is sometimes easy to think there's not much going on behind the scenes. Nothing could be further from the truth. I was part of an amazing team. We got the job done, but there were no high fives, no celebrations of another win. This was everyone's job and part of the quotidian. In an hour or so, the operations room was cleared and ready for the next kidnap as we all went back to our day jobs and business as usual, apart from the kidnap investigation team who would now deal with the case against the kidnappers and the fallout for our hostage and his side hustle as a minor league cannabis dealer.

CHINESE KIDNAP

A Chinese family had failed to pay the man who trafficked their son into the UK and was now taken hostage until they sent payment from China. Unsure of what to do, the China-based family managed to get some friends in the UK to report the crime. It was my turn on call and I commenced the routine of getting together with the family member conducting the negotiations with the kidnapper. We set up our negotiation cell, ready for a long night of cat and mouse games and the kidnap response team was fired up in the operations room as the crisis response got underway. We managed a couple of early calls, navigating threats and anger down the line, buying some time in the process.

We were two or three hours in when a call came in from someone speaking Chinese. I could tell there was a different tone this time, calm and following the more usual pattern of taking turns to speak and listen. The call was from the hostage. He was in a public phone box, having been released on a promise to pay the kidnapper/trafficker all the money he owed him. I was puzzled and wanted to understand how this was possible and why he hadn't done so before. I then received a lesson in Chinese culture and the value they place upon reputation and trust in someone's promise. The hostage had decided he didn't want to be detained any longer and signed an IOU for the full value of the debt. Both he and his family were now bound on principle to the promise to pay the debt making the police operation completely redundant. He was picked up by detectives from the kidnap unit who would take it from there, but for me it was an early end to the call out. If only all kidnaps could be resolved this way.

CHILD KIDNAP

Through the patterned glass the red jacket of the postman's silhouette was visible as the single mother of three children answered the knock on the door of her Walthamstow home. She found two postmen in Royal Mail uniform standing before her asking for her son, who wasn't at home. They charged past her, brandishing guns and knives, startling the mother, her teenage daughter, and ten-year-old son, whose older brother they were looking for. He wasn't at home, having taken up with a girlfriend and rarely stayed at the family home.

The raiders tied up the family, hands behind their backs and gags in their mouths, and spent around two hours searching the home. They slashed the furniture looking into the backs of sofas, dissecting mattresses, turning out every drawer and cupboard, tossing the contents into a pile. Whatever they were looking for they hadn't found. They had guns and threatened the mother to call her older son, but luckily for her and him, his phone was off. The raiders made their next move and told the ten-year-old to kiss his mother goodbye, as he was coming with them.

The phone rang to provide my first kidnap call out of the week. A ten-year-old boy had been taken from a family in East London and his adult brother was now receiving the calls demanding a ransom. The kidnap intelligence team gave me what they knew about the situation.

I called the brother, Michael, and arranged to meet him at London City Airport's check-in hall. You never know what you might be walking into, and where there's organized crime there's always a risk you might get caught up in the fight. Although I didn't suspect I was in danger, I wasn't armed, so this would be a way to manage risk as there are always armed police at UK airports, and if necessary, I could show out and ask for their support.

Michael was what I would call a plastic gangster—he was pretending to be something he wasn't. He swaggered out of the airport entrance toward my car full of himself. He fed me a load of nonsense about what had happened. He was overconfident, putting on the hard man act and giving off attitude. I could see through it and wanted to get straight to the point: 'Do you want to fuck around all night or get your brother back safely?' I asked. 'Tell me everything and cut the bullshit. His life is in your hands right now.' That was all it took to snap him out of his fake gangster persona. He broke down in tears saying, 'Please, please, please,' repeatedly. Gone was the arrogance. Now we could now start working together to come up with a plan.

We went to a safe location where we'd work and extract more of the story from Michael. I was joined soon after by my on-call detective sergeant, just in time for Michael to tell us everything.

He'd met someone at a party who told him how he was making a lot of money as an international estate agent laundering dirty money from various criminal entities through the purchase of properties overseas that were either vastly inflated in value or didn't exist at all. Michael was impressed by him and admired his entrepreneurial approach to making, what sounded like, easy money. They exchanged contact details that night and got on very well with each other, promising to keep in touch. Some months later, Michael was at a different social gathering and wanted to impress some people he'd met who were known to be successful criminals. He adopted the story of the international estate agent, boasting how he could launder money, explaining the method that had been told to him at the other party some time ago. He sounded so confident that one member of the group he was talking to suggested that they could work together. They began to have serious conversations about laundering money through his system. Michael was excited at the prospect of a big payday and a new line of work that could change his life. Michael contacted his international estate agent friend, and they agreed to terms, subcontracting the work to him for a decent share of the profits.

The day came and Michael was given around $400,000 in cash to launder. He passed it on to his partner in crime and, perhaps predictably, never heard from him again. Michael was in way over his head and receiving increasingly threatening demands from the owner of the cash.

The criminal who'd supplied the money to be laundered was a woman from London who had dealings with a New York gang that had stolen the money through mortgage fraud in the US. When the money was lost, they sent four gang members from New York to London to find Michael. He was going to be the target for the kidnap, but when he wasn't at the family home, the gang improvised and took the boy to a bedsit in Central London that they were using as the stronghold.

Michael found out what had happened when he turned his phone on. At home he discovered the ransacked house and his mother and sister tied up. There was no chance that the family could raise the money so they called the police, which is where I came in.

We went to a safe location and, by the time we'd settled in, some of the higher-ups at the Yard were all over the operations room. Everyone was nervous as this wasn't a regular kidnap—it was a child kidnap, and the ramifications would be huge if it went badly. One drug dealer kidnapping another wasn't going to make the headlines, but a kidnap involving a child was very rare and would be closely and critically reviewed if something bad happened to the boy. As usual, the clear message from the senior investigating officer to everyone involved in the covert operation was the safe release of the hostage as the number one priority. As the negotiator, it was for me to decide on the tactics and approach.

My first objective was to get proof of life. I prepared Michael for the call, telling him what to say, which we practiced a couple of times. When the call came, Michael asked to speak to his brother. There was a brief, but emotionally charged, exchange between them with assurances that he was OK. The kidnapper came back to the phone and said, 'See? We're not animals. He's a little boy and we're not going to hurt him. He's eating McDonalds and watching cartoons on TV. It's simple. You've got something we want, and we've got what you want. Get the money and he can come home.'

This was a significant statement to make and went a long way to calming everyone down, including the higher ranks at the Yard about the threat to the boy's life. It made the kidnap instrumental and transactional, meaning it was a barter for exchanging value between Michael and the kidnappers. With guidance on what to say, there were several calls between Michael and the kidnappers. He convinced them of his promise of a ransom payment the next morning. Overnight, intelligence work had narrowed down the location of the stronghold to a flat not very far from Scotland Yard on a local authority estate in Westminster.

From there, it was a simple matter of sending in the specialist firearms team (our equivalent of SWAT) who found the gang and discovered the boy unharmed and hiding in the bathroom. He was reunited with his mum and brother within the hour, but that was a reunion I wouldn't see. My job was done, and the kidnap investigation team took over the investigation.

Later that year, five gang members involved in the kidnap were sentenced to a total of sixty-two years in prison, and in commending the police for locating the stronghold where the boy was being held the trial judge said, 'It is very commendable how quickly they managed to target this particular address on a kidnap which could have gone on a great deal longer.' Passing a sentence of fifteen years on the woman who had planned the kidnap he said, 'It is no good expecting to be given a lighter sentence because you have a two-year-old daughter when you arranged the kidnap of somebody else's ten-year-old son.'

But I feel it is the mother of the kidnapped boy who deserves the last words in this chapter, which she gave in her victim impact statement to the court to describe how this evil crime had affected her family's lives.

Before the incident we were all happy as a family. My son was doing well at school and enjoyed going. My daughter was doing well in her studies, and I was happy at work.

My life changed when the incident happened. Things have not been the same since.

Since the incident I have been a very different person. Before the incident I was lively and outgoing but now I am very insecure and find it hard to make friends and start new relationships. I am very wary of new people, and I find it extremely hard to trust people, although it happened a while ago it still has a profound effect on my life.

I have had to move from my home and was living in temporary accommodation for a long time. I was happy living where I was but had to move. This has also had a profound effect on my son who has not only to deal with the incident but has had to move school, a new house and make new friends.

This is also the same for me. I now live in an area unknown to me and I am finding it very hard to adjust.

I had to give up work after the incident, as I was not well. I spent time in a mental health unit as I was unable to deal mentally with the effects of the incident. I am still taking medication and continue see the doctors due to ill health.

I have not slept properly since the incident. I have been unable to concentrate, and I am also very tired most of the time.

I have had regular nightmares since the incident. These include being left alone with the suspects. I wake up and I am crying and shaking and can't get back to sleep.

I have had anxiety attacks both at home and when I am out. I get very scared when I am around lots of people.

At first after the incident, I was afraid to answer the door. Every time the bell went, or the letterbox went my heart jumped a beat and I was too scared to answer the door.

My relationship with my children has at times since been difficult. I feel that sometimes they blame me for having to move house although I know it's not my fault. We have argued because of silly, trivial matters.

Things that before I would just ignore get to me and I can be very abrasive and touchy at times.

On occasions I have felt physically sick and faint when I recall the incident in my head. This has happened many times.

I don't think I will ever get over what happened to me. A mum is there to protect her children and I was helpless when they took my son. I find it very difficult knowing that there was nothing I could do to prevent them taking him.

The incident has caused massive heartache for the whole of the family. We have all had to basically rebuild our lives and start again. It was not our choice but due to our events we had no choice.

Life was fine before the incident but now everything seems so much more difficult.

I hope that one day I will be able to move on with my life and put this all behind me, although at this time I don't think that is possible.

I went back to Scotland Yard after finishing my notes at the safe location and decided I might as well put in an appearance at my day job and went to the SO10 office. I was met by the obligatory comments about how shit I looked in my somewhat unkempt, unshaven state and that I looked like I had slept in my clothes, which they knew I had, of course. It was welcome banter and light relief after a couple of days of negotiating. I needed to decompress a little and do something routine for an hour or two before heading home.

SO10 Covert Operations

Part II

I WADED THROUGH THE DAILY SWATHE OF EMAILS, WHICH CONSISTED mainly of people covering their backs about something they wanted an audit trail for and then looked through some of the proposals for new operations, which was always more interesting.

Among them was a proposal similar to Stardust Jewellers, the operation I'd helped with as a PC when I drove a battle bus as part of the arrest phase. The idea was to set up a shop buying secondhand goods to deal with a growing burglary problem in a part of Central London where the burglars were having a field day. I wanted to support this idea and thought about the undercover officers I could assign, but it wasn't looking good, as we were already committed to a high number of active cases.

When I went through our case load, it was obvious that we had too many of our officers on loan to operations outside of London for other police forces, which was getting in the way of serving our own communities. As the largest undercover unit, I was usually supportive of assisting other forces with UC operations as we would benefit in a quid pro quo arrangement when we needed help, but it had gone too far. In a perfect example of mission creep, the proportion of operations outside of London exceeded what would be acceptable as reasonable and justifiable.

Some of my staff liked to work away from London as it came with overtime and all expenses paid by the host force, but the salary and cost of employing the cover officers and UCs was for the Metropolitan force to pay. Even with the host force budget, officers were still working away from home for extended periods and were grumbling that the hours worked didn't match the overtime they were being paid. This had been a long-standing informal agreement, where UCs would submit a claim for a flat rate of hours for each day when out of force, regardless of the hours they worked. That might've worked as a temporary arrangement for specific circumstances in past operations, but it had now become accepted practice and was no longer sustainable. Officers wanted to be paid for the hours they worked. I didn't blame them. Long hours in a high-risk role, away from home and loved ones is a tough gig. Why bother if the pay isn't there.

Another challenge with operations away from our force area was that when I needed them, our own undercover officers were committed elsewhere and while these out-of-town jobs were all very worthy undercover operations, our own operations should have been serviced first. I began to turn around the long hours culture and address the reasonable concerns of our UCs.

I was accused of pulling up the drawbridge by some of my national colleagues and of pricing us out of the market by one of my sergeants when I suggested that other forces would have to pay more realistic costs if they wanted to use SO10 undercover officers on long-term operations. I replied that I wasn't in a market and wanted to ensure we could serve the communities of London more than we had been. This was a deliberate, strategic move. It began to turn the tide and enable us to use our capacity for London jobs as well as doing our bit to help out nationally and balance how we shared resources with other forces.

This change of direction enabled us to run long-term community infiltrations to tackle criminality and support frontline policing in London boroughs with a specialist resource they desperately needed. We were doing London-based, long-term operations one after the other, and we were still able to service the day-to-day serious crime cases.

ETHICS
There was both necessary and unnecessary secrecy in covert policing. The identities of undercover officers, informants, covert facilities, and

tradecraft are, of course, confidential. The nature and details of undercover operations are secret when they're underway, but the undercover tactic itself isn't a secret, per se. I think secrecy was alluring for some and useful in keeping scrutiny at arm's length.

I had already started to change the culture when we began to recruit and train officers in a way that would support our aim to improve diversity in our ranks and better represent the communities we needed to protect. Now I wanted to make us more accountable as a function of policing.

Before 1999, the law regarding undercover policing and other covert tactics followed the principle that if the law didn't prohibit a tactic, either through legislation or a stated case after a decision in a trial, it was fair to use. Then, in the late 1990s, the Human Rights Act took effect, followed by the Regulation of Investigatory Powers Act and a code of practice for covert human intelligence sources (CHIS), which included undercover officers in its scope. Now, unless the law allowed it, we couldn't do it unless we could show that it was proportionate, legal, accountable, and necessary.

This was an important change in emphasis and police soon became familiar with working under laws that gave some clarity to the way we worked. In many areas of policing, scrutiny and accountability came from engagement with independent advisory groups made up of community representatives, often volunteers. Borough commanders worked with their local authority executives and others in public and community services and the mayor's office provided checks and balances for the whole of the Met.

In covert policing, we had a regulator known as the Office of Surveillance Commissioners (OSC), a nondepartmental government body led by retired judges with a team of inspectors made up of ex-military or retired senior police officers.

The OSC would visit every year and trawl through our paperwork for undercover operations and then draw up a report for the commissioner of the Met. No matter what I did to engage the OSC as a partner, they resisted. If they had ideas about what we could do to improve our compliance with the letter of the law, I was open to it. However, their approach was completely stand-offish, and their critique would only emerge when they shared it with the boss.

I was totally in agreement with the idea of a regulator. I thought it was essential that our work should have checks and balances and that the public should have confidence in the powers of state, especially where they could use intrusive methods. My beef with the OSC was that they didn't seem interested in discussing the details of operations, whether our tactics were being used appropriately and not excessively. Rather, they just seemed to look for errors in the paperwork and their feedback was based on a check box examination of whether every T was crossed and every I was dotted.

One example was that the signed authority (license to operate) for an undercover officer should last no more than one year before being renewed. One of the inspectors discovered that our documents mentioned the same day and month, that is, began on January 1 one year and ended January 1 the next year. It should've been January 1 to December 31, of course. It was an error we could correct very easily but was included in their report as a serious error of concern. I started to believe that they were finding ways to justify their existence rather than perform a critical function in protecting the public from the potential abuse of law. I found their visits rather tiresome for the first couple of years, though some of the inspectors I met in later years were more collaborative in helping us to maintain compliance with very complicated legislation.

Other than the OSC, the only other scrutiny of undercover operations outside of policing would be in the courts when cases came to trial. The judge had the power to exclude evidence if it had been obtained unfairly, but that rarely happened in undercover cases coming to trial as their evidence was always corroborated in some way.

How would we know whether the average member of the public would agree with our judgment of what was proportionate? The use of undercover officers was a powerful technique and I thought we needed to establish a panel to provide external scrutiny.

I wrote to some people I thought might be willing to help, including academics, a chief crown prosecutor, an executive from a children's charity, a barrister, leaders from community groups, a parent of a disaster victim who started a charity. I also invited representation from the campaign group Liberty, Human Rights. To both my surprise and delight, they all accepted.

We presented some case studies from which we stripped out the details to leave the bare bones of the dilemmas facing decision-makers in covert policing.

For example, we discussed the use of juvenile informants and gave a couple of hypothetical examples. For example, a sixteen-year-old girl wants to provide information about her mum's new partner. Domestic abuse is now present in their household from a man who is an active drug dealer. Her mum won't report him to the police, and the house is used to host gatherings with men who are clearly involved in crime. The sixteen-year-old has asked a teacher for help, and police become involved.

If police use this intelligence, the legislation and code of practice govern how the informant should be managed and protected. Should we use the intelligence to mount an operation against her mother's boyfriend?

In another example, a fifteen-year-old boy is being pressured into joining a gang to work as a courier in a county lines drug dealing operation. He knows the name and phone number of the drug dealer and how the operation works. Should police accept help from the boy to investigate the gang?

Cases such as these spawn headlines about child spies and yet police deal with dilemmas like this all the time and usually make the decisions based on operational necessity, legality, proportionality, and accountability, as well as the imperative to protect the child. The anxiety is understandable, and it feels right that the ethics of such decisions should be more widely debated. I felt that the Covert Policing Ethics Committee was a very worthy exercise in keeping with legitimacy and the doctrine of policing by consent.

LAWFULLY AUDACIOUS

John Grieve was a legendary senior officer at Scotland Yard who was much admired by the rank and file, as well as stakeholders far and wide. He coined the phrase 'lawfully audacious' to explain, without apology, that all tactics and methods available would be used to fight crime, including those that took us to the very edge of our legal powers.

The local authorities in London make up the thirty-two boroughs to which police divisions were aligned in the late 1990s. Those Borough Command Units (BCUs) were led by the Territorial Policing Command. Each BCU would police its divisional territory, with uniform response teams, detectives, intelligence units, and an array of functions to manage local crime problems and demands, including a register of people wanted either on a court issued warrant or as named suspects in investigation that they had evaded arrest for. The names would be logged on the police national computer so they would show as being wanted if arrested on other matters or stopped in a roadside check, for example. These wanted dockets would build up, especially if no active efforts were currently being made to find long term wanted people, relying instead on their chance encounter with police, or international authorities if they were out of the country.

An enterprising detective sergeant on the Territorial Policing Crime Squad came up with a plan for the bulk capture of wanted people in an audacious covert operation, using a method that had been successful in the United States and portrayed in the movie *The Sea of Love* in which wanted criminals were lured to their arrest on a promise of meeting the New York Yankees.

With the help of SO10, an enterprise was formed and a letter on headed paper was posted to a thousand people who were wanted, offering them an opportunity to benefit from unclaimed prize funds. Of course, this was a little before the era of scam emails, but it gained some traction at the time in the early 2000s. The letter said:

Congratulations,

You have been selected at random to receive a one-off financial reward.
    We are an authorised clearing house company for the distribution of unclaimed prize monies and other awards. In this capacity we are

presently operating in this area in the distribution of a major financial fund.

Please be assured:

- This is not a sales promotion.
- This is not a lottery or prize draw.

You are guaranteed a substantial cash sum; this is calculated on the numbers that reply. You are expected to receive at least a fiftieth share of £200,000. We are authorised by government statutes to distribute this money as it is allocated as prize money and, as such must be given away!

In line with current government authorisation and related financial regulation there are certain stipulations that we must abide by in the distribution of this fund.

- Please return the enclosed registration acceptance form within fourteen days.
- Provide two acceptable forms of identification in order to receive your award.
- The award will only be made payable by means of personalised cheque in favour of the named person only.

Upon receipt of your completed registration acceptance form you will be notified of the arrangements for the collection of the award.

Please understand that we are only allowed 28 days from the correlation of registration forms, which allow us to determine the individual award payments.

Once again, may I offer you my congratulations, and look forward to meeting you in the near future.

Financial Director.

A helpline number was included in the letter. Undercover officers staffed the help desk, convincing doubtful callers of their good fortune. Greed works—350 wanted people showed up at the convincing-looking corporate offices of the company in London's West End. They were met by smartly dressed people and showed through to the collection point after they had presented their identification. On the other side of the door were police officers who arrested, among others, two men sought for rape, a suspected child rapist, muggers, burglars, drug dealers, and thieves.

It was audacious but lawful, as no evidence was being gathered; they were simply caught for matters they had already gone to great efforts to avoid being arrested for. In more than one example, the newly arrested person would still want to know how they were going to get their cash prize. You should've seen their faces!

LUCAN

An inquiry came in about deploying an undercover officer overseas to help solve a cold case murder investigation of some notoriety, involving Lord Lucan, the British peer who disappeared after being suspected of murder.

Lord Lucan married Veronica Duncan in 1963. They had three children together, but his mounting gambling losses had a dramatic effect on his life and personal finances, resulting in the collapse of the marriage in 1972. He moved out of the family home and an acrimonious custody battle followed, which he lost, after which he began to spy on his wife and record their phone conversations, apparently fixated with regaining custody of the children.

On the evening of November 7, 1974, Sandra Rivett, the nanny of Lucan's children, was murdered in the basement of the Lucan family home, having been struck by a blunt object. During the same incident, but in another part of her home, Lady Lucan was also attacked and later identified her former husband as the assailant. As the police began their investigation, Lucan telephoned his mother asking her to collect the children and then drove a borrowed car to a friend's house in Sussex, where he left the property and disappeared. The car was later found parked in Newhaven, with blood stains in the interior and a piece of bandaged lead pipe similar to one found at the crime scene in the boot. The inquest into Sandra Rivett's death named him as her murderer. Since that day, Lord Lucan has been wanted by the police.

It became a cause célèbre, with the press and public fascinated by the downfall of an aristocrat in such shocking circumstances. Over the decades, there have been many alleged sightings of him around the world, none of which has been substantiated. He was declared legally dead in 1999.

My involvement in the case was initiated by a new, unconfirmed sighting of a now elderly gentleman with an aristocratic bearing, suggesting Lucan was running a remote safari range in an African country and it was thought worthy of pursuing, if only to rule it out. A senior colleague at Scotland Yard asked whether it might be an option to deploy a covert operative to recover DNA, to which I responded cautiously as it could risk the officer being arrested as a spy if they were there without the authority of their government, which was unlikely to be granted. We consulted the Foreign and Commonwealth Office (FCO) for advice and I was invited to Whitehall to discuss the proposed operation. I was met by a very charming man who would be my point of contact. He was supportive in exploring options but would need to get the go-ahead from his boss, a senior civil servant who would see us that afternoon.

My host asked whether I'd been to the FCO before, and I confessed I hadn't, expecting a lecture on protocols and the dos and don'ts of acceptable diplomatic etiquette. It wasn't that at all, but an offer to give me a personal guided tour of a magnificent building once considered for demolition in the 1960s, when such architecture was seen as old-fashioned. It is a truly magnificent building with a grand staircase, vaulted ceilings, murals, and impressive meeting rooms where treaties were signed, and grand receptions held. It would've been criminal to have demolished it.

I remember being shown a landing between floors so that I could see two offices. The one below was the office of the permanent secretary, and the one above was the office of the foreign secretary. The most senior civil servant was located directly below the senior political leader, and that's the way it should be, he said.

We arrived at the office of the senior person who would sign off the undercover deployment overseas. In a grand, ornate room with a glazed mahogany cabinet framing the backdrop, I was introduced to a young man who sat alone at a large desk that would've had the experts from the TV series *Antiques Roadshow* salivating. I went through the outline of my request, assuming this young chap was the gatekeeper, only for him to give his approval and instruct my tour guide to offer Scotland Yard every assistance necessary. Shame on me. He was a truly impressive individual who couldn't have been older than in his late twenties, and here he was, clearly in charge of steering a significant part of a government department. I'll bet he didn't go to St. Bastard's comprehensive, I thought.

After all that effort, we did not need to launch an operation as the safari owner died and there was sufficient proof that it had been another unsubstantiated Lucan sighting. It was a loose end that needed to be tied. I'd had an interesting experience working in partnership with another part of the government machine and reading the files to acquaint myself with this historic case. One for my memoirs, I thought. QED.

SITTING DUCKS

Of all the unsung heroes in policing, a special mention is deserved for those brave covert operatives known as decoy officers. Decoys are specially trained police officers who are used as ersatz victims, providing firsthand evidence of crimes that usually involve some form of violence, including sexual assaults, punches, kicks, and threats with weapons. They deploy in operations to capture muggers, rapists, flashers, stalkers, and any other type of criminal that makes it less safe to walk the streets. Usually, other methods of detection have been tried, but they have failed to catch offenders known to be active in a certain area with the offender repeating their crime and causing increasing concern for both police and the community.

Decoy officers know that if their operations are successful, they are likely to be attacked in some way. They volunteer for the decoy role to catch criminals in the act and, by doing so, spare future victims from the ordeal.

Wood Green is a suburb of North London. It's known for its bustling High Street, has an underground station, and a vibrant shopping mall. There are leafy side roads and a mixed stock of housing, tower blocks, and estates. In the mid-1980s, the women of Wood Green did not feel safe to walk the streets, and with good cause. A serial rapist was at large, responsible for eight attacks and two attempts over twelve months. He would physically drag women off the streets and into alleyways to assault them. DNA technology hadn't been developed as a way to detect offenders and the investigation relied on more conventional analogue methods, such as descriptions from victims and witnesses. Senior detectives decided to be proactive, so they used decoy officers and sought the help of volunteers to catch him. Janet was a uniformed constable at Wood Green with a few years' experience, a dedication to the job, and a great judo throw, a sport that she'd practiced since a kid and was now proficient in. She didn't blink an eye and immediately put herself forward. Janet was assured that she could change her mind at any time if she had second thoughts. She didn't.

Janet was one of four decoys that would be deployed in a covert surveillance operation intended to catch the rapist in a defined area along High Road and the side streets leading from it. The area was kept under tight observation with officers never more than two hundred yards away from the decoys, who were sent out, one at a time, when a potential suspect came onto the plot. Night after night the operation ran, and weeks rolled by without success. Then a report of an attempted rape was made. It described an attacker who was frightened off by a passerby responding to screams from an alleyway. This happened just a short distance from the plot the covert operation had been working, much to the frustration of the team.

It would be another ten days before a suspect was spotted on High Road who loosely matched the description of a tall, well-built man. One of the decoys was sent to walk near the sighting. The suspect started to follow the decoy, her colleagues observing and drawing nearer to be able to step in if anything happened, but they got too close, and the suspect walked away in the opposite direction. They thought they'd blown it and had scared him off. The operation resumed the following week—attacks never occurred on the weekends. There were two more long, fruitless nights. Everyone was returning to the station in the early hours to close down when there was a call on the radio with a potential sighting of the same suspect. Janet wanted to go back out again, but the surveillance operation had been stood down and not everyone was able to resume where they'd just left off. It can sometimes take a few minutes to reposition and park up, if observing from a vehicle, or get back into premises if watching from a nearby building.

Janet persuaded her colleague to go back. They got into one of the unmarked cars and drove back to High Road and she spotted the suspect. He was wearing a pale crewneck top and dark jeans. He had cropped hair and was well-built, over six feet tall and definitely the man who'd followed the other decoy a few days before. He was some way ahead of where they stopped the unmarked car. Janet got out, leaving her colleague, which was risky and hasty, but she had a feeling that this was the moment. She lost sight of the suspect and thought she'd missed another opportunity, adrenaline rushing to prepare her for the fight. As she came to a traditional red telephone box, he came into sight from the other side of it. The blind spot had blocked her view. He was casually sitting on the back of a bench with his feet on the seat, watching Janet as she walked past. He stood and began to follow her and Janet hoped that her colleagues had been able to get back into position with the sudden resumption of the operation. A drunk on the other side of the street called out, and the suspect disappeared again. It was a dark summer night, and lighting was patchy as trees in full leaf provided pools of shadows, especially in the side streets that led off the main road.

Janet heard footsteps running toward her, and she braced herself, certain that she was about to be attacked. A hand came round from behind to cover her mouth and nose to stop her from screaming, and a kidney punch knocked the air from her body before she was grabbed with the same arm around the stomach. She was struggling to breathe. The attacker said, 'What's your name? Where you from? Calm down and I won't hurt you.' With that, he lifted her off her feet and carried her to a car park, out of sight behind a hedge. Her colleagues weren't back in position and hadn't seen the start of the attack. The colleague who dropped her off had lost sight of her in the same blind spot behind the telephone box and was now searching frantically to find her. Everyone on the team knew that risks could only be managed and reduced and not eliminated entirely. There is always that moment between the attack on the decoy and their rescue by colleagues, however close to the action they are.

However, at this moment, the operational plan wasn't being followed. The opportunity taken was beyond the risk measures that had been put in place and followed every day until now.

Meanwhile, out of sight, the attacker was trying to force Janet's legs apart, but she managed to wrap herself around a concrete bollard, clinging to it with every ounce of strength that she had. He punched her repeatedly in the head and face. 'Don't struggle and I won't hurt you.'

Her colleague was, by now, just on the other side of the hedge. The attacker leaned out and said it was a 'domestic' between him and his girlfriend who was upset with him. Janet managed to struggle free and called out, causing the attacker to get to his feet and make a run for it. The officer gave chase, followed by Janet who, despite being injured, sprinted after him with the last ounce of energy she had. She caught up with him and threw his six foot one stocky frame to the ground with a judo move. Other officers caught up with the action just at that moment, and he was arrested. Janet had two black eyes, cuts, bruises, and a dislocated finger, and that night she'd brought a mass rapist to justice. He was only seventeen years old, convicted of eight rapes, one attempted rape, and two indecent assaults, and was sentenced to thirteen years in youth custody.

From this successful operation, Janet became the acknowledged expert on decoy operations and went on to train over two hundred officers nationally, shaping operations and improving safety for decoy officers, using her near-miss experience as a case study.

Millennium Quay was a new private housing development in an up-and-coming area of South London, overlooking the River Thames. Apartments and townhouses here were expensive and home to young professionals on the upward curve of their careers.

The pathways and paved gardens in front of the development ran alongside the river, a natural route to the apartments walking from nearby transport links in Greenwich. Those smartly dressed and carrying the appearance of people worth stealing from made easy targets when walking alone or in pairs to the gang of street robbers who were working the area and using increasing levels of violence, which was completely unnecessary against those they outnumbered and overpowered. In one robbery, the victim was pushed so hard against the low railing fence of the walkway that he was hanging over the side and facing the drop into the tidal, murky River Thames where he would've been likely to drown.

At the last second before falling, the robbers fled, leaving the victim badly beaten and feeling like he'd had a near-death experience.

There had been several attacks in the area in recent weeks. Similar descriptions of the gang and the way they carried out the robberies were reported, which was of growing concern. Local residents called for police to act before someone was killed. Although local officers had a good idea of who might be responsible, there wasn't enough evidence to make arrests. This was a gang that had to be stopped, and catching them in the act looked like the only realistic way.

With the help of residents and businesses, the local crime squad borrowed rooms overlooking the area, staking out the routes toward the quayside where previous robberies had taken place. Decoy officers dressed as young professionals on their way home from a late night out would take it in turns and walk a predetermined route, under the constant watch of their colleagues concealed in observation posts, with an arrest team and dog handlers ready to pounce from unmarked vans and hiding places. They also drafted in the Marine Policing Unit, which provided coverage on the river in case anyone should go over the quayside and into the water.

Officers patiently observed the area for four hours, between 10:00 p.m. and 2:00 a.m. for two nights, covering the peak times for robberies. Nothing happened. However, the following day, news came in of a robbery that had occurred just after 4:00 a.m. about one hundred yards from the area being covered by the operation. This robbery was by far the worst of the series, so far. The male victim was floored, and a knife put to his throat. He had already given up his valuables and even told the robbers the PIN for his bank card, yet they repeatedly kicked him in the head. He was with his girlfriend who was also made to lie on the ground, face down and she too was assaulted. One can only imagine how terrified they were and the psychological trauma of such an ordeal. Due to this attack, it was decided to expand the scope of the covert operation and extend the geography and time window of the observation.

It was just after 2:00 a.m. on a dark September night, just cold enough for a light coat to cover a stab vest. It was decoy officer Chris's turn to walk through the area again, like a baseball player hoping for a home run, he set off toward the quayside hoping to make it safely back to base, knowing that a successful night would mean it wouldn't be entirely uneventful.

One of the posts reported a car pulling up a few streets away, and five youths got out and started walking toward the quayside. They were likely suspects, loosely matching the description of a group of young men in dark clothing, as reported by previous victims. It was around 4:00 a.m., and no one else was on the streets in this residential area except this group of young men and the police officers now paying full attention to them. Chris was carrying a briefcase and a mobile phone, both of which would signal he was worth a second look, should the robbers find him on their way through the area. He was instructed to go to the paved garden where there were benches overlooking the river where he could wait and pretend to be on a call. Each observation post eagerly watched the progress of the youths as they casually walked through the streets leading to the quayside, with each team handing over their commentary to the next, like the baton in a relay race. The team overlooking the paved park calmy gave everyone a second-by-second commentary over the radio, adrenalin rushing as everyone prepared for an imminent attack on Chris, who was now aware that he was about to be the next victim. Yet he had to hold his nerve and let events happen, trusting that his rescuers would reach him before he suffered too badly.

One of the youths spotted Chris on the bench and looked around, scoping out possible witnesses before giving a thumbs-up to the others. They ran toward Chris to attack him from behind as, simultaneously, the arrest team who had been hiding in wait, leapt into action immediately, knowing it would take a few seconds before they could rescue their colleague and detain the robbers. Without any conversation, Chris was punched in the head by one of the robbers. He was bundled and forced against the railing fence on the quayside, with the drop into the Thames one good shove away. The attackers punched him about the face and body, taking his briefcase and the mobile phone he'd been using.

They'd landed a few punches but were suddenly confronted by a group of police officers converging on the scene, causing the robbers to make a dash in the other direction, only to be confronted by dog handlers with two angry looking Alsatian police dogs (or 'land sharks' as they are sometimes affectionately referred to by colleagues). The robbers found themselves outnumbered and overpowered. Four of them were arrested and taken to the police station, though, in the chaos, one of the robbers managed to escape and was never identified. When they arrived at the station, robbery squad officers learned that another incident had occurred a couple of miles away, about twenty minutes before the attack on Chris. The victim of that robbery had been beaten around the face and body and hit several times around the head with a hammer. His description of the suspects matched those now arrested, and when the attackers were searched at the station, one of them had the victim's stolen mobile phone in his possession. Officers at the scene went to find the car the gang had arrived in earlier and discovered it was stolen and the hammer used in the earlier robbery was found inside. The suspects were just sixteen and seventeen years old.

After further investigation, they were charged with ten robberies in a series of attacks over the previous few weeks.

Chris was bruised, but otherwise OK. Once again, brave decoy officers put themselves in harm's way, knowing they would be assaulted, and in doing so, to protect the public and catch criminals who might otherwise have gone on to use higher levels of violence, and in this case, possibly kill someone. There is no danger money or promise of career advancement, in fact no advantages on offer for decoys except the satisfaction of being at the sharpest of the sharp end.

TEMPTATION

Suzy had been an undercover officer for a few years, and now in her late thirties was experienced, confident, and considered a safe pair of hands for a broad range of operational deployments.

There was something about her. She was enigmatic, possessing a personality that made her fun to be around and drew people to her as moths to a flame. If you walked in on a conversation she would be in the middle, holding court, and everyone else would be smiling or laughing out loud at her funny stories or clever put downs. As a charming extrovert, Suzy made a very good undercover officer.

She was assigned to work with a foreign law enforcement agency that wanted to deploy an informant on British soil. To ensure compliance with the law, Suzy would be the UK liaison officer and went to meet the visitors at a London hotel, where they would discuss the investigation and plans for the next few days in the UK.

The hotel was in a nice part of town, modern and business-like, its lobby immaculate with clean lines and floor to ceiling plate glass windows. It was light and spacious with enough class to be on the border between welcoming and intimidating if you felt a little out of place. Suzy walked in with a smile, and, after the formalities of a discreet introduction between them and the informant, they moved to a private meeting room.

The informant, Sam, was in his early forties. Tall and handsome, he wore a well-tailored suit, no tie, and the top two buttons of his shirt precisely undone. A corporate accountant by trade, he was as articulate as he was immaculate and spoke with confidence and a firmly held point of view. The agents were here with Sam to follow the money trail from an audacious attempted fraud against his employer, which had been discovered just before it was too late. The authorities were called in and they devised a plan to continue the fraudulent deal and bring out all the players with the lure of a big payday.

London was just one of several cities they wanted to move money through and Sam, acting as the intended victim, needed them to know he was in town. This wouldn't be a difficult or dangerous part of the investigation, but a crucial step to keep the fraudsters engaged with the fake deal.

There was a relaxed atmosphere in the room, and everyone listened when Suzy explained her role and the law they would have to comply with for the duration of the deployment. Suzy was her usual self. There was a spark between her and Sam, which generated a few flirty comments back and forth. The meeting ended with a plan to reconvene in the morning before Sam would meet a contact in the financial district, who had connections with the fraudsters.

By now it was around 10:00 p.m. Suzy left the hotel with the others staying behind, as they were residents. Suzy called her cover officer, a colleague assigned as advisor, supervisor, and to provide welfare and support.

She reported that all was well and that this was a low-risk operation that she had no concerns about.

At around midnight, Sam was in his hotel room when a firm knock at the door broke the silence along the second-floor corridor. Sam was awake and had music on in the background and an open bottle of wine. He hadn't ordered anything that would prompt a caller at the door, so he froze in the hope that whoever it was would go away.

Knock, knock, knock. This time it was louder and followed by a man's voice. 'Sam, open the door.' Slowly walking toward the door, Sam looked through the spyhole and saw his agents with a concerned look on their faces. Sam didn't want to entertain a visit from them right now, so he gently walked away from the door, hoping he hadn't given away that he was in.

The agents knew he was in and weren't going anywhere. They were in covert operations and knew everything about Sam, where he was and what he was doing at any given time during the trip. They were not taking silence as an acceptable response to their late-night call. They persisted, knocking on the door, and letting Sam know that they knew he was there. Those few minutes seemed like an eternity, the awkwardness of the quiet corridor being disturbed by the commotion and the obvious delay by Sam who eventually opened the door, saying he'd been asleep and asking what they wanted.

His handlers pushed past and walked into the room, noticing the bottle of wine and both glasses in use. The bed did not look slept in but had been unmade to look that way and it was obvious to them that their concerns had been justified. They looked behind the curtains and opened the cupboard doors, searching for something or someone. 'What's going on, Sam?'

He let out a sigh of resignation as one of the agents went into the bathroom. 'I think you'd better leave.' From behind the shower curtain, Suzy said, 'It's not what it looks like. Nothing happened,' as she emerged, ashamed at being discovered in a compromising situation.

'You'd better pack your bags, Sam. We'll be leaving ahead of schedule tomorrow,' the lead agent announced. No amount of apologies or explanations were going to cut it in this situation. It was unprofessional and embarrassing. Suzy left the room. Gone were the charming smiles, knowing as she did that she'd made a serious error of judgment. Undercover officers operate in a regulated, high-risk environment, and there is an expectation they can be trusted to work independently and with integrity. Anything that erodes that trust could endanger high-profile cases.

It was around 2:00 a.m. and my phone, always on, rang. It was my boss explaining what had happened and was convening a meeting at Scotland Yard very early the next morning.

'Did she not think his room would be wired by his agents?' he asked, before hanging up. Of course, they'd heard everything and were well aware of what happened between the Scotland Yard undercover officer and the married accountant.

Our foreign colleagues were disappointed as their case was now potentially undermined by the actions of their informant and the unprofessional actions of a colleague we had trusted to get the job done. They were going to speak with their prosecutor and hold a case review to establish whether they could proceed with an informant whose integrity was now in question.

Suzy was crestfallen. I'd never seen her like this, and I was worried about her, but there had to be consequences. Our foreign colleagues did not want to make a formal complaint and left it to us to sort things out on our side, but with an informal expectation that heads would roll. My boss deferred to me, and the heavy decision of a path forward with Suzy on the team was in my hands. We had a long discussion, and she denied that it had happened the way it was reported, but we soon got past that and came to the understanding that she would, at the very least, be taking a break from undercover work. She was eligible for promotion, but that wouldn't be happening now. I couldn't promote her out of this, and my recommendation would matter.

I decided she needed to return to local frontline detective duties, reconnecting with her purpose as a police officer and as a development opportunity in preparation for a deferred promotion, should that window open again a year or so down the line. I knew my opposite number at a North London station. We had an off the record conversation so she knew what she was getting. Despite this episode, Suzy was a good detective and an asset to any team.

Crisis averted, but with our reputation dented within the circle of knowledge at Scotland Yard and certainly with our international colleagues, we moved on without Suzy. I had no doubts about my decision to remove her from undercover work, but I didn't like it one bit. I liked her too, and she was a loss to the department.

She'd go on to be successful in her new role, and everyone there loved being around her, just as before. As I'd hoped, she was successful at her next promotion bid about eighteen months later, but never returned to undercover work again.

OPPORTUNITY, KNOCKED

A team had been established to prepare for the London Olympics. I was approached about a lateral move to take up the role as DCI for crime and intelligence, planning for 2012 and making sure we pick up lessons from other major events to prevent crime. All major construction projects are vulnerable to large-scale fraud, organized crime, theft and, potentially, human trafficking. After four years in SO10, two longer than I originally intended, it would be a good move, so I said I would apply through the usual channels for an open vacancy. The ink was barely dry on my application when I had a call from Matt telling me that HE was moving on in a reshuffle of management roles in the command.

Actually, it was a problem for me because I wanted to move on and, as suspected, my skip level boss, the chief of covert policing, wasn't going to endorse my application for the Olympics job. She said she couldn't let both of us move as this would be too much senior experience leaving a high-risk unit. I understood that, but I wanted my application to be registered and for the process to formally block my move rather than me agree to it. In negotiation, as I'd learned, it was always important to show pain when making a concession.

I said I'd like the paperwork to run its course and I appealed to the assistant commissioner (AC) on the basis that I'd served the command well and didn't want my career impeded in this way. It went to a meeting between my current AC and his opposite number with responsibility for the Olympic vacancy, refereed by the director of human resources for the Met. It was nice to know I was worth fighting over, but the outcome was that the covert command needed me to steady the ship, so I was going nowhere.

A week or so later, I saw my AC in the lift lobby of Scotland Yard. He said that he hoped I wasn't too disappointed in the outcome of my posting decision. 'I'm the head of Scotland Yard's undercover unit. How bad can that be?' I said, stoically. I could tell he liked that answer and we parted with a manly handshake.

At least I'd have unfettered leadership of the unit now, after the reshuffle, and some of my changes could be implemented without the veto previously available to those willing to go over my head.

Violence against Women and Girls

THERE IS INCREASING CONCERN IN THE UK ABOUT VIOLENCE AGAINST women and girls (VAWG), which has seen a focussed effort and dedicated resources to tackle it. The College of Policing defines it as the harm caused to victims and society by violence against women and girls in all its forms—including but not limited to harassment, stalking, rape, sexual assault, murder, and coercive control.

A woman is killed by a man every three days. Domestic abuse makes up 18 percent of all recorded crime in England and Wales, and there are around two hundred thousand reported sexual crimes per year, of which more than seventy thousand are rape.

VAWG is not a new phenomenon with plenty of historic and notorious cases such as Jack the Ripper in the late nineteenth century, the Yorkshire Ripper of the 1970s, Fred and Rosemary West, Levi Bellfield, and John Worboys.

Jack the Ripper was a serial killer who was active in the late 1800s, responsible for at least five murders, though there may have been more. His method involved disemboweling the women he killed, thus earning his descriptive name, which some modern observers claim glorifies him and his crimes. Despite the passage of time, there remains an interest in the mystery of the killer who has never been brought to justice and the mythology attached to his identity, which remains unconfirmed.

In the late 1970s, Peter Sutcliffe was a prolific serial killer in the north of England and became known as the Yorkshire Ripper. Sutcliffe's victims were all women, and many of them were found in red-light district areas. He claimed that God had sent him on a mission to kill 'prostitutes.' He was found to have killed twenty-two women and had attempted to murder seven others. He was sentenced to twenty consecutive life sentences and died in 2020.

Between the late 1960s to 1980s, married couple Fred and Rosemary West are known to have killed more than twenty young women between them and abused their own female children. Police investigating their crimes excavated the cellar and garden of their Gloucestershire home, where remains were discovered.

Levi Belfield is a serial killer serving a whole life sentence. In 2002, he abducted and killed thirteen-year-old Millie Dowler when she was on her way home from school in Surrey. In 2003, he killed nineteen-year-old Marsha Louise McDonnell by hitting her over the head with a blunt instrument after she got off a bus near her home in Hampton, and he attempted to kill eighteen-year-old Kate Sheedy in 2004 by running her over in his car, but she survived her injuries. A few months later, Bellfield killed twenty-two-year-old Amelie Delagrange in Twickenham.

Then there are cases that don't involve murder but are very serious crimes carrying the potential for a life sentence.

In London, the drivers of iconic black taxis are considered the best in the world because of the time and effort it takes to complete the Knowledge of London, the world's most difficult taxi driver qualification. It can take years of work to learn the multiple routes to get from one part of London to another, along with landmarks, key buildings, and institutions. The application process involves background and character checks, and the trade is highly regulated and supervised. Licensed taxi drivers stay in the role for many years because they've invested a lot of time to achieve the qualification and the green badge they wear while on duty. These attributes give the public confidence in the use of licensed taxis, which are generally considered a safe way to travel.

John Worboys was one such licensed taxi driver. However, he was also a predatory sex offender and serial rapist. There were times that when he had a lone woman in his taxi, he would get her to drink a glass of spiked champagne during the journey. He would begin by telling her that he'd had some good fortune, such as a large win at the casino or the lottery.

Sometimes this would include showing off a bag full of cash that he used as a prop. He would go on to say that she was his last pickup of the night and that he'd bought a bottle of champagne to celebrate and then invite her to join him. Inevitably, the victims trusted a licensed taxi driver and most let their guard down, accepting his offer of a glass of bubbly. Before long, they would start to feel drowsy and, eventually, were nearly or completely unconscious. He would drive to somewhere private and rape or sexually assault them. Some opportunities for police to respond to and link allegations were missed, but his crimes eventually caught up with him. In 2009, he was convicted for one count of rape, five sexual assaults, one attempted assault, and twelve drugging charges, all committed from July 2007 to February 2008. He was given an indeterminate sentence of imprisonment for public protection with the minimum custodial term set at eight years.

The judge said he would not be released until the parole board decided that he no longer presented a threat to women. A bid for parole was overturned in 2017, following a public outcry when news of his potential release became a major news story.

In 2019, Worboys was charged with four further sexual assaults alleged to have occurred between 2000 and 2008, following a review of evidence by the Crown Prosecution Service. He admitted to attacking four women and was sentenced to two life sentences. It was revealed in court that Worboys had confessed to a psychologist that he had pushed alcohol on ninety women, of whom one-quarter had been drugged.

There is another much larger private hire or minicab industry whose drivers do not need to learn the Knowledge of London, though they must complete background and safety checks before they and their vehicles are licensed. Although minicabs can't be hailed in the street like licensed taxis, many of the ride hailing apps used today use minicabs that take us on our journeys safely and without incident.

During my time in SO10, there were concerns about unlicensed minicab drivers. I should make the distinction here that these were essentially men using cars to lure women, making them vulnerable to unwanted sexual conduct and assaults. They weren't minicab drivers at all, so the term 'unlicensed minicab driver' needs to be understood in that context.

The mayor's office had funded and established a Transport Operational Command Unit (TOCU) within the Metropolitan Police to improve confidence in the safety of public transport, which included an initiative known as Safer Travel at Night, particularly focused on promoting safer travel for women.

In my role as the head of undercover and as the gatekeeper for training of covert operatives, I had learned that TOCU officers in plainclothes were conducting covert operations by acting as potential passengers to detect properly licensed cab drivers picking up fares from popular venues without a prior booking, which was a breach of the conditions of their license. By law, only licensed taxis can be hailed in the street, and private hire minicabs are only allowed to take pre-booked passengers who call an office or use an app, such as Uber or Lyft. Covert operations, where officers were acting in undercover roles, required approval from my boss, the commander of covert policing at Scotland Yard, so this TOCU initiative was working outside of that authority. This wasn't simply a matter of bureaucracy, but was a policy to ensure that legislation related to covert activity and codes of practice was observed, hence the requirement for senior oversight. I didn't have any objection to the enforcement of licensing infringements, though my personal preference would've been to pay attention to the more dangerous unlicensed minicab drivers who had not been through criminal background checks. These men were using their own cars, which had not been inspected as safe and roadworthy for use as a cab and were certainly not insured for the job. Operating completely outside the law and any regulation is where sexual predators were more likely to be found. As the head of the undercover unit, I was hoping I could support TOCU with covert operatives trained for this work and decided to take the initiative to propose a collaboration.

I had a brief call with one of their senior officers and arranged to meet with three members of their senior team a few days later. I arrived to find that the meeting room had been set up as if I was being interviewed for a job. An ambush interview was not an entirely unfamiliar experience, so I just went along with it, confident in my position. The unit commander, a superintendent, and chief inspector sat behind a desk and declared immediately that they weren't interested in doing the work of Scotland Yard's specialist crime command, and their key performance objectives were their business, not mine. I hadn't quite expected them to be so defensive, but I kept my cool. I pointed out that the senior responsible officer for covert policing was my commander in the specialist crime command who could stop their activity with immediate effect. In this 'my dad's bigger than your dad competition,' I won, and the discussion moved on to how we could work together. I felt a little deflated that it had been a rather negative experience, approaching this as I had with positive intent in the spirit of collaboration. It was no skin off my nose if they screwed up, and the easiest move on my part would've been to flag this up the command chain and put a stop to their work. After this meeting, and the arrogance from senior leaders I expected more from, they lost me. I'd do what was needed to fix the immediate problem and then leave them to it. Churlish of me, perhaps, but I didn't feel like a warm professional working relationship was likely to emerge and part of me wished I'd thrown a legal spanner in their works, but I knew that wasn't really going to help anyone, least of all the potential victims of crime. I got over myself fairly quickly after my initial reaction, and I offered to provide some covert training for the limited role their officers were performing and design a process for approving and documenting the activity by the senior command team.

My training staff picked things up from here and devised a training course, during which we learned that some of the TOCU officers in these covert licensing operations had placed themselves in great danger, with reports of officers being dragged along by cars when they revealed they were police officers and had tried to grab the keys from the ignition. The book of remembrance at Scotland Yard has several mentions of officers killed on duty by moving cars in exactly this way. It is a highly dangerous thing to do. In another example, an officer posing as a passenger had been taken away against her will when she produced her police ID to an offending driver, who sped off taking her a mile down the road. She was able to escape only when traffic blocked the car's path, and she jumped out. If ever there was a need for training to manage risk and improve safety, this was it. We put a few of them through training courses, gave them the means to train their own staff, and left them to pursue the low-hanging fruit—licensed minicab drivers who were breaching conditions of their regulations about picking up passengers in the street.

As TOCU senior leaders didn't want to collaborate, I supported a separate covert operation to respond to intelligence about a male predator using his own car as an unlicensed minicab. His objective was the opportunity to approach lone women. There had been a few complaints about a driver in a silver VW Golf with similar accounts of unwanted flirting, language, and physical touching, such as initiating neck massages. The most recent passenger to raise concerns was an astute woman who had noted the registration number of his car along with a description of him. From this report, he wasn't difficult to identify. A bus driver by occupation, Ali was married with young children and was the owner of a two-door VW Golf, an unsuitable car for use as a minicab. Neither he nor his vehicle were licensed for the role. He was put under surveillance.

Liz, a covert operative, was deployed to hang around bars where Ali was known to stalk his prey. On this night, if things went to plan, Liz would be his next intended victim, under the watchful gaze of a team who would respond to ensure her protection. If she needed help, she would speak a prearranged code word on her covert microphone or gave a physical signal.

It was a cold, late evening in February and just about the right time for people to leave the bars, restaurants, and clubs in Bishopsgate, a main road out of the city district toward North London. Liz had been dropped several times that night in areas with bars and night spots where Ali had been driving around, in the hope that he'd approach her, but these attempts had proven fruitless, so far, and Liz was hoping for the deployment to end soon. She was tired and worried that the covert radio link she was wearing was running out of power and starting to fail. She had a mobile phone as a backup, which was already connected to a call with the surveillance team who were watching her, so she summoned up the energy for one last try. She could see him in his car passing by in the street and side turns nearby. Finally, he drove up alongside her and she asked him, 'Are you a minicab? I need to get back to the Dorchester hotel.'

He quoted her a fare of £15 and she got in the front passenger seat next to him because it was a two-door. Liz thanked him for picking her up, explaining that she'd been out all day and had been looking for a cab, walking back and forth in Bishopsgate for about half an hour.

The journey started with standard small talk. Ali asked Liz if she'd had a good night and asked her name, introducing himself as Tony.

The first sign that the journey was going to be unusual was when he started to drive north toward Shoreditch, which was the wrong direction. The famous Dorchester Hotel in Park Lane was westbound. Any taxi or minicab driver with the most basic knowledge of London knew that. In fact, he continued driving in the wrong direction for about three miles, before stopping for fuel in Stoke Newington, unaware that he was being trailed by a surveillance team, watching him and listening to the conversation between him and Liz. It's also unusual to stop for fuel with a passenger on board, as most drivers would refuel between fares to ensure they can complete the journey for their customers. He said that he needed to get money from the ATM to pay for fuel, which was another sign that he wasn't a real minicab driver, as he would surely have some cash from his fares or a float to provide change to customers. He then suggested that Liz could pay her fare in advance rather than him drawing from the ATM. Liz agreed, asking him for reassurance that he was going to take her to her destination. 'Of course,' he said. 'Lend me a tenner, then.' Liz handed over a £10 note. He put fuel in the car and went inside the shop to pay. Music from the car stereo was playing lightly in the background and while she was alone in the car, Liz took the opportunity to check in with the surveillance team.

'Are you getting this?' she asked. The surveillance team confirmed they were through Liz's hidden earpiece.

Ali returned to the car with a not-so-smooth greeting. 'Alright, Lesley?' getting her name wrong. 'Liz!' she said, emphasising her name. He apologized, offering her a drink from an open bottle of Coke. She wasn't about to drink from the same bottle as him and certainly didn't trust that it hadn't been spiked with something.

'You should have a soft drink to sober up,' he said, but Liz made her excuses. 'No, I might be sick if I eat or drink anything right now.'

As they moved off from their unscheduled stop, Liz asked how long it would take to get to the Dorchester. Ali said it would be half an hour, which was about right. He was trying to keep the conversation going, asking about where she'd been and whether it was for work or pleasure.

Liz thought it would be helpful to confirm her location with the surveillance team and asked him if they were in Hoxton, which he confirmed, unaware that the conversation was being monitored via her covert device and in an open phone line.

The conversation took a slightly bizarre turn when he said he'd been clubbing earlier that evening.

'Clubbing?' Liz asked quizzically. 'I hope you haven't been drinking if you're driving me,' she said with humorous tone. The conversation and the journey were becoming stranger by the minute. Rap music was playing on the car's radio, which he suddenly turned up very loud. 'Wow, you're giving me a headache,' said Liz. 'But you're on a night out,' he said, turning the volume down. Liz thanked him. 'You know what it's like when you've been in a club all night. You need to give your ears a rest.'

He noticed Liz was wearing a ring and asked her about it, but really wanted to know whether she was in a relationship. 'Why you wearing that ring for?' 'Because I like it. Why do you wear anything?' she replied. 'You're not supposed to be wearing it on this finger though, are ya?' he asked, probing further. 'Cos it's for engagement, yeah?' 'No, that's the other hand,' Liz replied.

They talked about her work, with Liz giving a good account of the fictitious firm she worked for and her role in market research. Liz didn't know that the open call on her mobile phone had dropped, and she answered it when it rang, keeping up the act of it being from her friend that left the same function earlier, confirming she'd arrived home safely. Liz did a great job of sounding tipsy and cheerful in conversation with the very sober and alert detective on the end of the line. Liz pretended the call had ended with a cheery goodbye and kept her phone on and connected.

'She sounds worse than I am,' she said. He suggested that he and Liz go to another club, an idea that she nipped in the bud straight away saying she needed to get up in the morning. He turned the stereo up to full volume, laughing as he explained that he was creating club atmosphere in the car to change her mind.

Liz responded, 'Well, I'm the DJ and I'm gonna have to turn that down. It's alright, it's just a bit loud. I can still feel my ears thumping from the last place. You know what I mean when you get that *whoom, whoom, whoom?*'

He responded by turning it up again, the music now reverberating off the surfaces in the car.

'No. No. No . . . it's too loud,' Liz complained.

'Come on. Have it loud. You like it. Just imagine it's your club,' he said, going way beyond the boundaries of a normal minicab journey, but Liz was getting annoyed. 'No, it's too loud. I came out of the club for a reason.'

'OK,' he said. 'Get a massage, man.'

'Ah, no . . . what're you doing?' Liz laughed politely, finding it ridiculous as he fondled her neck. 'Give you a little massage,' he said. 'I'm very tired. I'm alright. I just wanna get home and sleep now,' she said, pushing his hand away from the back of her neck.

They drove on in silence, but with the stereo playing, now on lower volume in the background. The car came to a stop in traffic near King's Cross station, an area then under development with road diversions and temporary routes.

Liz broke their silence. 'Roadworks everywhere in London.'

'You don't like it do you?' he said, referring to the music playing in the car.

'No, I do. It's cool. It's fine,' Liz replied.

'Ha, you're just sayin' that . . . alright then.'

'No, it's nice. It's just like chart music,' she tried to assure him.

After a short pause he said, 'I'll put it up, alright?' cranking the volume back up again.

'No, turn it down. I've got a headache from it,' she pleaded, 'and that's gonna make it worse.'

This was the strangest cab journey anyone could experience, with a level of familiarity that was highly unprofessional and uncomfortable for any passenger. Boundaries had certainly been crossed, and Liz was doing a great job of staying in there and keeping her cover.

As the traffic lights changed to green, he went through the road-works alongside King's Cross station and pretended he'd taken a wrong turn and was confused by the changed layout. This weird minicab journey was about to take another bizarre turn when he decided he needed to drive down a service road at the side of the station to urinate. 'Oh, come on, I need to get home, what are you doing?' Liz complained.

He didn't reply and as the car came to a stop. He opened the door and got out. Liz wasn't sure what was going to happen next and hoped the team had seen them turn into the service road. He returned to the car after about a minute, having been disturbed as someone was coming.

'Can't we just go to the hotel, and you can go there, can't you?' Liz asked.

'What, you'll let me into your hotel?' he said, optimistically thinking his luck had changed. Liz explained that she meant he could use the gent's toilet there if the hotel would let him.

It was all clear again in the service road so he got out again to relieve himself. After a good couple of minutes, Liz called out, 'Come on!' to which he said, 'Coming man.' He opened the door and got in. He had trouble closing the door, or so it seemed, and sat there for about a minute.

'Oh, for fucks sake, come on let's go,' she said.

'Yeah, yeah, let's.' He slammed the door, but the car didn't move.

'Are we going or what?' she said.

'Yeah, yeah. We are, we're gonna go, don't worry,' he said, clearly distracted and not paying attention to the task of driving.

'Come on then, let's go.'

'You wanna drive instead?' he asked.

'No, I . . . I can't drive, I've had too much to drink, come on.' As she looked toward him, he exposed himself and began masturbating.

Liz announced loudly, 'You're fucking playing with yourself, you dirty bastard!'

'I'm not. I'm not, man,' he replied.

The surveillance team heard this and began moving in.

Liz got out of the car. 'Fucking hell, playing with your willie in front of me.'

To which he said, 'It's OK, I've finished.'

'What do you mean you've finished? You dirty bastard,' Liz said, walking away from the car. Her colleagues on foot were now approaching. Maintaining cover, she said, 'He's just got his willy out in front of me.' She knew it would be better to stay in role so that her real identity could be revealed, tactically, in the interview when Ali was back at the station.

The world suddenly changed around Ali as unmarked police cars skidded to a stop, and he found himself surrounded by plain clothed officers who arrested him. Other officers rushed Liz away to a waiting unmarked car.

Liz could now relax, but the adrenaline was rushing through her. She wanted reassurance that she'd made the right call by giving the team a signal to call in the arrest, which she had, of course, ending the most unusual minicab journey.

Even though this was a planned operation, with backup just a short distance away, the courage it takes for someone like Liz to put themselves in harm's way to bring an offender like Ali to justice deserves our admiration and gratitude. Thanks to an astute member of the public who noted his registration number and took the time and trouble to report him, police were able to devise an operation to gather unassailable evidence against him through the brave efforts of Liz, sparing other women a similar, if not worse ordeal.

Ali admitted this and several similar charges of indecent exposure and assault, resulting in a sentence of four years in prison.

There are more journeys like the one Liz experienced than there is capacity to deal with them in this way. Like all crimes, prevention is better than detection after the fact, but it's never the victim's fault. Why did she go out? Why did she drink too much? Why did she leave alone? Why did she get into that car?

Why shouldn't she be able to go out and celebrate without being endangered by creeps like him? Sadly, there are many like him out there, and often safety campaigns focus on cautionary tales and advice that implores women to take preventative care, which is hugely problematic from the inferred responsibility of women in these crimes.

Some of these predatory men, I'm sad to acknowledge, come from within the police service too. The murder of thirty-three-year-old Sarah Everard as she walked home from her friend's house through Clapham one March evening in 2021 sparked national outrage. Police officer Wayne Couzens used his police ID and handcuffs to detain Sarah on the deceitful charge of being in breach of lockdown rules, taking her away in his car before the horrors of raping and violently murdering her. The investigation into her disappearance found CCTV footage linking Couzens to the crime from a passing bus. Her body was discovered in a pond, just yards from land owned by him, which led to his arrest. He was convicted and is serving a whole of life sentence. Police were condemned for missing opportunities that may have resulted in his arrest for indecent exposure in other reported incidents. Convictions for these crimes would've resulted in his dismissal from the police service and may have prevented his illegal conduct from escalating.

In another case, David Carrick, a police officer for twenty years, was arrested when a woman reported that he had date raped her, deciding she would come forward following the Sarah Everard case. The investigation that followed revealed multiple cases of rape and abusive and degrading conduct toward women, many of whom he met through dating websites. He used his position as a police officer to gain their trust and exaggerate his importance, making them fear he was untouchable.

The woman described how she had met Carrick on a dating app. On their first meeting, he showed her his police ID and tried to impress her with claims that he had met famous people including the prime minister and boasted that he handled firearms.

After plying her with drink, he took her to a hotel room where, she said, he raped her. Carrick was arrested and charged. Appearing in court meant that he was publicly named, which led to more victims coming forward with allegations.

Carrick pleaded guilty to more than fifty charges, including twenty-eight cases of rape. In early 2023, he was given thirty-six life sentences and won't be eligible for parole for over thirty years. After his conviction, the Metropolitan Police re-examined allegations of domestic or sexual abuse by about one thousand employees, both officers and staff. Evident that more than weak signals were present, his colleagues had given Carrick the nickname Bastard Dave, knowing his supposed propensity for cruelty.

Carrick joined the Metropolitan police in 2001, after serving in the army. He was successfully vetted, despite having been implicated in allegations for which he wasn't charged, though should still have raised flags about his character. One of the allegations was said to have included a burglary at the home of a former partner he refused to accept had ended their relationship.

While still in his probationary period in 2002, he was subject to investigation by the Met police after being accused of assaulting and harassing a former partner.

There were other reports of assault, abuse, and domestic violence throughout Carrick's career, which had been made in Hertfordshire, Thames Valley, and Hampshire police force areas.

Yet, in 2017, he was vetted again and continued to serve without suspension, even following an allegation that he grabbed a woman by the neck in 2019 and following the allegation that led to his arrest in 2021. While the Met police were publicly making commitments to protect women after Sarah Everard's murder, Carrick continued to serve, albeit on restricted duties. These were not weak signals, but red flags frantically waving for attention. He should have been stopped much earlier.

Decent police officers share the public's outrage at the crimes committed by Couzens and Carrick, who were serving officers and whose duty it was to protect those they committed crimes against. My former colleagues are working hard to turn around the loss of trust in the police service, publishing a turnaround plan called a 'New Met for London.' The ongoing efforts to reduce violence against women and girls has set them an enormous challenge too and, not only as a former police officer, but as a father of girls and a husband, I hope they succeed.

Violent men who harm women and girls should be in no doubt that we are coming after them. We are going to increase the use of our unique police powers to relentlessly pursue perpetrators, manage offenders and disrupt their activities—whether in public spaces, online or behind closed doors. We want to help turn the tables so violent men feel under threat, not women and girls going about their lives. (Maggie Blyth, Deputy Chief Constable, National Police Coordinator for VAWG)

CHAPTER 13

Psychology in Undercover

I'D SPENT A COUPLE OF WEEKS HELPING WITH A TRANSFORMATION PROJ-
ect for the Met, working with a firm of consultants on some changes that
were going to affect the covert world. It was an interesting experience
in a strategic way, but quite distant from operational police work. I was
offered a temporary promotion to superintendent to take on the role for a
year, but it would mean that I would have to leave my post in undercover,
which would be backfilled.

I felt that a promotion would be welcome, as would the jump in pay
for this rank. It would probably lead to permanent promotion, but there
was a risk it wouldn't, and I'd find myself in my same middle rank as a
chief inspector somewhere mind numbingly dull. I decided I'd be better
off waiting for the promotion process and, if successful, go somewhere
I'd prefer to work.

The assistant commissioner called me and asked why I hadn't gone
for the post. I explained my rationale. It was quite unusual for such a
senior officer to call, and it was clear that he wanted me to take the job
as payback for having been prevented from taking the Olympics job. But
as I said to the AC back then, I'm the head of Scotland Yard's undercover unit, and I far preferred that to becoming a superintendent in the
transformation project.

NATIONAL WORKING GROUP
I was appointed as the national lead for undercover training and development, which I'd manage along with my day job, being a kidnap negotiator

on-call, and studying for a master's degree (because I was a glutton for punishment). I'd wanted to transform recruitment, selection, and training for some time, and now had a formal role in changing not just SO10's approach, but every UK law enforcement agency. I wondered if I'd bitten off more than I could chew.

The police staff college, known as Bramshill, was where the highfliers went to play Mah Jong and contemplate blue sky thinking, as we mere mortals liked to say. Bramshill was the closest thing the police service had to Sandhurst or Westpoint, and it was an impressive place, long since sold off as part of the austerity measures after the global financial crisis of 2008.

I'd approached the National Policing Improvement Agency (NPIA) and persuaded them to support me with a project team. This agency was responsible for Bramshill. They gave me accommodation and meeting rooms in support of the national UC training project. I convened a meeting of a sample group of undercover officers, supervisors, unit managers, and senior investigating officers and locked them in breakout rooms for a couple of days, punctuated by a good session in the campus bar. Their task was to come up with a list of tasks, actions, tactics, and requirements that enabled them to do their job. The results were taken away and crunched by the NPIA project team who distilled them into competencies from which my group created the training courses fit for modern policing.

To bridge the gap between test purchase officers and UCs used in higher level deployments, we created foundation and advanced undercover officers to encourage those in street level operations to follow a pathway we created to upskill them as rapidly as their aptitude would allow. These changes were designed to dissolve internal barriers between the different levels of covert operative and use our resources more effectively.

To pilot some of the changes in SO10, I initiated a mentoring scheme to give some control back to my experienced trainers and operatives so that they would have a stake in managing the changes that were now happening quite quickly.

This was a great move as the training sergeants developed a connection with those they were mentoring and, whereas the mindset had been to emphasise how difficult it was for candidates to pass the training course, they were now invested in their success. Using the same measures before and after a year of the new recruitment and selection process, we saw a 35 percent increase in the diversity profile of undercover officers. It had a real impact on our work and the outcomes we could provide through undercover operations.

It had long been my view that the undercover unit could provide a better service for all of London's diverse populations by providing more officers that looked, sounded, behaved, and blended within their communities. Some might think that sounds like we wanted to infiltrate those communities to attack them, and they should expect no apology if there are criminals in those communities that need to be caught. The reality is that most people want to live peacefully, and I saw it as our job to enable everyone to participate in public life without fear from crime. Our role was to protect all communities and sometimes, to do that successfully, we needed our officers to be among them, covertly.

PSYCHOLOGY IN UNDERCOVER POLICING

There is, without doubt, a romantic Hollywood view of the undercover officer (UC). The list of movies and TV shows where the undercover role is portrayed is endless and includes such epic titles such as *Donnie Brasco* (1997), *Rush* (1991), *Reservoir Dogs* (1992), *Point Break* (1991), *The Wire* (2001–2008), *Luther* (2010–2019), and the highly successful British TV series *Line of Duty* (2012–2021).

A typical undercover movie trope might include the mystique of the smouldering, brooding detective with endless courage, the sleuthing ability of Sherlock Holmes, and a maverick who doesn't play by the rules, usually harangued by a deskbound boss who gives them twenty-four hours to get results or they're off the case. We've been thoroughly entertained by these productions and, no doubt, will continue to be enthralled by their compelling stories and characters.

At the risk of sounding like that deskbound boss, the real world was different. It came with the daily challenges of leading people with strong personalities who had the ability to think several chess moves ahead. Even in the real world, undercover officers carry a certain cachet and colleagues from other parts of the police service can be a little starstruck in their presence sometimes. There is confidence in and respect for the work they do, which carries throughout the criminal justice system.

There had been some ad hoc undercover operations in the early 1980s, but it wasn't until 1986 that two pioneering detective sergeants were given authority to form SO10, Scotland Yard's undercover unit. With the support of intelligence agencies and military special forces, they designed and delivered some of the most challenging training, devised rules that kept UCs on the right side of the law, and created innovative evidence-gathering operations that enabled infiltration of previously impervious organized criminal groups. Undercover identities were underpinned by covert infrastructure, enabling officers to be deployed with a cover story that they would learn, practice, and test to ensure it was capable of being pressure tested by inquisitive and suspicious criminals.

Undercover operations can involve anything from a few deployments in street-level drug operations to long-term infiltrations of many months into organized crime, terrorism, online crime, or corruption investigations. Each operation is unique, requiring creativity, skill, and an appreciation of the risks that need to be managed to keep people safe and bring offenders to justice in cases that would be subject to the highest levels of scrutiny in court. This reality leaves little scope for tolerating the maverick who wants to do things their way, regardless of the rules, as sometimes portrayed on screen. Thankfully, few undercover officers were like that, and it was a privilege to work with them and to lead such a prestigious team. Often a tactic of last resort, UCs were deployed against those who thought they were untouchable and where other conventional tactics were unsuccessful. We owe UCs a huge debt of gratitude for their courage, determination, and resilience.

I felt a sense of moral obligation to them. They put themselves at risk, and I understood the importance of my leadership role in managing those risks to reduce the harmful effects of undercover work, even undertaking a master's degree to demystify the theories and practice of risk management. I had to hold a lot of confidences as the head of the unit, and I took it as a good sign that members of the team felt comfortable in approaching me and sharing their concerns. Sometimes it was about others they were working with, and the sort of personality clashes you might find in any profession, however, they could increase operational risks if tensions existed that affected communication and support, though they were usually resolved or managed to the extent needed until the natural conclusion of the operation. Sometimes, the concerns were more personal and needed to be managed in the same way any manager might need to provide support, such as a bereavement, a relationship breakup, an illness in the family, except in this high-risk environment the stresses that visit the lives of many people in their day to day add further to the psychological strain of working undercover. We needed to take extra care to find ways to ease their condition and come up with solutions so they could excuse themselves, even if temporarily, from undercover operations.

I became a strong advocate of the psychologists who worked with us in undercover policing. They helped us to select the right people for the job, or perhaps I should say they helped us to deselect the wrong people for the job. Not that those unsuitable candidates weren't good police officers in other roles, but this job needed characteristics that not all possessed. Successful candidates had a clear sense of why they wanted to be a UC, the challenges it would mean for them and their families if they were deployed, and the mental pressures involved in living with a covert identity. When in role, clinical psychologists would provide a safety net with frequent confidential consultations, enabling UCs to talk to someone independent of management. I would receive feedback from the psychologists, not about individuals, but about trends they identified, which I used as a bellwether for how people were feeling about their work and any indications of red flags I needed to take note of. I put a lot of effort into learning what I could about the psychological risks in undercover work, making visible my support of national and international psychologist groups by attending their meetings and contributing to the body of knowledge with case studies from contemporary operations.

It should be obvious that the more someone pretends to be something they're not, the more likely it is that they will identify with the characteristics of that identity, over time. Research in the United States and Canada reported some of the factors that contribute to job strain including exposure to criminal environments, blurring of social identity, and boundaries from having to move in and out of role. Surveys of UCs reported symptoms of work-related stress including increased anxiety, loneliness, depression, paranoia, and identity strain arising from long-term role playing.

No one could doubt that undercover officers were psychologically at risk, but it was tricky to address. UCs were often emotionally invested and committed to the task, sometimes resisting efforts from management to intervene and rarely self-disclosing when they were experiencing stress. When withdrawn from an operation, the excitement and positive emotion could be replaced by lethargy, low drive, and lack of motivation, making them more emotionally reactive, less stable and resilient to life experiences. Friends, family, and other interests could fall by the wayside. Many UCs invest themselves so deeply, that frustrations, problems, and setbacks would take on disproportionate significance.

I worked closely with psychologists to understand my leadership role in making decisions, introducing policy, and influencing national doctrine to mitigate the risks we were responsible for managing and which undercover officers and their families were the ones bearing.

There were, however, factions within covert policing that espoused the culture of the tough guy, capable of mixing with hardened criminals, mimicking the attitudes and acts that are criminal, sometimes violent, and the complete antithesis of the values, lives, and norms of most police officers. For some, there was an expectation that UCs would roll with the punches and then return to a normal life.

In truth, the work could be highly damaging. Some attitudes to the psychological screening process were that it sometimes deselected people whom existing UCs and managers saw as an ideal fit. They were friends or colleagues they'd found entirely dependable in previous postings in squads and departments where they'd worked together. Colleagues they'd recommended who failed the psychometric assessment would be seen as victims of frustrating inconvenience, rather than appreciating the valuable screening tool to protect those either unsuitable or not ready.

Psychologists provided more than a screening process—they carried out vital research about undercover roles and the long-term impacts on mental health, the potential for substance and alcohol abuse, and even corruption.

In one meeting, a psychologist from the US presented a case study about a covert unit in Philadelphia, which had made headlines in the city's newspaper the *Daily News*. It reported that raids on small stores by plainclothes officers, working with informants, were fraudulent, unethical, and in many cases, unlawful.

The target for drug raids were described as 'mom and pop' stores, independently owned, often by legal immigrants from places such as the Dominican Republic, South Korea, and Jordan. The store owners reported that they suffered significant losses in the raids through theft of property and damage, including smashed CCTV cameras. Some owners were arrested for no more than selling small plastic bags in the mistaken belief or deliberately false claim they were used for drug deals.

Similar experiences were described in statements from store owners who didn't know each other, adding weight to the accounts of the events, and providing evidence of the method used by the corrupt officers. In at least one instance, officers returned to a corner store to retrieve footage that recorded their previous raid. They held a gun to the owner's head and demanded the video tape.

The lines between confidential informants and their police handlers were more than blurred, they were deliberately crossed, with examples including one informant renting his home from his police handler and another informant being provided with bail money from their handler. Officers had lied on applications for search warrants and had sexually assaulted women conducting pat downs during raids, which took place in solitary areas. There was also a marked increase in violence by officers during raids.

Officers were described as narcissistic with no regard for others and as having a complete disregard for rules, process, and the law.

This case study was presented as a salutary lesson in the importance of supervision and control, where police officers operate with autonomy at arm's length from the routines of institutional accountability.

UCs are expected to fit into the criminal culture, language, and mindset and then turn that persona off at the end of the day. We should not expect people to do this work indefinitely.

It was universally appreciated that undercover work was dangerous, but the danger came not only from the criminals targeted by UCs, but even more so from the psychological pressures of the role and the long-term effects on mental health. This was the slow-burn creeping crisis that needed to be addressed.

Undercover units in other countries already had time limits, where the UK had none, not because there was a negligent attitude, but it hadn't arisen by then that there ought to be one.

Through my role in the national working group, I introduced limited tenure in SO10 and made recommendations that it should become national policy. It was an unpopular decision and quite a difficult policy to sell, but the alternative was for undercover officers to stay in-role indefinitely. The national working group lacked authority, and as a mid-ranking officer, I didn't have the power to direct the forty-three individual police forces and other law enforcement agencies in the UK to comply. Even the chief officer who chaired the national group wouldn't have been able to demand compliance unless the policy was signed off by the chief constable leading the national crime portfolio of the chief officer's group. I visited forces and regional covert unit meetings throughout the UK to present the changes in recruitment, training, psychological support, and tenure in a bid to use influence rather than authority. I think it's fair to say that some of the changes were received more warmly than others. It would take some time for change to be accepted and adopted everywhere.

SCANDAL

In the annals of undercover policing, few tales are as enigmatic and tumultuous as that of Mark Kennedy, an officer who spent seven years embedded within a group of environmental activists. By the time he came to notoriety in 2010, I'd known Mark for about ten years from the days when he deployed in Operation Strongbox and other street-buying drug operations. He was very effective in his role, not least because his appearance couldn't have made him look less like a police officer, due to a squint in one eye from a childhood injury. When he dyed his hair and wore the right clothes, he looked nothing like a cop and was always accepted without suspicion. I wouldn't ordinarily name a UC, but such was the publicity surrounding this case, his identity is already well-known and not least because of his self-disclosure.[1]

From that auspicious start in undercover policing, he was recruited into the National Public Order Unit (NPIOU), a standalone undercover unit aligned to the Association of Chief Police officers rather than a specific police force, with the remit to gather intelligence about domestic extremism and protest groups. Under an alias, Mark Stone, the role would result in his dramatic and emotionally charged exposure as an undercover officer that continues to provoke scrutiny and contemplation today. The narrative unfurls into a web of unresolvable moral dilemmas as he became entangled in a labyrinth of ethical quandaries while balancing his duty to law enforcement with personal convictions sympathetic to the activist cause.

Kennedy's double life involved a complex interplay between loyalty, betrayal, and a search for identity. His infiltration into the tight-knit activist community was marked by his own changing appearance and character, blurring the lines between his real self and the persona he had assumed.

Kennedy started a relationship with an activist, despite being married with children in his real life. He would say that his relationship with his wife was, by then, only serving to protect his children from a parental break up while they were still young. Regardless, he knew it was completely inappropriate to start an intimate relationship in his undercover persona, even if it was built on genuine emotions. The turmoil of sustaining duplicity and the toll it exacted remains a disturbing aspect of Kennedy's own explanation of the situation he created.

The turning point came when Kennedy's role as an undercover officer collided with the activists' plans to occupy a power station, leading to arrests and the exposure of his true identity. The partner he'd started the relationship with found his real passport in his belongings while they were away on break out of the country. She and other activists in the group confronted him, leading to his admission in a charged meeting that he was an undercover police officer, as by now they had suspected. The fallout from this revelation cast him adrift, estranged from the activist community, leaving him isolated and grappling with a shattered sense of self.

Subsequent attempts to reintegrate into mainstream policing proved futile, as Kennedy found himself ill-prepared and facing the stark reality of a life irrevocably altered by his undercover mission.

In the aftermath of exposure, media frenzy, and personal upheaval, Kennedy's journey toward reconciliation and self-understanding began. His introspection, plagued by questions of trust, identity, and the moral repercussions of his actions, reflects a tumultuous internal struggle.

Mark Kennedy resigned from the NPIOU and the police service. His complex saga entangled in conflicting loyalties serves as a cautionary tale, prompting reflection on the ethical boundaries and psychological toll inherent in covert policing. Beyond the headlines and controversies lies a poignant narrative of human frailty, moral ambiguity, and the lives that were negatively affected by a questionable mission where an undercover officer was in role for far too long.

The revelations from the Kennedy scandal led to ongoing inquiries about the nature of undercover policing and questions in Parliament: Was it proportionate and necessary to infiltrate protest groups in this way? Did undercover officers have the right to intrude into the private lives of people? Was some of the activity led or generated by the police?

The trial of the six activists accused of aggravated trespass at a power plant collapsed following the revelation of the undercover operation, with allegations of agent provocateur and withholding evidence that may have exonerated them. The NPOIU was disbanded in 2011 and responsibility for its operations transferred to the National Domestic Extremism Unit at Scotland Yard.

The story caught the popular imagination and severely damaged confidence in covert policing as more women came forward with claims that they too had been in relationships with undercover officers from a different unit known as the Special Demonstration Squad (SDS).

The SDS was part of Special Branch, created in the late 1960s following a protest that descended into a riot outside the US embassy in Grosvenor Square, London. It was disbanded in 2008. The squad's purpose was to infiltrate left-wing direct-action groups using UCs. The SDS used the names of dead children to create false identities for its UCs. Some members of the SDS engaged in sexual relationships with members of protest groups and in some cases fathered children by them. In 2013, former SDS undercover officer Peter Francis revealed that the SDS investigated the family of Stephen Lawrence to seek possible evidence to smear Lawrence with, in case of racially motivated public order issues.[2] The revelation of this information led to Home Secretary Theresa May announcing a public inquiry in Parliament.

The post-scandal inquiry is often deployed as a solution to crisis in the public sector. At the risk of being cynical, the announcement of an investigation gives politicians the opportunity to appear outraged and accountable while simultaneously shifting responsibility away from themselves. In practice, their recommendations are often ignored or diluted.

I was visited by senior officers from what was then called Her Majesty's Inspector of Constabulary (HMIC) (now His Majesty's Inspector of Constabulary and Fire & Rescue Services, to reflect the succession of the king and the expanded role of the inspectorate).

The two HMIC officers wanted to discuss the crisis and know more about how SO10 operated and the work I'd been involved with in the national working group. What they really needed was the documentation from the national training group, as it provided detailed analysis and recommendations for change that they could adopt into their own report. They left with a bunch of papers about the new advanced and foundation UC roles, training, tenure, and psychological support we had created. Where this work had once foundered through lack of universal support across national policing, it now became part of HMIC's recommendations and with their added bite and the need for a response to a crisis, they were implemented by the College of Policing as authorized professional practice.

The Undercover Policing Inquiry (which is ongoing at the time of this writing) is assessing the contribution that undercover policing has made to tackling crime, how it was and is supervised and regulated, and its effect on individuals involved—police officers and others who came into contact with them. This includes:

- Undercover officers adopting deceased children's identities
- Sexual relationships entered into by UCs
- UC participation in criminality and the criminal justice system
- UC deployments, and how they were managed
- Support for UCs

Following initial legal cases against the police, at least twelve women received compensation in the High Court of Justice. In November 2015, the Metropolitan Police Service issued the following statement:

> Thanks in large part to the courage and tenacity of these women in bringing these matters to light it has become apparent that some officers, acting undercover whilst seeking to infiltrate protest groups, entered into long-term intimate sexual relationships with women which were abusive, deceitful, manipulative and wrong. . . . Firstly, none of the women with whom the undercover officers had a relationship brought it on themselves. They were deceived pure and simple. I want to make it clear that the Metropolitan Police does not suggest that any of these women could be in any way criticized for the way in which these relationships developed.

> Second, at the mediation process the women spoke of the way in which their privacy had been violated by these relationships. I entirely agree that it was a gross violation and also accept that it may well have reflected attitudes towards women that should have no part in the culture of the Metropolitan Police.

> Third, it is apparent that some officers may have preyed on the women's good nature and had manipulated their emotions to a gratuitous extent. This was distressing to hear about and must have been very hard to bear.

Fourth, I recognise that these relationships, the subsequent trauma and the secrecy around them left these women at risk of further abuse and deception by these officers after the deployment had ended.

Fifth, I recognize that these legal proceedings have been painful distressing and intrusive and added to the damage and distress. Let me make clear that whether or not genuine feelings were involved on the part of any officers is entirely irrelevant and does not make the conduct acceptable.

In light of this settlement, it is hoped that the Claimants will now feel able to move on with their lives. The Metropolitan Police believes that they can now do so with their heads held high. The women have conducted themselves throughout this process with integrity and absolute dignity.

There's no doubt that some officer's conduct and practices were appalling and completely unacceptable, as the public inquiry will no doubt examine, so it won't end here despite the Metropolitan Police urging the 'claimants' to move on with their lives.

It is also worth examining the work of the units to understand why those operations were conducted at all. By doing so, I do not suggest the operational need justified what was revealed by the victims of this scandal. Not at all. Rather, I think it helps to understand what the operations were trying to achieve and how they differ from undercover operations intended to provide evidence for the courts and the level of scrutiny and oversight involved.

Most citizens support the fundamental right to peaceful protest, but few will be aware of the full extent of the dark side of some (but certainly not all) protest groups and the serious criminal activity a minority of protestors were involved in. It can include serious violence and tactics that not only attacked the targets they were opposed to, but anyone who worked for them, supplied them, or provided services for them. Violence, damage to homes and property, and in one case, digging up the buried remains of a woman whose family owned a research facility, were among the activities of radical protestors. Some of the UC deployments involved gathering intelligence about serious crime including threats to life, serious harm, and the acquisition of weapons including firearms and home-made bombs. It was for those types of criminal activity that dedicated units were established but would later suffer from 'mission creep'—a gradual shift in objectives often resulting in an unplanned, long-term commitment.

Both the NPIOU and SDS used UCs for intelligence development operations, which would provide opportunities for disruption and prevention of crime and disorder. Unlike SO10 operations, where the deployments were intended for outcomes in the criminal justice system and cases that would reach the courts, intelligence operations would not be open to the same scrutiny in criminal trials, so were not held to those standards. Professional boundaries and treading the fine line of legality were always carefully considered in undercover operations destined for trial, knowing that matters could be raised by defendants about undercover police officers who now became witnesses against them. Anything that defendants could present to undermine the credibility or trustworthiness of the undercover officer would be to the advantage of the defendants. Undercover officers involved in operations destined for trial are aware of this and are careful to consider how their conduct might look in court.

Section 78 of the Police & Criminal Evidence Act, 1984 provides the catch all clause for judges to dismiss evidence obtained unfairly. However, if the investigation is an intelligence-only deployment it will not be presented to the courts and there is no expectation that the information obtained will be assessed by a judge as to its fairness.

This is not to say that intelligence deployments are of lesser value as part of the tactics available to law enforcement agencies. The information they provide is often used to disrupt and prevent crime and serious disorder, saving others from suffering injury and damage to property before it can occur.

Those pioneering detectives that created SO10 wrote rules where none existed in UK legislation or in police procedures. They researched case law to develop a code of conduct for undercover officers and a system of control, which included appointing a cover officer to monitor, supervise, and advise each undercover deployment. Since those early days, undercover policing has enabled many successful investigations and prosecutions, leading to convictions where the most serious criminals would otherwise have evaded detection and not been brought to justice. Undercover work expanded over the years, but the rules, governance, training, and strategic implications hadn't kept pace with the changing demands for covert methods.

It was unfortunate that it took a scandal to provide the drivers for change, but practices that had evolved through innovation, successes, and failures of undercover work, case law and experience were now given a formality in professional doctrine that was right for modern policing.

In an unexpected turn of events, so concerned were senior officers with ensuring public support for undercover policing, the documents setting out standards for selection, training, psychological support, limited tenure for UCs, and renewed structures for covert units, were all published online for public consultation. The documents were originally classified as confidential to protect the information they held about the changes to the improved system for undercover policing. Now, they were declassified and published online in a transparent bid to repair the reputational damage that had been inflicted by the scandals. It was pleasing to know that our work had made such a valuable contribution, though I read that in a later development, the tenure policy recommendations were diluted to allow unit managers to decide how long an officer can be deployed using a risk-based approach, leaving this to their discretion. In effect, this means there is no tenure policy as each unit decides for themselves and thus potentially begins the incubation period of a future crisis if UCs are left in-role for too long.

CHAPTER 14

The Beautiful Game and Operation Peyzac

ONE FRIDAY EVENING I WAS ON CALL, ACTING AS THE DUTY SUPERIN-tendent for the covert policing command when I got a call from the assistant commissioner for specialist crime, Cressida Dick, who would later become the first woman commissioner of the Metropolitan police. I and another detective superintendent were to meet her near Tower Hill the following morning and accompany her to a meeting.

It was late August, and as the early Saturday summer day began, a few people were milling around, in no hurry, as they emerged from the nearby hotels, clutching coffee cups, maps, and other belongings that marked them out as tourists. Even at that time of day on a weekend this part of the city was already getting busier by the minute as visitors made for the nearby historic attractions of the Tower of London and iconic Tower Bridge. Meanwhile, our working day was just beginning.

I pulled up in a side road near the Tower Hotel and got into the back of the car that was already waiting. Cressida and Matt, a detective super-intendent I knew well from the economic crime unit, were already in the car. If she'd asked me to guess, I would have been right as we were just a few minutes away from the offices and print works of News International, publishers of *The Times* and the now defunct tabloid *News of the World*, the latter being well-known for exposing scandals in its Sunday-only newspaper. It was typical of the Sunday papers to hold back on involving police in stories they were going to print until the last possible moment, either late Friday or on Saturday, when the police wouldn't have time to do anything but react to the information the journalists chose to share.

It was also a good strategy to reduce the risk of someone in the police leaking the story and ruining their scoop, which was not unheard of.

Cressida told us she'd had a call the previous evening from the editor of the paper, revealing that they had been working on an undercover investigation to expose corruption in cricket. They had recordings of players on the Pakistani cricket team conspiring to fix matches.

We went to the building and were met by the newspaper editor and Maz Mahmood, a well-known journalist and specialist in undercover exposés. We met in a large open office with rows of work desks on which computer screens were mounted, with each workstation looking like it was the place of typical office workers with papers, notes, and personal effects around each pod. Except that today, the office was empty apart from the few that were in this meeting. This was the journalist's floor and I mentally noted that none of them were having their weekend disrupted, as we and a whole squad of Scotland Yard detectives were about to.

We were given the story they were going to print in *The News of the World* the next day and an evidential package that had been prepared and ready to hand over to us. They knew, from experience, exactly what the police would need to make progress in the investigation before the paper went to press.

Mahmood had secretly videotaped a meeting with bookmaker Mazhar Majeed as he counted out bribe money and explained that he had paid three of Pakistan's cricketers to bowl 'no balls' at specific times during the test match between England and Pakistan at Lord's cricket ground—information that was used by gamblers to place bets in a fraud known as spot fixing. The cricketers were team captain Salman Butt and bowlers Mohammad Asif and Mohammad Amir.

Matt took the lead on managing the reactive operation to arrest those involved and I talked with Mahmood, going into the details of his undercover investigation to ensure it could be managed as part of the evidential chain.

We returned to Scotland Yard and the investigation quickly gathered pace, starting with the arrest of bookmaker Majeed on suspicion of defrauding bookmakers and, subsequently, three others suspected of money laundering related to the allegations. The cell phones of Asif,

Amir, and Salman Butt were seized as part of their investigation and a file was sent to the Crown Prosecution Service for a charging decision.

In November 2011, Majeed, Asif, Amir, and Butt were found guilty at Southwark Crown Court of conspiracy to cheat at gambling and conspiracy to accept corrupt payments. Majeed and Amir were convicted after entering guilty pleas. Judge Jeremy Cooke dismissed Amir's mitigation plea, stating that evidence from submitted text messages suggested involvement beyond a single spot-fixing incident. Prison sentences were handed out, including two years and six months for Butt, one year for Asif, six months for Amir, and two years and eight months for Majeed.

The cricket community widely accepted and supported the convictions. Former Pakistan captain Aamer Sohail called it a 'shameful' day for Pakistani cricket and my colleague, Matt, had the last word after the trial: 'The defendants have let down the cricketing world, their fans and the hard-working people who buy tickets to watch. I'm not sure these men appreciated how much they were admired by cricket fans. They were role models to countless children around the world and have betrayed their trust.'

OPERATION PEYZAC

Mark, my fellow DI from Islington, was now a detective chief inspector at my old stomping ground Edmonton in North London, an area that had seen a surge in gang violence where firearms were frequently used. Young men were victims of life-changing and, in some cases, life-ending shootings that remained largely unsolved after thorough investigation. In these situations, public confidence is eroded when police seem incapable of bringing offenders to justice and police confidence is tested when the public doesn't come forward to provide information or witnesses. The term 'wall of silence' becomes part of a widening gap of trust between police and the community.

Mark came to SO10 to discuss a proposal for an undercover operation that would aim to take guns off the street and improve public confidence. Rather than trying to infiltrate gangs of people who had probably grown up together, lived in the same area, and knew everyone, Mark proposed setting up a music shop with a recording studio that would have a whiff of criminality sufficient to bring the gangs to us. It was a solid idea, and planning for Operation Peyzac began straight away.

The local authority supplied an empty shop on the Edmonton/ Tottenham border and undercover officers were assigned and began to appear in the shop, setting up the new business called 'Boombox' as the shopfitters knocked the place into shape. Before long, curiosity drew people to the shop and small, but significant, signals were sent out to suggest that things were bought and sold without too many questions.

Perceived disrespect, often generated through social media posts, was a driver for violence. Comments that challenged the status of other gang members would need a response to save face. If police knew who the current disputes involved, they could disrupt this tit-for-tat violence and Mark's idea was to provide a space where they could hang out, talk, and record some rap music, which often revealed who they had a beef with that day, so a recording studio and hangout space was built within the back area of the shop. If discussions developed to a clear intention to find someone they wanted to attack, police would have a duty of care to do something about it, or tell the person they were at risk in a procedure known as an Osman warning.

Police issue an 'Osman warning' letter, named after London businessman Ali Osman who was murdered by Paul Paget-Lewis, a teacher at his son's school in 1988, when there is intelligence of a threat to someone's life.

Courts heard Paget-Lewis had formed a 'disturbing' attachment to Mr. Osman's son, Ahmet, then fourteen, and at one point told police he was considering committing a massacre. In March 1988, he stole a gun, killed Mr. Osman, and shot and seriously injured Ahmet.

The Osman family successfully argued in the European Court of Human Rights that the Metropolitan Police had breached Mr. Osman's right to life because it had all the information it needed to deal with the threat. It was a significant ruling that led to police developing a complex methodology for assessing risks, and the formal 'Osman warning' letters were introduced.

The challenge for Operation Peyzac was that threats to life could emerge and disappear as quickly as a gang member's mood changed and the risks had to be managed to keep the operation going, rather than react too quickly to each new threat, triggered by a post on social media.

When the shop opened, the anticipated interest gradually came. The recording studio was used as a place to hang out and everything was captured evidentially on video and audio. The undercover officers were doing a fantastic job and began to build rapport with their new associates in the community.

Before long, the inevitable discussion was heard and an imminent threat to life needed to be addressed and, in a return on the careful investment of trust that the undercover officers had developed with the gang, they came up with a plan that would solve the problem. The undercover officers explained that they were meeting some people from out of town and needed a few people to keep lookout on the periphery. This occupied them for a few hours, diverting them from their planned attack on the individual they'd been heard discussing in the studio, obviating the need for an Osman warning. One of the undercover officers mentioned to his colleagues, in a way that the gang would overhear, that he needed a gun as he'd lent his to someone who needed some protection. After a thoughtful pause, one member of the gang offered to lend his and went to fetch it and, on seeing it, the undercover officer was so impressed that he said he would give him a good price for it if he was willing to sell. This was the first of many firearms that Operation Peyzac would take off the streets and later, this evidence would be presented to the court to secure his conviction.

The operation continued in the same vein for a few months, but took its toll on the undercover officers who were doing a great job working in stressful conditions. The operation reached the stage where they'd bought so many illegal guns that they were beginning to recover badly converted sports starting pistols, signalling they had exhausted the freely available supply of firearms in the area at the time. Where there are guns, there are drugs and often vice versa. Through the shop, Boombox had amassed evidence against thirty-seven subjects for gun and drug trafficking. It was decided to end Operation Peyzac with a mass arrest operation and over six hundred officers were sent to execute warrants in raids on addresses.

I wondered whether there was a PC out there driving a battle bus who would become my successor one day.

The resulting convictions led to prison sentences totalling over four hundred years and violent crime in Edmonton was cut significantly in the year following Operation Peyzac. The crime problem began in the borough and was seen to be resolved by police in the borough, with senior officers from their team responding in media articles, promoting confidence in local policing. I was particularly taken by one newspaper headline that referred to the investigation as 'The Hip Hop Cop Shop!'

It had been a challenging operation for everyone involved and would be my last in SO10. I'd finally move on from the department after eight years as I'd managed to get through another promotion process and was now looking for a permanent superintendent's post. I spent a few months in covert policing command as an acting detective superintendent as job after job came up for those awaiting promotion. There were some very intense looking jobs in the serious crime command, which I wasn't sure I wanted to do, given my recent experience. There were quite a few shiny arse jobs in strategic management roles, which I didn't fancy either. I had three years to go before I could finish my thirty years and go into management consultancy in my next career, if that's what I wanted. I still needed to be operational.

I also had a family and my children were still young, having started later in life than most in my peer group, so I felt I needed something with a little balance and decided to wait for the right post to come up.

In the meantime, I continued to run the department as my successor was identified and was able to start taking over as I acted in the superintendent role, leaving my old DCI post clear.

CHAPTER 15

Olympics and Beyond

I'VE REACHED THE AGE WHERE I AM SOMETIMES ASKED WHAT I WOULD say to my younger self. My go-to reply is that life's decisions sometimes seem like a crossroads, where a wrong turn represents an irreversible moment of fortune. In actuality, there is often another crossroads a little further along the way, where you can course-correct and get back on your preferred route. Sometimes the next crossroads comes quickly, and sometimes it's later. I left SO10 and took up a post as detective superintendent for the Olympics, serious and organized crime command that I'd missed out on four years prior, but now at the next rank, working from a shared office on the other side of Scotland Yard. It seems that it was just meant to be. It was weird. Overnight, my phone stopped ringing to the extent that I had it checked in case there was something wrong with it. I'd become so used to calls coming in morning, noon, and night, whether on- or off-duty or even on holiday. Then suddenly, they stopped.

When I left SO10, I knew the job back to front and had developed a level of expertise that was a comfortable place to be in my professional life. Now, I went from expert to novice as I started a completely new role and one for which there was no handbook. The London 2012 Olympic and Paralympic Games would be a blank canvass and I had to start learning a new job all over again. To cover my sensitivity at being a novice, I adopted a phrase that expressed my humility in my new leadership role when faced with a question I had no answer for: 'Forgive me, this is my first Olympics.' Of course, the London Olympics was a first for everyone else too and after a micro expression of confusion, most would smile and understand that we were all breaking new ground together.

As I became accustomed to my new role, I visited sites around the country that would be used as Olympic venues and established contacts with people who would be in leadership roles in their respective force areas during the games. Most of this seemed straightforward for UK policing, with Olympic venue forces sharing good practice in preparing for major events. With additional responsibilities for coordinating and planning to protect the games from serious and organized crime, I would be required to pitch my plans to the Home Office for funding then face a panel that would pick holes in my proposal. In anticipation of being bartered down, I decided to ask for more than I needed. To my complete surprise, they accepted everything I proposed and suggested that my figures lacked 'provision for optimism bias,' to which I nodded and pretended I knew what the hell that was. When they added 10 percent to my figures, they explained that most proposals were made based on a reasonable assessment but wouldn't cover any contingency if something didn't go according to plan. Therefore, they added this additional margin to allow for extra spending in the knowledge that most projects wouldn't need it and so it wouldn't be spent. It was part of a backup plan and would be accessible without having to ask for it. They were right and my budget was generous enough for me to return a seven-figure sum after the games.

For the first few months in my new role, I plodded along and tried to get some of my Scotland Yard colleagues interested in shaping their plans for 2012, but their attention was on present challenges, such as the riots of 2011, through which I felt something of a bystander. There were plenty of people dealing with that, and so, even though I had the capacity to do something—perhaps to backfill roles that were stretched—I was out of sight and out of mind.

Refurbishment of a dedicated office space was nearing completion at the Yard and all the teams working on plans for 2012 were to be relocated to one big open floor. I was apprehensive, having gone from having a private office in SO10 to a shared four-person office for the Olympic crime planning team to a space where I'd share an office with nearly one hundred people. I had to be 'Bobby Fantastic' in attitude and a role model working shoulder to shoulder with the whole team, even though I had reservations about it. I needn't have worried. It was a great experience and I enjoyed being surrounded by officers and staff at every level. I like to think they saw me as approachable and willing to take part in the esprit de corp. As the only detective on the floor, one uniformed sergeant would address me as 'Guv' in an over-the-top accent, reminiscent of characters from the 1970s TV series *The Sweeney*. He decorated my desk with *Sweeney* memes, adding his own text to the pictures and speech bubbles of imagined conversations from the era, involving me as the Guv. I pretended to threaten him with discipline, to which he would challenge me to prove he was responsible, which was all in good fun, of course. I think our exchanges helped those in junior roles get used to working within earshot of senior ranks. We soon got on with our jobs and got along with each other pretty well.

I was also part of the senior command team and worked with other superintendents, chief superintendents, and commanders who adopted me as their 'token suit,' meaning I was the only detective there. Without doubt, the connections with others in this open plan environment and the warm welcome I received as part of the command team made the whole experience one that I really enjoyed. To this day, the command team meets at least once a year for a long lunch, confirming the bonds we made in this role.

I was awaiting the appointment of a detective chief superintendent to report to, but both potential candidates had taken other jobs, which drew comment from the commissioner, concerned that this key post was vacant. As I'd been in post for a while and had a good grip of the brief, I offered to represent crime and intelligence in any meetings or reports until they found a chief, which they accepted. Within the command team was a chief superintendent I'd worked with way back at the beginning of my career. He was then my direct supervisor and the young sergeant who submitted my request to change my divisional number to PC 123. He was now the commander for the Olympic Park and part of the senior team.

He spoke highly of me and quietly recommended to the assistant commissioner that I was someone who was highly motivated and would be a good candidate for the chief role. And so, for the second time in my career I was awarded a 'battlefield promotion' to detective chief superintendent, which would see me out to the end of my thirty years of service. To say I was pleased would be an understatement. After the promotion, the uniformed sergeant in the shared office still called me Guv and continued his tongue-in-cheek defiance by saluting me in an exaggerated style every time we passed each other for the next week or so. Piss taker!

As plans for policing the games started to firm up, we used the Notting Hill Carnival event as a rough template for dealing with crime and crime scenes in a defined territory. We were aware that any incident that stood in the path of an Olympic event would create pressure to make way so that the 'show could go on.' However, I knew it wouldn't be acceptable to any victims, their families, or the courts to offer this as an explanation for doing half a job. Neither was it acceptable to me to do a poor job because of the need to get scenes cleared. Our solution was to create dedicated investigation teams, each with forensic capabilities, that were near every Olympic venue. They would operate as rapid deployment squads that could reach and attack a scene within minutes and complete the tasks thoroughly and to the high standards expected. Teams worked in shifts to ensure constant cover. I had meetings with all my teams, and I continually briefed them so that everyone knew their jobs and what success looked like. I didn't want the games themselves to make the headlines and we were there to ensure that 'crime is not the story.'

Scotland Yard's economic crime command established Operation Podium, which was part of the crime plan. It was led by Nick, a very impressive detective superintendent as part of my team during the games. Operation Podium was a groundbreaking initiative that was initiated before the games began. It was tasked with preventing and detecting criminal activity concerning the economy of the games. Some of the targets of Operation Podium included more than thirty international fraudulent websites created for the sole purpose of selling tickets that didn't exist and ticket touts trying to buy tickets in bulk to sell, which was made a crime under the 2006 Olympic Act.

We took up our command positions in the Special Operations Room (SOR) a few days before the games began so that we could soft test our systems and command structure. SOR is a vast command and control room, the largest in UK policing. It is used in over two thousand pre-planned operations every year, including large sporting events, protests, and ceremonial events such as the Trooping of the Colour. Commanders and their specialist functions work together in pods across a room the size of a football field, the walls partially made of TV screens monitoring everything from local traffic CCTV to images streamed from police helicopters.

We settled into SOR, the place we'd spend the summer, working extended hours, except overnight between 10:00 p.m. and 6:00 a.m., which was covered by a smaller 'caretaker' command team with some resources in reserve. Our soft launch was useful in knocking off some of the rough edges that only surface when tested, as we prepared for the opening ceremony, which promised to be a spectacular event. At the dress rehearsal the night before the real opening ceremony, Jane and I, along with a stadium full of other workers, were guests of the Olympic committee. It was the only event I'd see, and we made the most of the evening taking in the parade and the theatrical performances designed by the brilliant film director Danny Boyle. The only omission in the dress rehearsal was the entrance of Her Majesty the Queen. There had been a helicopter hovering overhead at the start of the dress rehearsal, and we were told that its presence would become clear the following evening at the real ceremony. When I saw the TV coverage of the opening ceremony the following evening, there was a clip showing James Bond supposedly escorting Her Majesty in a helicopter, followed by both parachuting into the stadium. Of course, it was an edited clip made to look as if the queen had actually jumped from the helicopter! How impressive that the queen should use a parachute, eh?

On the big night, everything was in place. I was looking forward to handing command over to night duty after an incident-free opening ceremony. There were thousands of officers in reserve and not too much going on that was of concern. There was one protest group that we were keeping an eye on, known as Critical Mass, a cycle campaign group concerned with safer conditions for cycling in London. There was good reason for their campaign, as cyclists were being killed and seriously injured in London's crowded streets. There weren't enough cycle lanes and larger vehicles, turning at junctions, were colliding with riders, with catastrophic results. Cyclists were good for the environment as an emission-free, space-saving, health-promoting way of commuting. It was easy to see their point and they were keeping themselves in the spotlight with quarterly protests in the Waterloo and South Bank area of London. This was about six miles by road to the Olympic stadium and far enough away from being a problem for the opening ceremony. This group had been compliant, working well with police liaison officers in previous events. We had thousands of officers in reserve, should there be a problem anywhere in London that night.

Given the usual compliant nature of the protest group, the distance from the Olympic Park, and the ability to deploy huge reserves, should they be needed, it was decided that the cycle protest could go ahead with the single condition that they were not to cross to the north side of the River Thames. As there were limited places to cross, we put cordons in at the nearest bridge crossings and liaison officers circulated among the assembling cyclists as they formed up prior to the protest, announcing the conditions and handing out notices. This would be used as evidence that the conditions had been published, should there be problems and arrests for noncompliance.

The protest began and cyclists started making their way around the streets of Waterloo, snarling up traffic, but otherwise peacefully wheeling their way along toward Waterloo Bridge, where a serial of officers stood to direct them away from a route north across the Thames. Suddenly, a few cyclists made a sprint toward the cordon, followed by a few more as officers tried to stop them. There were too many and soon a large group had rushed the cordon and was making progress across the bridge toward the city. My hopes of a quiet drink at the bar in the hotel I was staying were dashed as the command team sprang into action, deploying the police helicopter and reserves toward the peloton that was now heading east toward the Olympic Park. They had the advantage of being agile through the traffic, and more so than the police serials we deployed. I should add that the campaign group probably knew nothing about this and had been infiltrated by more radical protestors intent on causing disruption.

Images from India 99, the call sign of the helicopter, were beamed into SOR as the cyclists reached the last mile before the stadium. A quick-thinking officer had parked a vehicle across the carriageway, diverting the errant cyclists onto the Bow flyover above the main road, just as the queen's convoy of limousines and outriders passed through the junction and gracefully drove into the last road toward the venue, missing the band of cyclists by a few feet above on the flyover. We all breathed a sigh of relief, seeing our careers flash before our eyes, like an imminent death!

Reserve serials had arrived, and both ends of the flyover were blocked by traffic, penning the cyclists in. We commandeered some of the buses and the silver commander ordered that all the cyclists should be arrested and taken to temporary prisoner charge facilities around London for processing. We took their bikes, photographed them with their riders, and a lorry took the cycles away and buses took those arrested to be processed. In all, 184 cyclists were arrested. I was tasked with finding cell space for them, as this fell within the crime command. It took twelve hours, and I never did get to use the hotel room.

Each day of the games was busy, and luckily our worst fears never surfaced. The rocket launchers mounted on high-rise buildings and the warship moored in Greenwich weren't used for anything other than presenting a robust military posture to warn off a terrorist attack.

My role as the commander for crime and intelligence was to represent the detectives, intelligence officers, and forensic staff, providing 'top cover' from interference by well-meaning but unhelpful seniors outside the chain of command. Small things could become a big deal, especially when reported through the liaison officers from competing nations to government officials. This would escalate through one part of the security directorate in government, to ministers, and then senior police officers. I was fortunate in having an assistant commissioner and commanders who trusted me to get things done. The challenge would come if incidents were picked up elsewhere and other senior officers would start to direct officers or begin questioning whether they had done this or that. I would apply my 'cold February morning test,' asking whether the incident needed anything beyond that which would resolve it on any other routine day. For the most part, the incidents that arose would be well within the abilities of detectives and their frontline supervisors and wouldn't get the same level of attention they did during the games. The Olympics had a magnifying effect so that ordinary, everyday police activity sometimes drew a higher reaction and more people than necessary would want to get involved. However well-intended, this interference could add stress and worry where our well-established routines were all that was necessary, so it was helpful that I had my own senior team to step into these types of conversations and we all understood our role in providing this 'top cover.'

A call came in about a shot fired at a bus that was being used to transport athletes near the Olympic Village. It was starting to get out of hand with suggestions that someone was trying to assassinate an athlete, and I'm sure you can imagine the excitable calls that were flying around with demands for urgent updates from different stakeholders. I sent a detective sergeant and a crime scene examiner from one of the teams embedded at the Olympic Park to investigate. They examined the windscreen of the bus and found a hole and a shattered windscreen caused by a stone thrown up by a passing vehicle during their journey. The stone was found inside the coach on the floor behind the first row of seats. They went through the motions looking for ballistic traces, but unsurprisingly, none were found. All was calm once again.

One of the main sponsors of the games was BP, the global energy giant. It had installed a huge billboard in West London on the approach to London on the main highway from Heathrow Airport. Overnight, the panels had been seriously defaced by protestors who had daubed the adverts with black paint, mimicking oil slogans. It was part of a concerted attack on BP property, including service stations, art exhibitions connected with the games, and other celebratory events. All the protests used the same method of daubing property with black paint. I met with representatives of the company to share knowledge about what was happening and who might be responsible. There wasn't much to go on, but sometimes you make your own luck. I knew there were serials of officers patrolling in vans visiting every train and underground station overnight. I asked them to swing by BP garages and advertising sites on their routine patrols. In the early hours of the following morning, one of the serials pulled into a BP garage that was closed for the night. Their headlights picked up a figure in dark clothing running across the forecourt, which was freshly daubed with a slogan in black paint. He was caught with rolled-up stencils bearing slogans and paint all over his hands. He was arrested and his home searched, where further stencils were found, providing incriminating evidence of the criminal damage he was responsible for. There were no further incidents, and the sponsor was relieved and happy that we'd stopped the mischief.

Between the Olympics and Paralympics, we had the annual Notting Hill Carnival to police and rather than stand us down and insert a team to manage this over the bank holiday weekend, we rolled on to be the command team for that too. Carnival weekend is a big public event that takes place in a small geographical footprint celebrating Caribbean culture, music, and heritage. Originating in the late 1950s, it has grown into one of the largest street festivals in Europe, featuring vibrant parades with costumes, lively music, and traditional Caribbean food and drinks. Notting Hill Carnival attracts millions from diverse backgrounds who come together to enjoy the festive atmosphere, dance to the rhythms of steel drums and live bands, and revel in the rich cultural experience it offers. However, over the years, concerns about safety, crowd management, and issues related to the event's scale have also been raised, prompting ongoing efforts to ensure a balance between celebration and public safety.

The event's massive crowds and the lively, often-congested streets can present challenges for police in managing security and preventing criminal activities such as theft, disorderly conduct, and occasional instances of violence. Despite concerted efforts by organizers and authorities to ensure a safe environment through increased police presence, crowd control measures and community engagement initiatives, incidents have sporadically occurred. These incidents, although not reflective of most attendees, have led to ongoing discussions around enhancing security measures, community involvement, and managing the balance between preserving the carnival's spirit and ensuring public safety for all participants. These measures include considerations about crowd surges that can lead to crushing, with so many people in a small area. There have been suggestions that the whole event should be relocated to somewhere like Hyde Park where large events and music concerts are held and where there is more open space and transport facilities surrounding it to ease congestion, but this is unthinkable for those that want to preserve the tradition and cultural home of the event. It is called Notting Hill Carnival, after all.

For the Metropolitan Police, Carnival is the worst event for crime on the annual calendar and so much more severe than other events. Several stabbings occur at this event every year, and since 1987 there have been six deaths caused by violence. Possession of weapons, sexual assaults, and assaults on police officers (some of those being sexual assaults) are common. The final evening of the celebration often spirals into a small riot, with youths throwing missiles at police in pitched battles on the streets.

In the weeks leading up to Carnival, a proactive crime operation disrupts gangs intent on using the event to settle scores with their rivals. Police know that if they can arrest gang members and apply bail conditions that specifically exclude them from attending Carnival, they can be arrested on sight if they show up for breaching bail. This is preferable than dealing with the aftermath of violence that has clouded what, for most who attend, is one of the greatest street parties in the world. Sometimes, police receive intelligence about individuals they know are intending to meet at Carnival to 'sort things out.' The pre-emptive arrests sometimes give gang members a face-saving way out of an inevitable confrontation if they have a good reason for staying away.

Some commentators have suggested that police activity before Carnival is motivated by police racism and that the same activity doesn't take place before similar large events, such as the Glastonbury music festival, where reported crime is higher. Using the number of arrests or crimes reported during carnival and comparing them with other large events is an oversimplistic view, in my opinion. Recorded crime at Glastonbury involves mainly theft and drugs, but it is the severity of the crimes such as stabbings, other assaults, and gang activity that are the cause for concern at Carnival.

I had a staff officer to assist me during the Olympics, Carnival, and Paralympics, which is a colleague appointed to assist a commander with both administrative and operational matters. Deb, a detective sergeant I knew from my Islington days, was my staff officer for the Olympics and Tony, a detective inspector from covert policing, covered the Paralympics. They both worked during Notting Hill Carnival to share the role and hand over the baton, meaning I was grandly walking about with two sidekicks for the weekend. For my role in Carnival, I was referred to as Bronze Crime, using the Gold, Silver, and Bronze command system.

There was a temporary base near the Carnival footprint where police serials from all over London would rendezvous, receive their briefings, and be fed a decent meal (referred to as operational feeding) prior to what could be a very long day. I remembered the experience from when I had been a uniformed constable, spending the weekend on aid to Carnival. I suggested to Deb and Tony that we should go for breakfast at the operational feeding facility for old time's sake. It would also be a good leadership move to be seen as representing detectives at this mainly uniformed policing assembly. The temporary canteen was vast and the Met's catering department was in their element, feeding hundreds of police officers and staff all at once. It was a marvel of planning. We took our turn in line and gathered our breakfast, being directed by a member of the catering staff to join a table of uniformed colleagues on a serial. We engaged in polite conversation, though they weren't sure who we were. I played my part as leader, asking questions about which division they were from, whether they'd been to Carnival before, and generally showing interest, giving off my best self-important vibe. After breakfast we said our goodbyes to our new friends, dropping our dirty plates and utensils off at the waiting tray holders, like the good corporate citizens we were. At that moment, a constable in uniform with an unimpressed look on his face and a full tray of recently served breakfast items approached me. 'Hey mate, I've got a complaint. Are you in charge of catering?' In an instant, my grandiose status as leader of detectives was punctured and I knew my two sidekicks would love this moment. 'No, I'm the detective chief superintendent—Bronze crime,' I said a little indignantly. 'Oh, sorry guv. This breakfast is cold, that's all.' I suggested that he go back to the canteen staff and he turned back from where he'd came. I turned to see Deb and Tony barely holding themselves together at the comedic misidentification and the contrast with my efforts at looking leader-like. In fairness, the head of catering is in a leadership role, so there.

We returned to SOR, taking about twenty minutes to get back from Notting Hill. To my astonishment, there was already a large banner hanging over my desk with the legend 'Bronze Catering.' A covert observation had been mounted on the other side of the room awaiting my return and the look on my face. My fellow commanders henceforth referred to me as Bronze Catering and, when we meet socially all these years later, the name has stuck. Thanks Deb and Tony for keeping a secret. You'll never make it as a spy, either of you!

On the final day of Carnival during the summer of 2012, intelligence reached me in SOR that a gang carrying weapons was boarding a train on London Underground's Victoria Line, headed for Carnival. Fortunately, we had a representative from Transport for London in SOR and this would prove to be vital in cutting down the time taken to communicate with the right Underground control room and, ultimately, the train driver.

I found out which train they were on, and which carriages. I knew they would have to change at King's Cross, so I asked for the train to stop in the tunnel just before arriving there, sending serials of officers to line the platform. When we were ready, the train rolled slowly into the station and the gang members were located and detained. Weapons were found and arrests made, which were sent to the temporary Olympic charge facility in Blackheath, some distance away from Notting Hill. By the time they were processed and released, in dribs and drabs, they were in no mood to go anywhere but home. We'll call that effective crime prevention, shall we?

Carnival went by with lower than usual crime, probably due to the high police presence in London that summer and so, after a successful weekend we transitioned to resume as the police command team for the Paralympics. The pace was calmer and as a police team we were comfortable with the few incidents that happened, most of which were easily dealt with by our teams on the ground.

On the day of the closing ceremony for the Paralympics, I received a call from a deputy assistant commissioner I had known through the ranks for many years. She congratulated me on being appointed to my next posting, immediately after the Paralympics was over. This was news to me, as I was anticipating remaining in post for a couple of months, at least, to debrief, document the lessons learned, and manage anything postgames that needed tidying up. We knew we had been protected from austerity cuts up to now because of the Olympics, but we also knew it was going to bite quite soon afterward.

As a result, I was to move straight away to the deputy commissioner's command and a team called Met Change, which was a management role charged with taking half a billion pounds out of the Met Police budget, in the first phase of cuts. Approaches had been made by consultants to some of the departments at Scotland Yard that had covert assets, only to be refused access on the grounds of confidentiality and security clearance. As this was familiar territory for me, I would be the door opener to ensure those units could be included in the reckoning for budget cuts. It was a difficult move after the high of the Olympics to work on dismantling an institution in which I'd only ever known growth. It's fair to say my heart wasn't really in it and although I did my best, I was a few months away from my career finish line and it confirmed in my mind that I would now plan my exit. It only took a few meetings with covert units, where I knew my senior colleagues who were running the departments, and I could speak the same language. They accepted that they would have to be active participants in the change process and be part of the redesign of their own workforce. I'd opened the doors and the main reason for my appointment to this command was soon achieved. However, I'd continue working with external consultants and had a small team of police officers and police staff working on the redesign of headquarters' functions. They were a delight to work with and very capable, so I was mainly there to provide a senior officer if they needed a bit of rank to help in meetings. They did all the heavy lifting and deserve all the credit for helping the service manage through a very tricky mission.

The work was like being a management consultant, and I should have been more engaged in it than I was. It was certainly a challenge and I liked that in my work, but being sent there before I'd had a chance to fin-ish the Olympic posting properly and the fact that I'd gone into a highly contrasting administrative role from something so operationally dynamic and enjoyable dented my spirit and enthusiasm for the job.

I recalled that, in preparation for the Olympics, we were visited by representatives from Vancouver Police to transfer their learning from being the host city for the Winter Olympics in 2010. I distinctly remem-ber a presentation that described how the torch relay team, responsible for escorting the Olympic torch around the country in a symbolic ritual of continuity between games, had developed a strong esprit de corps. There was such a positive response everywhere they went. The team had bonded, working together away from the routine challenges of their regular police jobs. When the torch reached the opening ceremony, their job was done and they returned to their stations, going back to business as usual. We were told that members of the team reported post-event depression, feeling a real sense of loss from the sudden removal from the positivity of the experience and separation from colleagues they'd grown professionally attached to. We were warned to be aware of this for police teams across the Olympics and to be prepared for it. Of course, we lis-tened carefully to their advice and then in a typically British response, we privately scoffed at the very idea that we should be bothered by such 'touchy-feely' emotions. Well, they were right. I think I had a mild case of depression after the games, and I suspect some of my colleagues in the command team had similar experiences. When we met up for a social event a couple of months later, all the fun seemed to have been squeezed out of us. We'd all been sent to new postings that most of us hadn't anticipated or welcomed. Chief superintendents that had been told they would return to their commands after the games found their positions backfilled, and we were posted to any gaps that were left open, none being our preferred choices. I didn't expect to be carried on the shoulders of colleagues through the halls of Scotland Yard as a hero, but I thought we'd done a good job and might at least be consulted about what was next for us in our careers. I'm not too proud to say I lost my mojo for a while.

During those last few months, I signed up to the role as commander for crime and intelligence for Notting Hill Carnival again, which would be in addition to my day job. It kept me sane having a hand in operational policing, and I could easily manage both.

Eligibility for retirement from the service came at thirty years, but many officers would stay on if it suited them. If I'd been in a more enjoyable post, I might've considered it, but I was an expensive employee at the top of my career on a senior pay band and the austerity mood music was encouraging retirement for old boys like me. I appreciated that I'd enjoyed a fantastic career, and it wasn't going to get any better. I had a business opportunity to pursue and decided that the time was right to call it a day. I did my last day on duty in SOR with Notting Hill Carnival, ending my career with my operational boots on, so to speak. And that was that. After burning through a couple of weeks of annual leave, I went back to Scotland Yard for the last time and handed in my warrant card, leaving with my certificate of service as a civilian. It was a quiet anticlimax. I went to the pub with my friend and now business partner Mick for a few beers, never to return to Scotland Yard. Not that there were any hard feelings; on the contrary, I remain a staunch supporter of the institution that gave me such an interesting life and a job I loved. It's a job that keeps on giving in a new career I'm enjoying very much, using my knowledge and experience to help executives and business leaders to thrive in a volatile, uncertain, complex, and ambiguous world.

CHAPTER 16

Hunted

IT WAS JUST OVER A YEAR SINCE I'D LEFT THE JOB, AND THINGS WERE going well with the transition from a lifetime career in policing to being a business owner and consultant. It carried far less risk and responsibility than my senior roles in the police, paid better, and afforded me international travel working with a growing list of clients on interesting projects. Life felt considerably easier and less stressful.

Someone I'd worked with called and asked if they could introduce me to a TV producer regarding a series about police investigations they wanted to make. They needed someone with experience in running police operations that would help take it from a raw idea to a developed proposal.

Part curiosity and part courtesy to the friend who'd asked, I took a meeting with the production team of Shine TV at their offices in Primrose Hill. Shine TV is an independent production company, then owned by a multinational media giant. Its niche area of TV was in popular factual series such as *MasterChef*, *The Island with Bear Grylls*, *The Force* ('fly on the wall-type' police documentary), and a swathe of reality shows.

Primrose Hill is one of London's most desirable postcodes with historic properties valued in the multimillions and home to celebrities, musicians, bankers, and titans of industry. To get there from the Underground station requires a walk-through nearby Camden Town, a vibrant cultural destination where the smell of cannabis pervades the air. Shine's offices were nestled among the period properties in a modern office block. There was a youthful and cool vibe about the place with its casual dress code, funky decor, and furnishings that included a door to an airplane casually leaning against a wall.

I met the producers, Tom and Lucy, who were both charming and disarming in equal measure. I relaxed once they explained they wouldn't be asking me to spill any trade secrets. The idea, which was no more than a broad concept at that stage, was to create a reality TV series that was, in part, a social experiment that examined whether it was possible for a fugitive to evade capture from a pursuing group of former police and military personnel, armed with the powers of the state in today's digital age.

We agreed to what I was willing to talk about, and what I couldn't. They explained what the regulator of the Office of Communications (OFCOM) was and the rule that prohibited broadcast of any material likely to encourage or incite the commission of crime. The easiest way to avoid this was by not talking about anything I considered sensitive. We moved on to the substance of the meeting and discussed the powers of the state in the modern digital world of policing. In my thirty-year career much had changed. I had seen the introduction of DNA as a forensic tool, the internet, mobile phones followed by smartphones, SMS messages, and instant messaging tools such as WhatsApp, digital payments, contactless payment on public transport, Voice Over Internet Protocol (VOIP) calls, and every map, bank, newspaper, service, or form of entertainment becoming an app. In truth, we increasingly live two lives—our physical, real-world life and our digital life, passively scattering digital breadcrumbs as we go about our daily existence, leaving clues for investigators to follow. Like athletes passing the baton in a relay race, our devices hand our connections and transactions to the service provider enabling investigators to locate the user. When mapped to other data it's possible to re-create an individual's pattern of life—the starting point for tracing a wanted or missing person.

I sketched out for the producers all the possibilities, showing both conventional and digital opportunities for investigators, all of which were open source and freely available.

Tom and Lucy looked at each other. 'That's our TV series right there,' said Lucy. 'And I think we've found our chief.' In that short meeting, we'd made enough progress for the production company to start the ball rolling with the broadcaster, Channel 4, and make a pilot to test the concept of a TV series called *Hunted*. On my advice, they agreed that the concept should reflect the powers of the state as they apply to serious and organized crime investigations. All the powers at this level are 'open source' and described in legislation and codes of practice the public can readily access. Using these powers would mean that we could explain to the viewers how the fugitives were caught. If we tried to emulate the powers available to counterterrorism investigations or those techniques used by the security services, we'd be unable to be as transparent and prove, through open-source information online, that such techniques really exist. We wouldn't be able to explain those techniques to the viewer and we might find ourselves in hot water with the institutions that need to protect that tradecraft.

A few months later, in a makeshift studio fitted out to look like a police operations room, I met my team of 'hunters' who were made up of active and former police and military personnel who would use simulated and real investigation techniques to find their fugitives. There was a gentle rivalry between blue and green, with a boastful former soldier expressing his desire for abseiling down buildings and smashing through windows to make an entrance. Making fun of his overdramatic approach, I replied that we keep things simple and knock on the door and say, 'It's the police.'

The production company recruited a cast of volunteers to evade my team over a week for a successful run to an end point.

Although it was never intended for broadcast, the action was filmed to create a teaser episode for the broadcaster to decide whether they would commission a full series.

Acting as the chief of the hunters, I used my own experience to direct the operation and ran the team as I would in a real investigation, staying calm and making sure we gathered and shared intelligence frequently to stay in the game. The producers were enthusiastic about the twists and turns of a fast-paced operation, encouraging discussion on set about what we were thinking as a team and what we would do next to catch our fugitives. Sometimes, I found myself having to step out of role and be the police adviser, explaining to the producers how things would work in a real investigation before rejoining the set and acting out those directions as the chief. We'd work out how we could simulate police techniques in a TV series, such as accessing phone data or financial records to make it look like the real thing in the action.

I had always admired operational commanders who remained calm, gave people an opportunity to share what they knew, and listened to their point of view. I once heard one of my bosses described as epitomizing 'laconic competence' because he was able to articulate his grip of a situation clearly and simply, especially when under pressure. He was much admired and a role model to me. I tried to emulate him throughout my career and replicate his steady hand in the pursuit of fugitives. In this light, I could grandly picture myself as the stoic character Air Chief Marshall Dowding played by Sir Laurence Olivier in the *Battle of Britain*, with his calm acknowledgment of the dire lack of pilots in the face of a prolonged attack by the enemy. He had some great lines. In a phone call to a minister asking him to verify figures being disputed in the press, he replied, 'I'm not very interested in propaganda. If we're right, they'll give up. If we are wrong, they'll be in London in a week!' His deadpan expression unchanged. Yes, that would be how I'd play it. Laconic competence with a touch of Olivier's Air Chief Marshall Dowding, imagining myself looking wistfully at the intelligence board and saying something like, 'Either our investigation gets close enough to capture them, or the fugitives make it to extraction.'

Idiot! I couldn't have got it more wrong! What they needed for TV was someone considerably more animated, vocal, and who would be far more entertaining than I had been in the pilot episode. They needed energy and action, creating tension, excitement, and pace.

Channel 4 loved the test episode, and the series was picked up. We were in business! The producers were very kind to spare my feelings, emphasizing how important the adviser role was and how they really needed me to be part of the production side rather than on camera. 'You're telling me I have the face for radio?' I joked, making it easier for them to break it to me. One of the producers in a later series said that she'd seen the tapes from the pilot and was more honest in her feedback. 'You were shit!' Brutal, but I think I took it well.

In all honesty, I think it was the right decision. I would be able to help shape the series and run things in a central role, off screen.

We created a clearing house we called TV Command (TVC) for the information coming from fugitive activity on the ground and the leads being generated or followed by the hunters. As part of the senior production team, I would lead a small group of researchers monitoring what the fugitives were doing and gather information that would be shared with the hunters if (and only if) their investigation had identified the lead deserving of the information they would need to move their investigation forward. I decided what was shared and when, replicating the real-time delays in acquiring data from the various sources the fugitives were interacting with.

Having no previous experience working in TV, I had nothing to compare it with, but it was intense. Fugitives were going in all directions, followed by a camera crew, ground hunters trying their best to catch up also followed by a camera crew, and the hunters in HQ being filmed as they fired off hundreds of requests to my team for data, trying to make sense of everything that was happening.

There were frequent tensions between TVC and the hunters: Everyone had an opinion on how things should've happened. There were challenges from hunters about how investigations worked 'in the real world' and demands that TVC should be providing more information, more rapidly. The problem was that I couldn't explain why the hunters were wrong in their assumptions because it would reveal what I knew and what they needed to find out. So, we just had to suck it up and, in most cases, the matter would pass with no hard feelings. It was far better to take a little heat and accept that they were passionate and competitive in their roles than not have all this energy bouncing around, which made for a more tense and exciting TV show.

Series 1 was broadcast in 2015 and became an instant Channel 4 ratings winner. At the time of this writing, the show has filmed thirteen seasons, of which six have been celebrity versions, which raises funds for the charity Stand up to Cancer to which all the celebrities donate their fees, adding to generous public donations.

When the first season concluded, I met with the executive producers and senior officers from a law enforcement agency to discuss the investigative techniques we'd replicated in the series and those we avoided due to their sensitivity. There is a misunderstanding sometimes about covert techniques, suggesting they are secret in and of themselves. Yet, the outcomes from covert operations are often played out in court and their use openly discussed by investigators in post-trial media interviews and documentaries.

My former colleagues explained that it was the 'tradecraft' that was secret; those techniques that would enable criminals to understand the way certain methods were applied. Provided we didn't reveal tradecraft, they were supportive of the series as it demonstrated the way police powers are used and why they are needed, especially to a younger demographic.

We discussed one such technique that we didn't simulate in the first season: phone tapping. In the UK, phone tapping, or lawful intercept, is used sparingly and only in serious and organized crime cases or counter-terrorism investigations, with a warrant issued by the home secretary. We did, and still do, use serving officers in the series, alongside former police and military personnel. I knew the sensitivities with lawful intercept and thought it best to avoid references to it. However, in this meeting we were advised that they were relaxed about it being portrayed in *Hunted*, provided we didn't show the tradecraft and specific details about how it was deployed. This encouraged us to further shape the simulation of techniques used in the series to show the viewers more action. *Hunted* got better with each season and became one of Channel 4's highest rated series, winning a British Association of Film and Television Awards (BAFTA) nomination and a Grierson Award in 2018 for the Celebrity format. I went to both award ceremonies. BAFTA was a grand black-tie occasion—a publicity-grabbing photo opportunity for both the famous and not so famous. On arriving, the organizers badgered everyone to move along the red carpet and get inside for the awards ceremony, sounding anxious that their timeline was under constant threat of slow-moving arrivals hogging the limelight. I missed the point, keen to be helpful and walked at a pace that looked like I was the protection officer for the

Hunted production team, clearing the way ahead. They knew the score and took their time a few steps behind me. Although we didn't win a BAFTA, we did win a Grierson Award. There was an array of worthy TV formats highlighted before ours, with short video clips showing some very impressive and noble efforts that shed light on difficult subjects and challenges for humanity. When we reached our category, Best Entertaining Documentary, I'm sure I heard a resigned groan from one-quarter of the audience, in aloof judgment that *Celebrity Hunted* should be mentioned in the same awards event as Sir David Attenborough's *Blue Planet II*. The awards jury said, 'The winning film paired a good cause, joyous characters, and a solid format to create a film that was tense and surprisingly gripping. Not a millisecond was wasted as every bit of entertainment was squeezed out in an expert example of high-quality filmmaking.' We gathered on stage, the production team along with the celebrity contestants, safe in numbers to receive our award to polite applause.

Around this time, I was also involved in a spin-off series, *The Heist*, which ran for two seasons, based in the beautiful towns of Thirsk and Alnwick. The first season featured local residents cast in the roles of members of a criminal gang with the task of breaking into a parked and unattended cash in transit van and stealing £250,000 in cash. They divided the spoils in a remote barn and then had to evade detection with incriminating evidence for two weeks, keeping their share if successful. An old building in Thirsk was made into a film set as the police station and the base our detectives used to conduct the investigation.

The series was commissioned for another season and moved to Alnwick in Northumberland. This time, an old shop was converted into a bank, complete with a vault in the basement. Again, residents were invited to take part as the criminal gang as they planned a nighttime raid on the bank vault, using a core drill to bore a hole in a concrete wall to access the treasures within. This time, a million pounds was at stake as the prize money. An empty warehouse was the gang's hideout where they shared the loot before trying to spend the next two weeks going about their normal business to avoid the suspicion of the detectives. Both Thirsk and Alnwick provided a cinematic backdrop to a daring and fun crime caper that was a joy to work on. Unlike *Hunted*, these towns in the north of England meant the whole crew was away for the shoot and it was like a working holiday with a fantastic bunch of people.

After a pause in filming during the pandemic, *Hunted* returned and continues to attract a strong following. It has been a privilege to be part of these TV productions. Each year they return are gifts because I get to work with people I have grown close to and where I am affectionately known as Uncle Kev by some and the character Winston Wolf from *Pulp Fiction* by the executive producers because of my ability to untangle problems and quietly clear up the mess the production sometimes creates. I feel very lucky to be involved, not only in my role in the UK series, but advising those making international versions of *Hunted*. Eleven other countries have bought the format and made their own versions in Italy, the Netherlands, Australia, the United States, and Germany, among others. The UK series has been broadcast in over one hundred countries to date and on Amazon Prime as well.

CHAPTER 17

Epilogue

I'M OFTEN ASKED WHETHER I MISS MY OLD JOB, TO WHICH MY GLIB answer would be, 'I don't miss the circus, but I do miss the clowns.' It's true, at least to some extent. I worked with some fantastic people I remain friends with to this day, and there are others I'd be delighted to see if our paths crossed again, as sometimes happens. Although I love what I do now, working in leadership development and TV production, it is hard to compare it with the strong sense of purpose that comes with public service.

Of course, everyone has good and bad days, but I have no regrets and look back on my thirty years as a police officer fondly. I would do it again in a heartbeat. However, as you'd expect, things change and what I miss probably isn't there anymore. I think police officers today have a tougher time than I did. There is more confrontation, more violence, more bureaucracy, and more politics.

In writing about my career, the arc of societal change is clear. I've often said that I joined a post-war police force, operating as it had since the early twentieth century when Scotland Yard was arranged in four large departments:

A: HQ functions, complaints and discipline, solicitors

B: Specialists—dogs, traffic, prisoner transport, mounted

C: Crime

D: Personnel and training

The Metropolitan Police District, as the force boundary was known, was further divided into twenty-four districts, each of which was subdivided again into divisions. Each division had a leadership team consisting of a chief superintendent, a superintendent, a chief inspector (operations), a chief inspector (personnel), and a detective chief inspector. Quite top heavy when compared to the wide span of control these ranks cover in a flatter hierarchy today.

Each was its own fiefdom with four uniformed shifts (or reliefs) covering three eight-hour periods each day with one shift on rest day at any time. Investigations were conducted by detectives in the divisional criminal investigation department (CID), supported by investigators from uniformed teams who would be responsible for less serious crimes.

The divisional intelligence function was carried out by two old hands either close to or beyond retirement age who would manage thousands of cards indexed in plastic pouches and filed alphabetically in metal cabinet drawers. Each card had a mugshot of a named criminal and typed entries relating to arrests, convictions, sightings, and suspicions about their activity. This system was only searchable if the card was put back in the drawer it came from in alphabetical order. This was a time of pins on maps as our version of analysis.

My first posting was to North London's 'Y' district, which was a pilot for a system to manage calls, known as computer aided despatch (CAD), featuring green characters on a black screen and noisy dot matrix printers pushing out messages for attention. Otherwise, information was passed via landline phones and on paper messages. On an early career visit to the emergency call room at Scotland Yard, I witnessed handwritten paper message forms traveling along a conveyer belt system between rows of call handlers to the despatcher who would radio out the call to the area cars patrolling on the ground.

Back then, there were no dedicated murder teams. When required, the district detective superintendent would create a murder investigation team by abstractions from divisions—a detective from here, another two from there, a detective sergeant and a typist from the next and so on. They would form a temporary squad to investigate the murder and return to their home divisions when the work was done. There were no specialist child protection teams, and the first dedicated domestic violence units were only established in 1987.

Suddenly, from the late 1980s, the structural changes in the Met began and then accelerated, remaining in a state of constant change, chasing our evolving society, businesses, and the world's institutions. A once analogue workplace became electronic, digital, and faster. Manual typewriters, once found in every corner of every station gave way to word processors and email. CCTV footage became available in more and more crime scenes along with advances in DNA, mobile phone, and computer records, collecting passive data we could use in evidence-gathering. Calls went from a few thousand to ten thousand or more per day as mobile phones made an emergency call convenient and instant.

The challenge for policing is keeping up with it all, along with recruiting and retaining people that have the skills to stay ahead of the growth in available data from technology. Investigations are becoming more complex, with more channels open to exploitation by criminals who use and abuse data and carry out crimes in one territory when they are thousands of miles away in another. Artificial intelligence will change everything, with deep fakes already making life difficult to tell what's real and what isn't. No doubt, it will bring great advantages too, as technology tends to do, but it will require new thinking and skills for policing to adapt to it.

Some of the challenges from changes in society are more fundamental than the technical advances that affect our lives. The challenge of legitimacy for the police has changed since the death of George Floyd in Minneapolis, Minnesota. It raised questions about racism in society and trust in the police, and not just in the United States. Meanwhile, the murder of Sarah Everard and the convictions of police officers such as Wayne Couzens, David Carrick, and other high-profile cases in the UK, including those of errant undercover officers, have damaged trust in the British police service, which manifests itself in more confrontation and challenge for police officers doing their job.

Every citizen is a journalist, with phone camera video footage instantly streamed and posted on social media, sometimes with narrative or comments of the owner's point of view. This democratizes information, enabling everyone to witness what is happening in the world, where such online platforms are permitted. It has many advantages, providing a witness and a record of events where there might not have been such detailed information before. It can also influence the way people behave in public, knowing that actions might be documented for all to see. However, it can also mislead or raise tensions when the context isn't available or properly understood either by the commentator or the people viewing it.

Some interactions between police officers and the public seen in phone footage are presented in a suspicious light, questioning the intentions of officers responding to calls or being professionally curious about something that doesn't look right to them. Officers will have the context that may have come from a call from the public, the previous history of a person in mental health crisis, or about a suspect wanted for a previous crime that hadn't taken place in the moment that the video was created. Policing can involve physical confrontation and restraint, which never looks good for the uninformed observer. The challenge for the police is in making the context known when possible, responding quickly to social media posts that cast police action in a bad light, or admitting to errors when they occur. Context is everything and better communication is needed to address concerns of trust and legitimacy. In fairness, at the time of this writing, I have noticed a change and hope that police communications teams can keep up with the pace of social media, responding in those places of immediacy where many get their news and information.

Potential recruits form opinions about the police service as a potential career from a range of sources, including whether the tone of public discourse makes the role and the institution seem like a good place to be. Police are competing with other employers for the same candidates and will have to work very hard to keep up with the demand to maintain police officer numbers. For some years now, many have not viewed single employer careers in the same way as previous generations and there is evidence of higher rates of churn as officers tend to serve for shorter terms rather than complete a full career. Recruitment is one challenge, retention another. I spoke with someone who had recently left the service after less than two years, citing bad pay and endless paperwork as key reasons for his early rejection of a career in policing. He said that, after he'd paid for travel and food, he was left with around £350–£400 per week to live on, which just doesn't cut it in London today.

I remember when the then-Commissioner Sir Paul Condon met with a few of us when he visited Enfield police station where I worked as a detective in the late 1990s. The conversation came round to discussing an imminent change that would shift oversight of the Met to the newly installed mayor of the Greater London Authority, making the commissioner jointly accountable to the mayor and the home secretary. He said that it should be seen as an opportunity to have an elected official helping to support and influence the direction of the service, which I thought was typically diplomatic of him, though I eyed the powershift with suspicion foreseeing greater political interference ahead. In fairness, the Met went through a significant period of growth and Sir Paul was right–there did seem to be a mostly positive alliance between Scotland Yard and the mayor's office back then.

Until 2012, police forces outside of London were governed by a local authority policing committee when the appointment of elected Police and Crime Commissioners (PCCs) began, whose role was to be the voice of the people to hold the police to account. These PCCs were empowered to hire and fire the chief constable, creating a new power dynamic that was, in some cases, unproductive. If you give someone a hammer, they will eventually seek out a nail. So, in the early years of PCCs there were unprecedented sackings of chiefs. I can't say whether any or all of them deserved it, but it was clear that the preferences of these new political officials would influence the chiefs who relied on their support to keep their jobs. PCCs are elected every four years, and chief constables eye the horizon weighing up whether the candidate likely to succeed has views aligned with theirs or more likely to want to bring a new chief in, on whom they will be able to exert their influence more readily. A higher degree of churn is inevitable.

For the Metropolitan Police Service, there isn't a PCC, as such, but the same function is performed by the mayor of London, who delegates the day-to-day work to a deputy mayor. As an outsider looking in, I see political interference and criticism more than I see confidence and support for the Met police. It didn't help me warm to Mayor Sadiq Khan when he allegedly engineered the resignation of Cressida Dick, the first-ever female commissioner.

His public criticism of her grew rapidly after toxic messages between junior ranking officers in a WhatsApp group were exposed, producing yet another in a series of scandals and reputational issues for the Met, placing responsibility and accountability firmly on her shoulders. The mayor did not give her a chance to turn things around, using his position and influence in a way that meant she was unable to continue in post. A review by the former chief inspector of Constabulary, Sir Tom Winsor, examining the resignation of Dame Cressida Dick found that the mayor ignored due process and failed to respect her dignity:

> Those acting on behalf of the Mayor told the Commissioner that the Mayor intended publicly to announce his loss of trust and confidence in her, and that he intended to commence the statutory removal process, on the afternoon of 10 February 2022. The Commissioner was given a very short period in which to consider her position following that news. She was left in a position whereby she felt, even if others might have felt differently, that she had no option but to announce that she would step aside, in part to protect the Metropolitan Police itself. The circumstances in which she reached that view had been largely created by the actions of the Mayor and his staff. No good reason has been identified as to why such a resolution had to be reached on 10 February 2022 itself. The Mayor's actions on 10 February 2022 failed to respect the dignity of the Commissioner as an individual, and as the holder of high public office. He did not act, in particular on 10 February 2022 itself, in accordance with the legislative scheme, still less its spirit.[1]

We are amid a more acute arc of societal change today with huge global shifts in migrating populations fleeing conflict, climate change, disaster, and poverty. Current unrest around the world is generating divisions in society with higher levels of tension between communities and a surge in public demonstrations and protest marches, often requiring huge numbers of police, which takes them away from their normal duties, straining capacity and adding significant costs to an already stretched budget. However difficult to police, the fundamental right to peaceful protest is an inalienable right in the UK and must be defended. It can foster change through public agency and is a way to express dissent, disapproval, or objection. Periods of high demand always ease with time and the police service will have upheld an important human right by enduring through it.

We also have an epidemic of knife crime among our youth. Police figures for England and Wales from over a twelve-month period showed that 261 people were murdered with a sharp instrument.[2] Ninety-nine murder victims were under the age of twenty-five and thirteen victims were under sixteen. Over a ten-year period, police have recorded an increase of 76 percent in crimes involving a knife or sharp instrument. Over one-third of these occurred in London.[3]

According to work carried out by the Ben Kinsella Trust, children as young as nine say 'protection' is the reason they carry a knife.[4]

How on earth has it come to this? Well, I certainly don't have all the answers and it can't be for the police alone to solve this crisis, though they have their part to play. The public and political discourse reported in the media calls for new legislation, more police powers, longer sentences, and banning the sale of weapons, all of which is laudable, but there has to be a realistic prospect that knives will be taken off the streets.

Stop and search has been criticized as being overused, ineffective, and disproportionate and, on face value, the statistics show that only 29 percent of searches result in a police outcome, which means that two-thirds of searches find nothing.[5] Are police over-reliant on the 'copper's hunch,' that gut feeling that motivates enquiry? Or are they using data from crime reports in which victims have reported who attacked them or other intelligence that drives action? This is a complex topic, with many studies on unconscious bias reporting how our reactions, suspicions, and actions tap into our societal upbringing and ideas of cultural norms.

Police guidance on stop and search was reformed by then home secretary Theresa May, acknowledging in Parliament the damage caused to police/public relations when an innocent person was searched, especially in the case of younger people and ethnic minorities. She said,

> In London, thanks to the leadership of Sir Bernard Hogan-Howe, changes to stop-and-search show that it is possible to reduce the number of stops, improve the stop-to-arrest ratio, and still cut crime. Since February 2012, the Metropolitan police have reduced their overall use of stop-and-search by 20%, and they have reduced no-suspicion stop-and-search by 90%. In the same period, stabbings have fallen by a third and shootings by 40%. Complaints against the police have gone down and the arrest ratio has improved.[6]

These are very impressive claims and the guidance that followed continued to encourage searches based on robust intelligence and information. As a result, stop and search did decline by over two-thirds by 2018.

However, by 2022, government and police leaders were arguing that stop and search should be part of the response to an increase in violent crime. The Home Office, now led by a different politician, revised its guidance to encourage more forces to use it and also removing the restrictions imposed in previous policy, which led to an increase in its use by about 30 percent, though still far less than had previously been the case.

I spoke with a serving officer who told me that stop and search remained problematic, with some officers preferring to avoid the backlash that can follow from a search that doesn't yield an illegal item and an arrest—criticism that can come from some of their supervisors as well as those stopped and searched.

New legislation is being drafted that will be useful, but the police need empowerment through backing from the public, politicians, and senior leaders, more than they need new laws and longer sentences. The law can sound as robust as lawmakers care to draft it, but it is useless unless there is an effective way to apply it. Police are better and more professional in their approach to stop and search. Body cameras record what happens during encounters, which protects officers from unfounded complaints and ensures they are professional with those they interact with.

Police officers and staff don't get rich doing their job and few join the service for the salary alone, in fact it is lagging in real terms as inflation bites and pay reviews award low or zero percent annually. Many do it as a vocation, to serve with purpose in the hope of enjoying a rewarding and fulfilling role. With all the problems and scandals that have eroded trust by the actions of a few, the decent, hardworking police officers and their staff colleagues urgently need active, vocal, and visible support to help restore pride in the service.

I don't want it to sound hopeless. It isn't. We have a long tradition of public inquiry in a democratic-free country, a free press, a moderate and mostly peaceful public that is supportive of policing by consent. The British police remain a largely unarmed service, which is remarkable in the twenty-first century where very few of the world's police forces do not routinely carry guns. I still believe we have the best police service in the world.

I'm proud to have been a part of it and grateful that I had the opportunity to serve and enjoy the adventure of a lifetime. Thank you to the Metropolitan police.

I leave a few pearls of wisdom for those doing the job I used to do:

1. Leadership can come from anywhere, not just the higher ups.

2. You won't always see people at their best.

3. You will always be held to a higher standard.

4. Rank is not a barometer of wisdom.

5. It might make you feel better to blame 'the job,' but remember, you are 'the job.'

6. Fortify!

7. Nothing stays the same for long. Expect and embrace constant change.

8. Conflict is inevitable. You are the professional in that exchange.

9. Society needs you. It relies and depends on you.

10. The British police service is the best in the world.

Notes

Chapter 2

1. "Bottle" is a British idiom meaning courage. To say that someone has lost their bottle is to say that someone was cowardly.

Chapter 3

1. A bollocking or to be bollocked is a British coarse reference to being admonished.

2. A term used for those noncombatant office-dweller types who prefer doing administrative police roles rather than dealing with angry people on the front line. So called because the material in the police uniform trousers becomes shiny with wear if you sit on your backside too much.

Chapter 7

1. The Stephen Lawrence Inquiry. Report of an inquiry by Sir William Macpherson of Cluny, accessed March 30, 2024, https://assets.publishing.service.gov.uk/media/5a7c2af540f0b645ba3c7202/4262.pdf.

2. The Stephen Lawrence Inquiry. Report of an inquiry by Sir William Macpherson of Cluny, Chapter 1, para 6.34, accessed March 30, 2024, https://assets.publishing.service.gov.uk/media/5a7c2af540f0b645ba3c7202/4262.pdf.

3. The Stephen Lawrence Inquiry. Report of an inquiry by Sir William Macpherson of Cluny, accessed March 30, 2024, https://assets.publishing.service.gov.uk/media/5a7c2af540f0b645ba3c7202/4262.pdf, chapter 1, para 6.46 and 6.47.

4. The Stephen Lawrence Inquiry. Report of an inquiry by Sir William Macpherson of Cluny, accessed March 30, 2024, https://assets.publishing.service.gov.uk/media/5a7c2af540f0b645ba3c7202/4262.pdf, pp290—91.

5. College of Policing, Critical Incident Management, accessed March 30, 2024, https://www.college.police.uk/app/critical-incident-management/introduction-and-types-critical-incidents.

6. London Emergency Services Liaison Panel (LESLP) Major Incident Principles, Version 11.5, December 2021. https://www.london.gov.uk/sites/default/files/leslp_mip_v11.5_dec_2021_-_public.pdf Accessed 30 March 2024.

CHAPTER 8

1. Balmer, Delia, *Living with Serial Killer* (London: Ebury Press, 2017).

CHAPTER 10

1. Albert Camus, *The Myth of Sisyphus, and Other Essays*, trans. Justin O'Brien (New York: Vintage Books).

CHAPTER 13

1. Mark Kennedy: Confessions of an undercover cop. The Guardian, 26 Mar 2011. Accessed online 23 November 2023 at https://www.theguardian.com/environment/2011/mar/26/mark-kennedy-undercover-cop-environmental-activist

2. Police 'smear' campaign targeted Stephen Lawrence's friends and family. The Guardian 24 June 2013. Accessed online 23 November at https://www.theguardian.com/uk/2013/jun/23/stephen-lawrence-undercover-police-smears.

CHAPTER 17

1. Sir Thomas Winsor WS, special commission on the resignation of the commissioner of Police of the Metropolis, 2022.

2. Knife crime statistics: England & Wales (October 2023), Research Briefing, House of Commons Library.

3. "Knife Crime Statistics," The Ben Kinsella Trust, accessed January 9, 2024, https://benkinsella.org.uk/knife-crime-statistics/#.

4. Ben Kinsella Trust, "How did we get to this place?" *The Ben Kinsella Trust* (blog), January 9, 2024, https://benkinsella.org.uk/how-did-we-get-to-this-place/.

5. "Stop and search in the Metropolitan Police," accessed January 9, 2024, https://www.police.uk/pu/your-area/metropolitan-police-service/performance/stop-and-search/?tc=E05000362.

6. Hansard, daily commons debate, Wednesday, April 20, 2014, column 831, https://publications.parliament.uk/pa/cm201314/cmhansrd/cm140430/debtext/140430-0001.htm#14043038000002.

Bibliography

Balmer, Delia. *Living with Serial Killer* (London: Ebury Press, 2017).

The Ben Kinsella Trust. *Knife Crime Statistics.* January 2024. https://benkinsella.org.uk/knife-crime-statistics/#

The Ben Kinsella Trust. Blog: *How did we get to this place?* November 2020. https://benkinsella.org.uk/how-did-we-get-to-this-place/

Camus, Albert. *The Myth of Sisyphus, and Other Essays*, trans. Justin O'Brien (New York: Vintage Books).

College of Policing, Critical Incident Management, accessed March 30, 2024, https://www.college.police.uk/app/critical-incident-management/introduction-and-types-critical-incidents.

Hansard, daily commons debate, April 2014, column 831.

Police.uk. *Stop and Search in the Metropolitan Police.* Accessed January 2024. https://www.police.uk/pu/your-area/metropolitan-police-service/performance/stop-and-search/?tc=E05000362

Sir Thomas Winsor WS. *Special commission on the resignation of the Commissioner of Police of the Metropolis.* August 2022. https://assets.publishing.service.gov.uk/media/6311cacdd3bf7f4cb23bbf61/2022_08_24_-_Winsor_Commission_-_Report_ _TC_.pdf

The Stephen Lawrence Inquiry. Report of an inquiry by Sir William Macpherson of Cluny, accessed March 30, 2024, https://assets.publishing.service.gov.uk/media/5a7c2af540f0b645ba3c7202/4262.pdf.

The Stephen Lawrence Inquiry. Report of an inquiry by Sir William Macpherson of Cluny, accessed March 30, 2024, https://assets.publishing.service.gov.uk/media/5a7c2af540f0b645ba3c7202/4262.pdf, 290—91.

The Stephen Lawrence Inquiry. Report of an inquiry by Sir William Macpherson of Cluny, accessed March 30, 2024, https://assets.publishing.service.gov.uk/media/5a7c2af540f0b645ba3c7202/4262.pdf, para 6.46 and 6.47.

Thoreau, Henry David. *Indeed, Indeed I Cannot Tell* (1840-44). *From Troubles of The World.* Accessed January 2024. https://fromtroublesofthisworld.wordpress.com/2012/03/10/indeed-indeed-i-cannot-tell-by-henry-david-thoreau/

UK Parliament. *Knife crime statistics: England & Wales*, Research Briefing. House of Commons Library. October 2023. https://researchbriefings.files.parliament.uk/documents/SN04304/SN04304.pdf

Index

80; development operations,
204; gathering, 182, 199, 203,
243; point of contact, 104. *See
also under* cover officers; *specific
intelligence*
intelligence team/unit, 64, 65, 66,
95, 144, 146
internal investigations, 107
international estate agent, 150–51
Interpol (international criminal
police organization), 120
interviews: ambush, 125, 127, 129,
180; board for, 124–25; with
criminals, 5; with recruitment
office, 10–11; with suspects,
72–73, 75–76
invading privacy, 146
investigations: challenging, 127;
classification of, 99; internal,
107; target for, 52; transformation of, 84
investigation teams, 107
investigative journalist, 121–22
investigators, accountability of, 84
Islington: Chapel Market, 61–62;
DCI, 133–34; detective inspector, 95–104, 124–25. *See also
specific topics*

Jack the Ripper, 177
Jarrett, Cynthia, 33
Jarrett, Floyd, 33
The Job (in-house newspaper), 95
journalist(s), 35, 108, 121–22; citi-
zens as, 240; Mahmood as, 208

judge, Operation Polar Bear, 6, 7
jury, Operation Polar Bear, 5–7
"jury knobbling," 66
juvenile informant, 159

Kaden (criminal), 4–5
Kennedy, Mark, 198–200
Khan, Sadiq, 242
kidnap cases, 143–47; child,
149–52; Chinese, 148–49
kidnap intelligence team, 149
kidnap investigation team,
144, 148
kidnap operation, 129–30
kidnapper, negotiations with, 148,
151–52
kidnapping scams, 145
King's Cross, 48, 54–55, 57–58,
97, 136, 224; mounted branch
officers from, 53; Railway
Station, 59, 60; Road Division,
49–50; Road Police Station,
50, 95; station, 185–86; streets
of, 51
Kingston, 137
knife crime, 243–44
knifepoint robbery, 9–10, 41–42
Knowledge of London (taxi driver
qualification), 178, 179
Kray twins (London gang-
sters), 62

lack of diversity, 130
Lambrianou, Tony, 62
laundering money, 150–51

About the Author

Kevin O'Leary, a former senior detective at New Scotland Yard, served as the operational commander for crime and intelligence during the London 2012 Olympic and Paralympic Games. Within a distinguished career, he led Scotland Yard's Covert Operations Unit and excelled as a hostage and crisis negotiator, successfully resolving various life-or-death incidents. Kevin spearheaded a team combating serious and organized crime, implementing modern practices, and driving change. Internationally recognized, he chaired an alliance of senior leaders across forty countries aligned with Interpol. Kevin now designs and delivers immersive leadership development programs and serves as the series consultant for acclaimed UK TV shows, including *Hunted* and *The Heist*. His website is kevinoleary123.com.

Printed in the USA
CPSIA information can be obtained
at www.ICGtesting.com
LVHW040225021024
792664LV00002B/35